Betting Thoroughbreds

A Professional's Guide for
the Horseplayer

Betting Thoroughbreds

*A Professional's Guide for
the Horseplayer*

Steven Davidowitz

A Dutton Paperback *E. P. Dutton / New York*

*This paperback edition first published in 1979 by E. P. Dutton,
a Division of Elsevier-Dutton Publishing Co., Inc., New York*

*For information contact:
E.P. Dutton, 2 Park Avenue, New York, N.Y. 10016*

Library of Congress Cataloging in Publication Data

*Davidowitz, Steven.
Betting thoroughbreds.*

Bibliography: p.
1. Horse race betting.   I. Title.
SF331.D36 1977   798'.401   76–30458

ISBN: 0-525-47620-2

*Published simultaneously in Canada by
Clarke, Irwin & Company Limited,
Toronto and Vancouver*

Designed by The Etheredges

10 9 8 7 6 5 4 3 2 1

Acknowledgments

To my father,
my mother,
my wife,
and my son

Contents

Foreword

by Andrew Beyer

One of the luckiest moments in my life as a horseplayer occurred in 1971 when, by sheer chance, I sat next to Steve Davidowitz on a bench at Saratoga Racetrack. At the time I viewed racing the way many readers of this book probably do now. I desperately wanted to be a successful handicapper. But I wasn't convinced that this was possible, and I had no idea how to achieve my goal.

After striking up a conversation with Steve, I associated with him throughout that Saratoga season and got the opportunity to watch a consummate professional in operation. I was impressed not only by his success at the betting windows but also by his unique understanding of the nature of the game.

One aspect of Steve's approach to racing struck me as original and helped show me the way to win at the track. Steve was not a dogmatist. Most handicappers, even the good ones, define themselves by the primary methods they use. There are speed handicappers—pace handicappers—class handicappers—angle handicappers—and so on.

Steve perceived that there is a time and place for all these approaches. He swore by none and discarded none. The key to winning at the track was not to find one all-powerful secret, but to learn the right tools to use at the right time.

Most handicapping books purport to offer their readers all-encompassing formulas that will work anywhere. But, in practice, the horseplayer at Aqueduct and the horseplayer at Cahokia Downs are playing very different games. *Betting Thoroughbreds* recognizes their different needs and helps them both.

Steve's chapter on class at minor tracks explains an approach to the game which, as far as I know, has never appeared in a book before. Steve explains that the $1,500 claiming ranks at a cheap track may in fact include a half dozen different class stratifications. A handicapper who appreciates those differences will be able to find outstanding bets that elude almost everyone who reads the *Daily Racing Form*. For the bettor at any minor racetrack, that chapter alone is worth the price of the book.

For the handicapper who follows major-league racing, Steve's perceptions about the bias of the racing surface and his analysis of the way good trainers handle their horses are both invaluable. Those were the first things he taught me that summer at Saratoga. We examined a set of past performances and Steve said, "Let's train this horse." He then reviewed the horse's record race by race, considered what the trainer was trying to do with the animal, and determined whether the horseman was succeeding. By the time we came to the most recent race we had a very good idea of what the horse was likely to do that day, as well as insight into the trainer's methodology and competence.

This is a far cry from the approach of the dogmatists who distill the art of handicapping into neat, inflexible rules. But it is the only intelligent, realistic way to tackle the game. Steve's guidance pointed me in the right directions and ultimately enabled me to become a winning horseplayer and to beat him into print as the author of a handicapping book.

A book that examines all the complexities of handicapping may not sell in Peoria. Casual racetrack gamblers generally want systems and rules that will enable them to get rich quick without expending much effort. *Betting Thoroughbreds* offers no such simplistic strategies. But Steve's teachings will be a revelation for the handicappers who, like me in 1971, truly want to learn how to beat the game.

Introduction

For some horseplayers, the romance of the track is linked only to the number of trips made to the cashier's window. For others, it is the spectacle of a Secretariat or a Saratoga or the chance to root away the frustrations of daily living in 1:11⅖.

But for numerous racing fans—the ones for whom this book is written—Thoroughbred horseracing is all of the above and one of the most intellectually challenging pastimes man has ever invented. Through the art/science of handicapping and the wagering instrument, the fan in the stands is as much a participant as the horse itself. Armed with a copy of the *Daily Racing Form*, the horseplayer becomes a detective, and there are many mysteries to be solved.

How important are speed-pace-class-distance-track condition-weight-jockey-and-trainer? What role do they play in determining the outcome of a race? Are there patterns of predictability? Is the game based on logic or ruled by chance? What about drugs and year-round racing? And, at rock bottom, is it possible to play the game well enough to overcome the stiff 20 percent betting tax and still show a profit for the effort?

Virtually every serious or semi-serious fan has endured periods of frustration and self-doubt while trying to find workable answers to these and other racetrack riddles. The path is littered with thousands of torn-up pari-mutuel tickets. The clues are complex, sometimes contradictory. The secrets of the game are subtle and elusive. And there is just so much bad advice floating around.

Dozens of ads promise to make the racing game easy pickings but in every instance fall way short of the mark. Indeed, the racetrack experience is such that there are no absolute truths to memorize, no ironclad list of dos or don'ts, no simplistic three-rule systems that do your thinking for you.

It may sound like good advice to avoid playing a filly against colts, or to demand a recent race from a potential contender; but it has been my experience that the people who give such advice, and sell it too, have rarely had a winning season in their lives.

Along every step of the handicapping process the player must learn to make well-thought-out judgments: to separate contenders, to eliminate also-rans, to detect relevant information hidden in the hieroglyphics of the *Daily Racing Form*'s past performance records, and to glean valid insights from the fast-paced action on the track.

To acquire that kind of reality-based insight, most successful horseplayers have had to discard the majority of popular handicapping notions, substituting in their place more flexible concepts gained through practical experience, intensive private research, and conversations with the best players in the game.

I would love to assure you that reading this book will automatically make you a winner. But I can't. The truth is you may not have the competitiveness, the patience, or the inclination to follow the steps necessary to improve your game sufficiently.

It is my belief, however, that thousands, perhaps even tens of thousands, of racing fans could win at the races but are presently unable to do so because they do not know what skills are important, what sources of information are reliable, and what tools are most useful for the task. Thousands more, maybe millions, gain considerable pleasure in their initial outings to the track but for lack of good teachers and other aids find the experience too expensive to pursue. And there are others, too many in fact, who continue to play the game without knowing some of the strategies that could reduce the cost considerably.

The purpose of this book is to lend a hand and fill the void. It is a sourcebook, not about Thoroughbred horseracing per se, but about ideas, concepts, tools, and suggestions taken from seventeen years of personal and professional racetrack experience. It is designed so that any player, regardless of past history or present skill, can gain sufficient insights to build a solid plan of attack. Good luck, and I hope it helps your game.

Betting Thoroughbreds

A Professional's Guide for
the Horseplayer

1.
Through the
Looking Glasses

Secretariat X — Ch. c (1970), by Bold Ruler—Somethingroyal, by Princequillo.
Breeder, Meadow Stud, Inc. (Va.). 1973 12 9 2 1 $860,404
Owner, Meadow Stable. Trainer, L. Laurin. 1972 9 7 1 0 $456,404

Oct28-73 8WO	mc 1⅝	2:41⅘ fm	1-5	▲117	2 1½	1 5	1 12	1 6½	MapleE 12	WfaS 96	Secretariat117 BigSpruce GoldenDon	12
Oct 8-73 7Bel	Ⓣ 1½	2:24⅘ fm	1-2	▲121	1 1½	1 1½	1 3	1 5	T'c'teR 3	WfaS 103	Secretariat 121 Tentam Big Spruce	7
Sep29-73 7Bel	1½	2:25⅘ sy	1-3	▲119	2 1½	1 h	2 1½	2 4½	Turc'teR 5	WfaS 86	ProveOut126 Secretariat CougarII.	5
Sep15-73 7Bel	1 1-8	1:45⅖ ft	2-5e	▲124	5 4	3 ½	1 2	1 3½	T'rc'teR 7	InvH 104	Secretariat124 RivaRidge Cougar II.	7
Aug 4-73 7Sar	1 1-8	1:49⅕ ft	1-10	▲119	4 4	2 ½	2 h	2 1	Turc'teR 3	AlwS 94	Onion 119 Secretariat Rule by Reason	5
Jun30-73 8AP	1 1-8	1:47 ft	1-20	▲126	1 3	1 2½	1 6	1 9	Turc'tteR 4	InvA 99	Secretariat 126 MyGallant OurNative	4
Jun 9-73 8Bel	1 1-2	2:24 ft	1-10	▲126	1 h	1 20	1 28	1 31	Tur'teR 1	ScwS 113	Secretariat126 Twice aPr'ce MyGal'nt	5
May19-73 8Pim	1 3/16	1:54⅖ ft	1-3	▲126	4 5½	1 2½	1 2½	1 2½	Turc'teR 3	ScwS 98	Secretariat 126 Sham Our Native	6
May 19—Daily Racing Form Time, 1:53⅖.												
May 5-73 9CD	1 1-4	1:59⅖ ft	3-2e	▲126	11 8¾	2 ½	1 ½	1 2½	T'tteR 10	ScwS 103	Secretariat 126 Sham Our Native	13
Apr21-73 7Aqu	1 1-8	1:49⅘ ft	1-3e	▲126	7 5½	5 5½	4 5½	3 4	T'rc'teR 6	ScwS 83	Angle Light 126 Sham Secretariat	8
Apr 7-73 7Aqu	1	1:33⅖ ft	1-10	▲126	3 1	1 2	1 ½	1 3	T'rc'teR 3	AlwS 100	Secret'riat126 Ch'mp'gneCh'rlie Flush	6
Mar17-73 7Aqu	7 f	1:23⅕ sy	1-5	▲126	5 6	5 3	1 h	1 4½	Tur'tteR 4	AlwS 85	Sec'tar't126 Ch'pagneCh'lie Impec'n's	6
Nov18-72 8GS	1 1/16	1:44⅖ ft	1-10e	▲122	6 9½	3 3	1 1½	1 3½	Tur'teR 6	ScwS 83	Secretariat122 AngleLight StepNicely	6
Oct28-72 7Lrl	1 1/16	1:42⅘ sy	1-10e	▲122	6 14	5 3	1 5	1 8	T'rc'teR 5	ScwS 99	Secretar't122 St'p t'eM'sic AngleL'ht	6
Oct14-72 7Bel	1	1:35 ft	2-3e	▲122	11 13	5 3½	1 ½	1 2†	Tur'teR 4	ScwS 97	Secr'tar't122 St'p theM'sic St'pNic'ly	12
†Disqualified and placed second.												
Sep16-72 7Bel	6½ f	1:16⅖ ft	1-5	▲122	6 5½	5 3½	1 2	1 1¾	Turc'teR 4	ScwS 98	S'cr't'r't122 St'p t'eMusic Sw'tC'rier	7
Aug26-72 7Sar	6½ f	1:16⅕ ft	1-3	▲121	9 6½	1 h	1 4	1 5	Turc'teR 8	SpwS 97	Secretariat121 Fl't toGl'y St'p theM'c	9
Aug16-72 7Sar	6 f	1:10 ft	3-2	121	5 4	4 2	1 ½	1 3	Turc'teR 2	SpwS 96	Secr't'riat121 L'da'sCh'f N'thst'rD'c'r	5
Jly 31-72 4Sar	6 f	1:10⅘ ft	2-5	▲118	7 3¾	3 ½	1 h	1 1½	TurcotteR 4	Alw 92	Secretariat 118 Russ Miron Joe Iz	7
Jly 15-72 4Aqu	6 f	1:10⅗ ft	6-5	▲113*	6 6½	4 3	1 ½	1 6	Felic'noP 8	Mdn 90	Secret'riat113 M'sterAch'v'r BetOn It	11
Jly 4-72 2Aqu	5½ f	1:05 ft	3	▲113*	10 7	10 8¾	7 5½	4 1¼	Felic'noP 2	Mdn 87	Herbull 118 MasterAch'v'r Fl't 'nR'y'l	12

Oct 5 Bel tc 5f fm :56⅘h **Sept 25 Bel tc 1m yl 1:38h** **Sept 21 Bel tc 4f sf :48⅗b**

Thanks to television's coverage of the 1973 Triple Crown races, almost every person with the vaguest interest in horse-racing knows that the horse whose lifetime record is shown above was one of a kind, a champion of his age, if not, in fact, one of the greatest racehorses ever to appear on this planet.

As a two-year-old, before the TV cameras discovered him, Secretariat was just as spectacular to watch, officially winning eight races in ten starts, including a defeat only the stewards could hang on him in the Champagne Stakes. But it is his other defeat I want to tell you about. His first lifetime start.

Secretariat **113** Ch. c (1970), by Bold Ruler—Somethingroyal, by Princequillo.
Breeder, Meadow Stud, Inc. (Va.). 1972 0 M 0 0 (——)
Owner, Meadow Stable. Trainer, L. Laurin.
June 29 Bel 3f ft :35h **June 24 Bel 6f sly 1:12⅘h** **June 15 Bel 5f ft 1:00⅕hg**

One, two, three strides out of the starting gate with inexperienced Paul Feliciano barely able to stay in the saddle, Secretariat was welcomed to the sport of kings with a bang. Make that two bangs. One from the left and one from the right.

"Forget *that* horse," I said to console myself and made a mental note to see him a bit later in the race. Ten lengths to the front, a pack of expensively bred two-year-old maidens were trying to win the first race of their careers. It was time to see how the race was taking shape.

I love two-year-old racing. I'm fascinated by its freshness and its promise, and I've gained valuable insights about speed, class, distance potential, and trainers through watching these young horses progress from race to race. Besides, the better ones run fast, very formfully, and provide some of the best bets in all of racing.

When the great filly Ruffian, for example, made her debut in 1974, I was absolutely astonished to get a $10.40 payoff. Her trainer, Frank Whiteley Jr., is one of the deadliest trainers of first-time starters in the history of racing— a man who wins upward of 40 percent of all such attempts, a man who trains horses like they are put together with Swiss-clockwork efficiency.

Not only did Ruffian score by fifteen lengths in track record time, but she was the third straight first-time starter Whiteley put over in three early season attempts. It also turned out to be a typical Ruffian performance.

THIRD RACE
Belmont
MAY 22, 1974

5 ½ FURLONGS. (1.03) MAIDEN SPECIAL WEIGHTS. Purse $9,000. Fillies, 2–year–olds, weights, 116 lbs.

Value of race $9,000, value to winner $5,400, second $1,980, third $1,080, fourth $540. Mutuel pool $144,330, OTB pool $47,785. Track Exacta Pool $182,574. OTB Exacta Pool $83,829.

Last Raced	Horse	Eqt.A.Wt PP St			¼	½	Str	Fin	Jockey	Odds $1
	Ruffian		2 116	9 8	13	15	18	(115)	Vasquez J	4.20
	Suzest		2 113	3 3	3hd	24	25	25	Wallis T3	1.50
	Garden Quad		2 116	10 9	52	41½	43	31½	Baltazar C	26.20
	Fierce Ruler		2 116	7 5	61½	51	31	43½	Rivera M A	20.80
	Flower Basket		2 116	8 6	83	7½	5½	5½	Turcotte R	45.30
	Curlique	b	2 116	5 7	7½	84	63	6nk	Maple E	14.10
4May74 6CD12	Funny Cat		2 116	6 10	10	10	8½	75	Hole M	32.70
14May74 4Bel3	Merrie Lassie		2 116	4 4	96	95	94	84½	Gustines H	13.90
	Precious Elaine		2 116	1 1	2hd	31	7½	96½	Castaneda M	4.50
28Feb74 3GP2	Great Grandma Rose		2 116	2 2	42	61½	10	10	Cordero A Jr	4.60

OFF AT 2:32 EDT. Start good, Won ridden out. Time, :22⅖, :45, :57, 1:03 Track fast.

(Equals track record.)

$2 Mutuel Prices:

9–(L)–RUFFIAN	10.40	4.60	3.80
3–(D)–SUZEST		3.20	3.00
10–(M)–GARDEN QUAD			7.00

$2 EXACTA 9–3 PAID $35.20.

dk b or br. f, by Reviewer—Shenanigans, by Native Dancer. Trainer Whiteley F Y Jr. Bred by Janney Jr Mrs & S S (Ky).

RUFFIAN, rushed to the front from the outside at the turn, quickly sprinted away to a good lead and continued to increase her advantage while being ridden out. SUZEST, prominent from the start, was no match for the winner while easily besting the others. GARDEN QUAD hustled along after breaking slowly, failed to seriously menace. FIERCE RULER had no excuse. FUNNY CAT was off slowly. PRECIOUS ELAINE had brief speed. GREAT GRANDMA ROSE was through early.

Owners— 1, Locust Hill Farm; 2, Olin J M; 3, Irving R; 4, LaCroix J W; 5, Reineman R L; 6, Calumet Farm; 7, Whitney C V; 8, T-Square Stable; 9, Brodsky A J; 10, Five Friends Farm.
Trainers— 1, Whiteley F Y Jr; 2, Stephens W C; 3, Johnson P G; 4, Toner J J; 5, Freeman W C; 6, Cornell R; 7, Poole G T; 8, Cincotta V J; 9, Conway J P; 10, Donato R A.
Scratched—Cross Words; Footsie (14May74⁴Bel⁴); French Rule.

Throughout her two-year-old season Ruffian was never defeated, never threatened, never pushed to race any faster than she was willing to give on her own. But I'm not at all sure that pushing would have produced anything more than she was already willing to give.

Ruffian's striding action was very much like that of Valery Borzov, the Russian "doctor" of the sprint who won the gold medal in the 1972 100-meter dash at the Munich Olympics. Perfect rhythm. Maximum efficiency. Ruffian just came out of the gate running and never stopped, never missed a beat. Indeed, at six furlongs (three-quarters of a mile), I am convinced she could have beaten any horse that ever lived, including Secretariat, the fast-working son of Bold Ruler I had come to watch and bet in his debut, the colt we left in a tangle three steps out of the starting gate.

A few inches more to the left, a few more pounds of pressure, and we might never have heard about Secretariat. My notebooks are full of horses whose careers were terminated by less severe blows. But somehow this greenhorn kept his balance and settled slowly into stride far back of his field in the run down the backstretch.

On the turn I could see all the horses clearly at once, but the image I remember is that of the reddish brown colt going by three horses so fast it made me blink. Twice he changed gears to avoid further trouble. Twice more Feliciano choked him down to avoid running up on the heels of a tandem of horses that looked cloddish by comparison.

At the top of the stretch he moved again, into a higher gear, angling sharply to the inside, looking for room, shifting leads to gain better traction, losing precious time in the bargain. "A freak," I said to myself, but I had barely completed the thought when the red colt exploded in midstretch with a force that jiggled my binoculars right out of focus. He finished fourth, beaten by one and a half lengths. But it was the most electric exhibition of acceleration power I had seen since the mighty Kelso exploded seventy yards from the wire to gobble up Malicious in a stakes race eight years earlier.

It was only the beginning, only the tip of the iceberg; but being there, watching the race, knowing WHAT I was watching was a thrill—the kind of thrill that reaches the mind bringing awareness and awe.

Maybe your aim is to become a successful handicapper. Or perhaps you are reading this book just to improve your understanding of horseracing, putting it on a par with your comprehension of other hobbies and sports. In either case, the quickest, straightest line to the goal begins with the race itself and how to watch it. Unfortunately, all too many racing fans, it seems to me, do not know how to do that.

There are three simultaneous disciplines involved.

For one thing, you must see as much of the race as possible—the development of it, the flow of it, and the battle to the wire down the stretch. For another, your mind controls a switch for a focusing device like the zoom lens of a camera. You must train your mind to operate that switch—to zoom in and zoom out—the moment anything unusual hits the retina.

Combining these two disciplines into a smooth two-gear

transmission takes practice. You will have to learn when to switch away from the action in the front of the pack or away from the horse your money is riding on.

There are different ways to facilitate the learning process; but because the inclination of most horseplayers is to watch their bet, I suggest starting with that.

When the field hits the turn, when your grandstand vantage point makes it easy to see the entire field, without moving your binoculars, pull back on the zoom lens in your mind and see if you can spot the fastest-moving horses, the horses in trouble, the horses on the rail, the horses stuck on the outside.

Don't be concerned if you are not able to identify more than a couple of horses at once. Later you can use the videotape replays and result charts to put it all together.

In my judgment, the turn is the most important part of the race. It is the place where the majority of races are won and lost, the place where jockeys show their greatest skill and commit the most atrocious errors, the place where the fan can glean the most knowledge for the future.

Horses get into the most trouble on the turn. Centrifugal force pulls them naturally to the outside, and the ones that are weakly ridden, out of shape, or hurting are unable to hold their line as they turn the corner into the stretch.

Even more important, as I will describe in greater detail later, the action on the turn will reveal the true nature of the racetrack as the track itself influences race results.

There is no need for me to describe any further steps in the process of learning how to watch a race properly. If you master the turn, your ability to focus and shift focus to significant happenings will be firmly established. You will be able to use that skill anytime—at the start or in the stretch —at any stage of the race. After some practice you will even find yourself doing it automatically. Believe me, no other racetrack skill will ever be more useful.

The third discipline you need to master while watching races has nothing to do with the function of sight. And in all sincerity it is what the rest of this book is about. It is the discipline that all your racetrack judgments are based on—the discipline of enlightened insight.

Watching a race properly is only one of the ways you can acquire greater knowledge about particular horses. But to make maximum use of the skill, to put yourself in a position to recognize the unusual, important things that take place, you must first have some clear ideas about the limits of Thoroughbred performance, some understanding of the relative importance of track condition, trainers, class, and all the other pieces that make up the racetrack puzzle.

As I hinted in the introduction, most of the better players in the game have acquired that kind of knowledge only after many years of struggle. For some the effort was roughly equivalent to the pursuit of a college-level education. My own education was a case in point. And I mean that literally.

2.
A B.A. in Handicapping

The first race in my life took place at Aqueduct on April 18, 1960. I was an eighteen-year-old freshman at Rutgers University and I needed $100 to make it to Fort Lauderdale for spring recess. But I only had $42.

A few of my friends paid for the bus ticket, pushed me through the turnstiles, and armed me with a program and Jack's Little Green Card (a tout sheet). I bet $5 to show on Jack's best bet of the day—Happy Lion in the first race—but when I realized that wouldn't get me past the Delaware Memorial Bridge, I went back and bet a wheel in the daily double. Twice.

Of course, when Happy Lion sent me and my crazy friends barreling down the pike to a week of girl chasing in the Florida sun, I thought I had found the secret to a rich and easy life. Naturally, I became a devout believer in Jack's Little Green Card.

But the romance didn't last very long. Every time I skipped classes to go out to the track, Jack's Card would surely have three or four winners listed; but who could figure which of the three choices per race would turn out to be the right choice. It was my misfortune that the winner was rarely the top choice.

So I switched cards; bet the secret code selections of Ken Kling in the New York *Daily Mirror;* made a system founded on *Racing Form* consensus picks; bet repeaters; bet the top speed rating; followed the "horses to watch" list in *Turf and Sport Digest;* bought an assortment of systems and other gadgets at $5, $10, and $20 a pop; and then began to bet with a bookie.

At minus $1,200, it didn't take much of a handicapper to predict where I was headed; but the final straw was a last-place finish by my old friend Happy Lion. The irony of it all did not escape me.

My father, bless his heart, picked up the tab with the New Brunswick bookie and made me promise never to bet another horserace again. It was a promise I wasn't sure I wanted to keep, but I knew there wasn't much future in going out to the track just to lose. I was determined to find out if, in fact, it was possible to win.

For the next six months I stayed away from the track and bought, borrowed, and read everything I could find about the inner workings of the sport.

The history of it was fascinating enough: the stuff about Man O' War and Citation, Arcaro and Shoemaker. But I was appalled at the lack of good material in the field of handicapping. So much of it was so badly written, so illogical, so poorly documented that I became discouraged and abandoned the project. I was convinced that racing was nothing more than a game of roulette on horseback, a sucker's game of pure chance, and I might very well have held that view forever. An assignment my statistics professor handed out a few weeks later changed my mind. "Analyze the winning tendencies of post positions at Monmouth Park," he said. And the irony of *that* did not escape me either.

The task, simple enough, revealed very little useful information the first time through. But when I introduced track condition and distance into the equation, there were powerful indicators that suggested the need for more intensive research. My statistics professor—no fool, to be sure—probably took the hint and spent the rest of the summer buried in his *Racing Form*.

He wasn't the only one.

I looked up horses', trainers', and jockeys' records. I studied result charts and workouts diligently and kept a file on all the best horses and stakes races on the East Coast. I made endless comparisons and was not surprised when some patterns began to emerge, patterns that were never mentioned by the so-called experts who were publishing and selling their empty-headed systems and books to a starved racing public.

I discovered that each type of race had its own set of

key clues, its own major factors. I discovered that some trainers were consistently more successful than others and that most successful trainers were specialists who tended to repeat winning strategies. These strategies, I found, were frequently revealed in the past performance records of the horses they trained. By comparing these horses—comparing the dates between races, the workout lines, the distance and class manipulations—I began to gain some important insights into the conditioning process. The effort also cost me a failing grade in German 201, and I damn near flunked out of school. But it was worth it. I had begun to realize that there was a logic to the sport, and I suspected that I would be able to put all this time and effort to good use in the not-too-distant future. And I didn't have to wait very long to test out my thesis.

In late spring 1961 I spotted a horse named Nasomo in the past performance charts for Gulfstream Park. The half-mile workout from the starting gate attached to the bottom of his chart (.47bg) leaped off the page at me.

Nasomo hadn't shown such gate speed in any of his prior workouts, a deficiency he was content to carry over into his races. By habit he was a slow-breaking, Silky Sullivan-type whose late burst of speed had earned him absolutely nothing in eight tries. But my research into workout patterns had already convinced me that such a dramatic change in behavior on the training track invariably meant a vastly improved effort in competition. Barring bad racing luck—which is something that frequently plagues slow-breaking types—I was sure Nasomo would run the race of his life.

At 28–1 Nasomo turned in a spectacular performance, a nose defeat by the stakes prospect Jay Fox. Although that didn't score too many points with Nasomo's betting friends at the track, it was the first time I had ever felt confident about the performance of a horse before a race, the first time I began to think seriously about racing as a career.

Several weeks and several silent winning picks later, I broke my maiden on a horse called Flying Mercury. He was a retread sprinter that had once met top-class stock, but few people in the stands were able to appreciate his virtues (six outstanding workouts stretching back over a four-week period, all but one missing from the past performance records). Flying Mercury paid $78 to win, and I bought back my promise to my father with the proceeds of a $40 wager.

For the next two years I continued my studies into the mysteries of handicapping, keeping my losses to a minimum and my bets in perspective. But the Rutgers Dean of Men was not very pleased about my ragged classroom attendance, and he gave me a year off from school in September 1962, at the beginning of my senior year. In the true sense of the cliché, it turned out to be a blessing in disguise.

I visited racetracks in West Virginia, Louisiana, Ohio, Florida, New England, Michigan, Arkansas, Illinois, Maryland, California, New York, and New Jersey. Through those varied exposures and continued research, I detected two basic racetrack realities that seemed fundamental to handicapping. Yet I was sure that too few people in the stands were giving either of them the thought they deserved.

In the first place, I was surprised to learn that at many racetracks there was no way to measure the true class of horses by the claiming prices or race labels.

At most minor tracks, for example, a careful reading of result charts and race eligibility conditions suggested that there were five, six, or even seven separate class levels lumped into each claiming price. Moving up in company within a particular claiming price was frequently more difficult than ascending to the next claiming level.

At the major one-mile racetracks I frequently observed variations of this phenomenon in lower-level claiming events, maiden races, and nonclaiming (allowance) races. Very often these observations pointed out winners that were not otherwise discernible.

Secondly, because each racing surface—man-made and considerably different—had specific peculiarities, some race results were predetermined, or at least heavily influenced, by those characteristics.

In sprints at Monmouth Park, for example, post positions were of no consequence on fast-track racing days, but following any rain the track did not (and still does not) dry out evenly.

On days like that the rail was so deep and tiring that posts one, two, and three were at a terrible disadvantage. Stretch runners breaking from the outer post positions won everything. (At the Fair Grounds in New Orleans, where water can be found less than ten feet below the surface, the drainage system created precisely the opposite effect.)

Indeed, at every racetrack on my itinerary I noticed an influential track bias at work at one or more distances. And at some tracks a particular bias was so strong and so predictable that all handicapping questions had to be directed toward finding out which horse would be helped, hurt, or eliminated by the peculiarities of the running surface.

Of course, most handicappers seemed well aware of the difference between sloppy, fast, and other moisture-related track conditions, and a few even knew that Aqueduct in July favored speedy, front-running types while Belmont in September seemed to be deeper, slower, and kinder to stretch runners; but my observations about track bias suggested a stronger relationship between the track and actual horse performance. What I discovered was a relationship that sometimes eliminated the best horse in the race from contention, or else helped to promote an otherwise modestly qualified contender into a logical race winner.

By thinking first in these terms, before trying to compare the relative talents of the horses in a specific race, I found myself consistently able to recognize solid horses at every racetrack, horses that frequently went to post at generous odds. *It was also possible to interpret results and past performance lines more accurately when these horses ran back at a later date.*

With the first consistent profits of my handicapping career, I returned to Rutgers full of confidence.

On May 24, 1964, I finally did graduate from Rutgers, with a B.A. in psychology; but in truth it was only through the grace of my music professor, who raised my cumulative average to the passing level by changing a C to a B on the final day. Three weeks earlier the two of us accidentally met at Garden State Park, and he had a $280 reason to remember the event.

"I'm not doing this as a reward for your touting services," Professor Broome said while making the change of grade, "but I think you deserve some academic credit for your racing studies and this is the best I can do."

It was just enough.

3.
The Horseplayer's Bible

In the early morning hours at racetracks coast to coast, from January to December, thousands of horses of varying abilities are out on the training track. In the afternoons and evenings thousands more compete in races for fillies, colts, sprinters, routers, maidens, claimers, allowances, and stakes.

Some races are on the grass course, some on the dirt. Some tracks are fast; some are sloppy, muddy, or something in between. The possibilities are endless, the data voluminous. And at $1.25 per copy, most of it is all there in black and white.

Frankly, I'm not in the habit of endorsing the editorial policy of the *Daily Racing Form.* I think it could surely provide more pertinent investigative reporting and give sharper focus to issues affecting the plight of the player; but for hard racing news, statistics, and daily track poop, the *Daily Racing Form* is unequivocally the best publication of its kind in the world. Properly used, it is more valuable than the rest of racing literature put together. And they can quote me on that if they like.

Henrietta Sue **109** **Ch. f (1973), by Royal Trio—Cavangal, by Cavan.**
Breeder, Garrett & Carter (La.). **1976 6 1 0 1 $3,788**
Owner, T. Hickman. Trainer, B. Flint. **$5.000** **1975 9 M 3 0 $10.993**

16 Feb76	^{4}FG	5½ f	:22	:47	1:06^{2}ft	7¼	109	$5^{2\frac{1}{2}}$	5^{5}	$5^{2\frac{3}{4}}$	3^{3}	SpiehlerG^{9}	5000	83	SecondPolicy112	Dantlss Joe	12
11 Feb76	^{1}FG	6 f	:22^{2}	:45^{4}	1:11 ft	6½	112	$8^{6\frac{1}{2}}$	8^{11}	7^{8}	4^{11}	SphielrG^{10}	6500	79	AprilMoon120	JoustingRulah	12
29 Jan76	^{7}FG	1^{40}	:46^{3}	1:12	1:41^{2}ft	37	112	10^{15}	10^{18}	10^{28}	9^{39}	SoirezW^{7}	10000	47	LeCrack 119	ElChris	10
17 Jan76	^{3}FG	6 f	:22^{2}	:46^{4}	1:12^{3}ft	5¼	109	$5^{4\frac{1}{2}}$	$4^{4\frac{1}{2}}$	$4^{5\frac{1}{2}}$	5^{12}	SpiehlrG^{4}	12000	70	Shannon's Goal 115	Cosgin	7
11 Jan76	^{9}FG	6 f	:22^{1}	:46^{4}	1:13^{1}ft	13	109	$3^{1\frac{1}{2}}$	$2^{2\frac{1}{2}}$	$3^{\frac{1}{2}}$	4^{3}	SpehlerG^{9}	HcpS	76	ⒻItsYourProblem112	Tagita	12
5 Jan76	^{4}FG	6 f	:22^{3}	:48^{2}	1:14^{4}gd	9-5	▲1115	$2^{1\frac{1}{2}}$	$1^{\frac{1}{2}}$	1^{3}	$1^{6\frac{1}{2}}$	ClrkK^{10}	cM6500	71	ⒻHrttaSue111	Run to theFt	12
20 Dec75	^{9}FG	6 f	:22^{3}	:46^{3}	1:12^{4}ft	13	122	3^{3}	4^{3}	$3^{2\frac{1}{2}}$	2^{6}	LeBncAR^{3}	ScwS	75	Kitassy122	HenriettaSue	11
11 Dec75	^{3}FG	6 f	:22^{3}	:47^{1}	1:13^{2}ft	2¼	114^{5}	3^{1}	2^{1}	1^{h}	2^{4}	ClarkK^{7}	Mdn	74	ⒻMissyRed 119	HenritaSue	12
3 Dec75	^{1}FG	6 f	:22^{4}	:47	1:13^{2}ft	8¾	107^{5}	$4^{3\frac{1}{2}}$	$2^{\frac{1}{2}}$	1^{h}	2no	ClarkK^{8}	5000	78	CityDevelomnt115	HnrtaSue	12
24 Nov75	^{1}FG	6 f	:23^{2}	:48^{3}	1:13^{3}ft	50	108^{5}	$6^{3\frac{1}{4}}$	$6^{6\frac{1}{2}}$	4^{5}	$5^{9\frac{1}{2}}$	ClarkK^{12}	M7500	67	TryThs frSze119	SwngngE.J.	12

Feb 12 FG 3f ft :36bg **Jan 21 FG 3f ft :36⅖bg**

Most racegoers have no trouble recognizing the importance of past performance profiles. The pp shown above is a season's worth of racing history at a glance. The date, distance, track, and track condition for every start; the fractional times of the leader and finishing time of the race winner; the odds, the weight, the running line, the beaten lengths, and finishing position; the jockey, post position, class of race, speed rating, top two finishers, and size of field. An incredible amount of information. But it is not enough. Indeed, it is not even the complete picture provided by other sources of information published in the very same newspaper. The result chart is far more comprehensive, far more valuable.

While every race is being run in North America, a sharp-eyed *DRF* employee known as the "Trackman" gives a horse-by-horse call of the fast-paced action on the track to an attentive assistant. Presto, the result chart is born. Flash, it's over the wires to Hightstown, New Jersey; Los Angeles, California; Chicago, Illinois; and other cities where editions of the *Form* are put together.

At the chart desk at *DRF* offices each horse's running line is extracted from the chart and then added to its past performance profile.

What many fans do not realize about this process hurts them every time they go out to the track.

Because of space limitations much important information is lost in the transmission from chart to profile. And even more of that information is lost if the profile is scheduled for publication in the *Form*'s tabloid-size Western editions. But whichever edition we consider (in this book all past performance examples are taken from the smaller Western editions), there is no reason any of this information should be lost to the player.

Saving a set of chronologically dated result charts for the track(s) in your area is all that's required to fill in the spaces. While each edition of the *Form* publishes complete result charts for all tracks covered by the past performances, the cost-conscious, once-a-week horseplayer can still keep pace with doings at his favorite track through the condensed charts appearing in the sport section of a good local newspaper. Moreover, by not paying some attention to these charts, you will forfeit your best chance to advance your game.

Foolish Pleasure **126** **B. c (1972), by What a Pleasure—Fool-Me-Not, by Tom Fool.**
Breeder, Waldemar Farm Inc. (Fla.). **1976 6 3 0 1 $127,260**
Owner, J. L. Greer. Trainer, L. Jolley. **1975 11 5 4 1 $716,278**

5Jly76 ^{8}Aqu	$1\frac{3}{16}$	:47^{4}1:11^{2}1:55^{2}ft	$2\frac{3}{4}$	125	$1^{1\frac{1}{2}}$	$1^{1\frac{1}{2}}$	1^1	1no	MapleE^4	HcpS 85	FoolishPleasure125	Forego	4
20Jun76 ^{8}Hol	$1\frac{1}{4}$	:45^{4}1:10 1:58^{4}ft	9-5	126	$6^{9\frac{1}{2}}$	$7^{4\frac{1}{4}}$	7^6	$5^{6\frac{1}{2}}$	PincyLJr^1	HcpS 90	PayTribute117	Avatar	8
6Jun76 ^{8}Hol	$1\frac{1}{8}$	:46^{2}1:10^{2}1:47^{1}ft	2-3	▲128	3^3	$4^{2\frac{1}{2}}$	4^2	$3^{3\frac{3}{4}}$	PincyLJr^2	HcpS 92	Riot inParis122	PayTribute	5
27Mar76 ^{9}GP	Ⓣ $1\frac{1}{16}$	:46^{4}1:09^{4}1:40^{1}fm	3-5	▲129	$2^{1\frac{1}{2}}$	2^2	$3^{2\frac{1}{2}}$	$8^{4\frac{1}{4}}$	BaezaB^3	HcpS 99	StepForward117	LordHenham	9
6Mar76 ^{9}GP	7 f	:22 :44^{3}1:21^{2}ft	1-3	▲129	4^3	$6^{3\frac{3}{4}}$	$1^{\frac{1}{2}}$	$1^{3\frac{1}{2}}$	BaezaB^2	HcpS 97	FoolishPleasre129	PackrCaptn	10
4Feb76 ^{7}Hia	7 f	:23 :45^{4}1:22^{2}ft	1-3	▲119	$4^{2\frac{1}{4}}$	4^3	1^h	1^7	BaezaB^4	Alw 93	FoolshPleasure119	Dashboard	7
10Oct75 ^{8}Bel	$1\frac{1}{16}$	:46^{4}1:11 1:41^{3}ft	1-5	▲120	$2^{1\frac{1}{2}}$	$1^{1\frac{1}{2}}$	1^h	2no	CordroAJr^6	Alw 94	Stonewalk126	FoolishPleasure	6
13Sep75 ^{8}Bel	$1\frac{1}{4}$	:47^{2}1:10^{4}2:00 ft	$2\frac{3}{4}$	121	5^4	$6^{6\frac{1}{2}}$	6^6	5^{10}	CrdroAJr^4	InvH 89	Wajima119	Forego	7

July 22 Bel 4f ft :46⅖h **July 19 Bel 7f ft 1:26⅗b** **July 15 Bel 4f ft :46b**

When Foolish Pleasure invaded the West Coast in late spring 1976, he was probably unaware of his unpopularity with the top stock at Hollywood Park. Maybe they remembered the way Avatar and Diabolo were "bounced" right out of contention during the stretch run of the 1975 Kentucky Derby. Maybe they wanted to chase Leroy Jolley and his horse back East on the next plane. In any case, Foolish Pleasure's first race at Hollywood Park, on June 6, was much like his second race at Hollywood, on June 20. I think the chart and the Trackman's comments for the latter race tell the story quite graphically.

EIGHTH RACE
Hollywood
JUNE 20, 1976

1¼ MILES. (1.58⅘) HOLLYWOOD GOLD CUP. Purse $250,000 Guaranteed. A handicap for 3-year-olds and upward. By subscription of $150 each, to accompany the nomination, $750 to pass the entry box and $2,000 additional to start, with $150,000 guaranteed to the winner, $40,000 to second, $30,000 to third, $20,000 to fourth, and $10,000 to fifth. Weights, Sunday, June 13. Starters to be named through the entry box by closing time of entries. A Gold Cup of original design will be presented to the owner of the winner. Trophies will be presented to the winning trainer and jockey. Closed Wednesday, June 9, 1976, with 21 nominations.
Value of race $250,000, value to winner $150,000, second $40,000, third $30,000, fourth $20,000, fifth $10,000. Mutuel pool $372,617. Exacta Pool $285,230.

Last Raced	Horse	Eqt	A	Wt	PP	¼	½	¾	1	Str	Fin	Jockey	Odds $1
6Jun76 ^{8}Hol^2	Pay Tribute		4	117	7	$3^{1\frac{1}{2}}$	3^1	$3^{\frac{1}{2}}$	3^1	$1^{1\frac{1}{2}}$	$1^{3\frac{1}{4}}$	Castaneda M	13.90
12Jun76 ^{6}Hol^1	Avatar	b	4	123	8	5^2	5^1	6^{hd}	$6^{1\frac{1}{2}}$	$2^{\frac{1}{2}}$	2^2	McHargue D G	7.50
6Jun76 ^{8}Hol^1	Riot in Paris	b	5	123	3	4^{hd}	4^1	4^1	4^1	5^2	$3^{\frac{3}{4}}$	Toro F	a-2.40
31May76 ^{8}Hol^1	Dahlia		6	121	4	2^1	$2^{2\frac{1}{2}}$	2^1	$2^{\frac{1}{2}}$	4^1	$4^{\frac{1}{2}}$	Shoemaker W	a-2.40
6Jun76 ^{8}Hol^3	Foolish Pleasure		4	126	1	$7^{2\frac{1}{2}}$	6^{hd}	$7^{1\frac{1}{2}}$	7^3	7^4	$5^{2\frac{3}{4}}$	Pincay L Jr	1.80
23May76 ^{8}Hol^1	Ancient Title	b	6	127	5	6^1	$7^{3\frac{1}{2}}$	$5^{\frac{1}{2}}$	5^{hd}	6^1	6no	Hawley S	1.70
29May76 ^{6}Hol^1	Our Talisman	b	4	115	6	1^2	1^4	1^1	1^{hd}	3^{hd}	$7^{3\frac{1}{2}}$	Olivares F	a-2.40
31May76 ^{8}Hol^6	Top Command		5	116	2	8	8	8	8	8	8	Mena F	a-2.40

a–Coupled: Riot in Paris, Dahlia, Our Talisman and Top Command.
OFF AT 5:53 PDT Start good, Won ridden out. Time, :23⅕, :45⅘, 1:10, 1:34⅗, 1:58⅘ Track fast.

$2 Mutuel Prices:				
	4–PAY TRIBUTE	29.80	9.40	3.40
	5–AVATAR		9.00	3.60
	1–RIOT IN PARIS (a–entry)			2.40
	$5 EXACTA 4–5 PAID $360.00.			

Ch. c, by High Tribute—Drummer Girl, by Tompion. Trainer McAnally Ronald. Bred by Elmendorf Farm (Ky).
PAY TRIBUTE taken in hand after a clean break dropped behind the early leaders went up gradually into the far turn, attended the pace to the three sixteenths pole, drew out and into a clear lead under coaxing then stretched his margin in the last sixteenth under a hand ride. AVATAR raced unhurried early, moved nearer leaving the far turn, entered the stretch from between horses in the middle of the track to rally and prompted the winner then lost his full punch. RIOT IN PARIS saving ground raced close enought to the three furlong pole, remained inside pointing for a hole approaching the furlong pole but had to take up when blocked, steered out and around but could not regain his full momentum. DAHLIA broke alertly to be closest the early lead, rallied on the far turn to share the lead to the upper stretch and faded. FOOLISH PLEASURE placed on the rail while being outrun early, checked when blocked into the far turn, remaned without room passing the quarter pole, swung wide for a clear path then could not make up the needed ground. ANCIENT TITLE showed little early speed and came out from the quarter pole while perhaps in light contact with AVATAR and lacked a late rally. OUR TALISMAN set the pace and faltered. TOP COMMAND was always outrun.
Owners— 1, Elmendorf; 2, Seeligson A A Jr; 3, Bradley & Whittingham; 4, Hunt N B; 5, Greer John L; 6, Kirkland Ethel Estate Of; 7, Murty Farm & Schwartzman (Lessees); 8, Martin Mr-Mrs Q & Murty Farm.
Trainers— 1, McAnally Ronald; 2, Doyle A T; 3, Whittingham Charles; 4, Whittingham Charles; 5, Jolley Leroy; 6, Stucki Keith L; 7, Rettele Loren; 8, Whittingham Charles.
Scratched—Mateor (23May76 7Hol10).

Bettors at Aqueduct on July 5, 1976, probably needed no introduction to Foolish Pleasure. When you win a Derby and $1 million in two racing seasons it's hard not to make an impression. But only chart savers at Aqueduct would have known that Foolish Pleasure's two California races were not as bad as they appeared in the past performances. The Hollywood Gold Cup chart, along with many of the nation's most important stakes race result charts, appears regularly in all editions of the *Daily Racing Form*. I strongly recommend saving these charts too. You will pick winners from them. In the modern age of Thoroughbred racing a trainer will not hesitate to ship a good horse 3,000 miles and back again for a weekend shot at a stakes-class purse.

Fine-line decisions are intrinsic to the handicapping process, and result charts invariably present more clues to the right side of the line than the "p.p.'s." Sometimes these additional clues provide an insight or an excuse for a recent defeat, or force a reappraisal of a horse's physical condition. And sometimes they point out an extra dimension of quality not otherwise detectable from the past performances. The following two race result charts speak volumes to the point I am making. The first is one of my personal favorites. The salient points are underlined.

SIXTH RACE
Garden State
NOVEMBER 9, 1972

1 $\frac{1}{16}$ MILES. (1.41) ALLOWANCE. Purse $6,000. 3-year-olds and upward which have not wontwo races of $5,200 at a mile or over since June 15. 3-year-olds, 119 lbs. Older 122 lbs. Non-winners of three races of $4,225 at a mile or over since May 15 allowed 3 lbs. such a race of $3,900 since then, 5 lbs. such a race of $4,225 since April 15, 7 lbs. (Maiden, claiming and starter races not considered). (Originally carded to be run at 1 1/16 Miles, Turf.)

Value of race $6,000, value to winner $3,600, second $1,200, third $660, fourth $360, fifth $180. Mutuel pool $114,235.

Last Raced	Horse	Eqt.	A.	Wt	PP	St	¼	½	¾	Str	Fin	Jockey	Odds $1
23Oct72 ^{8}GS^5	Laplander	b	5	119	5	5	6	5^{hd}	5^6	4^4	$1^{3\frac{1}{2}}$	Barrera C	2.70
21Oct72 ^{9}CT^5	Test Run		6	119	3	1	2^2	2^3	4^{hd}	2^{hd}	$2\frac{1}{2}$	Keene J	20.50
21Oct72 ^{8}Lrl^2	Seminole Joe		4	119	4	3	$3^{1\frac{1}{2}}$	4^5	$1\frac{1}{2}$	$1\frac{1}{2}$	3^1	Iannelli F	7.30
21Oct72 ^{6}Lrl^1	Duc by Right	b	5	119	2	2	1^2	1^2	$2\frac{1}{2}$	3^{hd}	$4\frac{1}{2}$	Moseley J W	4.40
27Oct72 ^{8}GS^6	Warino	b	4	119	7	4	4^2	$3\frac{1}{2}$	$3^{1\frac{1}{2}}$	5^8	5^8	Hole M	3.30
27Sep72 ^{8}Atl^6	Roundhouse	b	4	119	1	6	5^2	6	6	6	6	Tejeira J	16.70
23Oct72 ^{5}Aqu^3	Prince of Truth	b	4	122	6	7	—	—	—	—	—	Blum W	2.20

Prince of Truth, Lost rider.

Time, :23⅘, :47⅕, 1:12⅘, 1:39⅕, 1:45⅘ Track slow.

$2 Mutuel Prices:				
	5-LAPLANDER	**7.40**	**4.20**	**2.80**
	3-TEST RUN		**11.00**	**4.60**
	4-SEMINOLE JOE			**4.20**

B. g, by Assemblyman—Reindeer, by Polynesian. Trainer Kulina J. Bred by Fowler A (Md).
IN GATE AT 2:55; OFF AT 2:55 EASTERN STANDARD TIME Start Good For All But PRINCE OF TRUTH Won Driving

LAPLANDER, forced to steady and steer wide to avoid a loose horse inside of him entering the clubhouse turn, fell back, recovered gradually nearing the end of the backstretch, circled rivals rallying into the stretch, again steadied and moved inside to miss the loose horse, gained command leaving the furlong grounds and gradually drew clear. TEST RUN pressed the early pace, reached close contention from the inside in upper stretch was in tight a furlong out and faltered. SEMINOLE JOE was forced to check lightly by the loose horse entering the clubhouse turn, recovered quickly, reached the lead from the outside nearing the stretch, came in when intimidated by the loose horse a furlong out, was straightened away and faltered. DUC BY RIGHT went to the front at once, drew clear and was tiring when placed in close quarters between horses by SEMINOLE JOE in the drive. A claim of foul lodged by the rider of DUC BY RIGHT against the rider of SEMINOLE JOE was not allowed. WARINO was forced wide into the first turn, was taken in hand, rallied to reach close contention from the outside entering the stretch and tired. ROUNDHOUSE was never a factor. PRINCE OF TRUTH stumbled and unseated his rider at the start, raced with his field and caused repeated interference.

Owners— 1, Buckingham Farm; 2, Oliver & Stanley; 3, Sugar Mill Farm; 4, Haffner Mrs H Y; 5, Nesbitt H J; 6, Brandywine Stable; 7, Tucker J R.
Trainers— 1, Kulina J; 2, Oliver D; 3, Stirling W Jr; 4, Wahler C; 5, Cocks W; 6, Raines V W; 7, Jennings L W.
Scratched—Best Go (18Sep72 ^{8}Atl^6); Vif (27Oct72 ^{8}GS^8).

On the day Laplander was playing tag with a riderless horse at Garden State Park, a claiming horse named Third Law was giving Maryland racing fans a first-class impersonation of O. J. Simpson.

FOURTH RACE

Laurel

NOVEMBER 9, 1972

7 FURLONGS. (1.22½) CLAIMING. Purse $7,150, of which $650 to breeder of winner. 3-year-olds, Registered Maryland-Breds. Weights, 122 lbs. Non-winners of two races since September 18, allowed 2 lbs. A race since then, 4 lbs. A race since September 11, 6 lbs. Claiming price $12,500; for each $1,000 to $10,500, 2 lbs. (Races where entered for $9,500 or less not considered.)

Value of race $7,150, value to winner $3,900, second $1,430, third $780, fourth $390; $650 to Breeder of Winner. Mutuel pool $87,225.

Last Raced	Horse	Eqt.A.Wt	PP St	¼	½	Str	Fin	Jockey	Cl'g Pr	Odds $1
20Oct72 ⁴Lrl⁶	Third Law	3 116	7 2	7ʰᵈ	7½	4½	1¹	Jimenez C	12500	40.60
29Sep72 ⁸Bel⁶	Admiral Kelly	b 3 118	1 8	2½	1ʰᵈ	2²	2½	Turcotte R L	12500	4.10
24Oct72 ⁵Lrl¹	All Above	3 119	3 1	1ʰᵈ	2¹½	1ʰᵈ	3ʰᵈ	Feliciano B M	12500	1.40
24Oct72 ⁵Lrl⁷	Rigel	b 3 116	4 6	5½	3½	3ʰᵈ	4½	Passmore W J	12500	6.10
4Nov72 ⁴Lrl¹	Gunner's Mate	b 3 113	8 3	6⁴	6²	6³	5¹	Cusimano G	10500	4.90
24Oct72 ⁵Lrl⁸	Go Bet	3 116	2 4	3½	4ʰᵈ	5ʰᵈ	6²½	Kurtz J	12500	22.70
2Nov72 ⁸Lrl⁵	Hoosier Grand	3 116	6 7	8	8	7³	7³½	Wright D R	12500	6.40
3Nov72 ⁵Lrl⁷	Sky Flight	3 116	5 5	4½	5²½	8	8	Alberts B	11500	12.90

Time, :23⅗, :47, 1:13, 1:26 Track fast.

$2 Mutuel Prices:

7-THIRD LAW	83.20	20.60	5.80
1-ADMIRAL KELLY		5.80	3.60
3-ALL ABOVE			3.20

B. g, by Quadrangle—Flighty Jane, by Count Fleet. Trainer Green P F. Bred by Kelly Mrs L C (Md).

IN GATE AT 2:28; OFF AT 2:28 EASTERN STANDARD TIME. Start Good. Won Driving.

THIRD LAW, away in good order but without early speed, had to check stoutly behind horses on the stretch turn, went to the rail entering the stretch, responded strongly when set down, had to pull sharply outside ADMIRAL KELLY for racing room a furlong out but continued strongly to gain command and draw clear in the final seventy yards. ADMIRAL KELLY, away a bit slowly, was hustled up to force the pace inside all above before a quarter, got the lead leaving the backstretch, lost and regained it inside all above in the stretch, then could not resist the winner's closing bid while tiring near the end. ALL ABOVE set or forced the pace outside ADMIRAL KELLY throughout but hung slightly near the end. RIGEL, always in contention, responded between horses in the final quarter but was not good enough. GUNNER'S MATE did not threaten with a mild closing response. GO BET gave an even effort. HOOSIER GRAND showed little. SKY FLIGHT had only brief early speed.

Owners— 1, Master's Cave; 2, Audley Farm Stable; 3, Lee C; 4, Leonard R A; 5, Green Lantern Stable; 6, DiNatale J; 7, Hunt R R; 8, Berry C T Jr.

Trainers— 1, Green P F; 2, Thomas G; 3, Lee C; 4, Hacker B P; 5, Delp G G; 6, Bannon J T; 7, Vogelman R E Jr; 8, Simpson J P.

Overweight: Gunner's Mate 1 pound.

Armed with the Trackman's notes about the winner in each of these two races, we should have no difficulty imagining that Laplander and Third Law were able to step up sharply in company and win with ridiculous ease shortly thereafter. It is not stretching the point to say that a few equally revealing charts a season could more than pay for the cost of a subscription to the *Form*. Frankly, I could fill the rest of this book with four-star Trackman comments that pointed out horses who gave better showings than the past performance profiles revealed. But there are other important result chart clues that never find their way into the past performance profiles. Let's go back to Hollywood Park for an everyday example.

Wool Jacket **113** **Ro. f (1973) by Try Sheep—French Jacket by Short Jacket.**
Breeder, Middle Ranch (Calif.).
Owner, J. Morjoseph. Trainer, G. Jones. **$13,000**

1976	9	2	2	0	$12,035
1975	4	M	0	0	$1,115

11Jly76 ^{5}Hol	Ⓣ $1\frac{1}{16}$	:47^{4}1:12^{3}1:44 fm	$8\frac{1}{4}$	113	$6^{3\frac{1}{2}}$	2^1	$6^{5\frac{1}{2}}$	5^6	MenaF^{10}	13000	73	ⒻWhyMreWrry116	NvrLetGo	12
27Jun76 ^{1}Hol	Ⓣ $1\frac{1}{16}$	:46^{4}1:11^{2}1:43^{2}fm	20	114	$7^{9\frac{1}{2}}$	$5^{3\frac{3}{4}}$	4^3	$5^{4\frac{1}{4}}$	RamirzR^9	13000	78	ⒻDallasMiss116	HisBoy'sPia	10
18Jun76 ^{1}Hol	$1\frac{1}{16}$	:47 1:12 1:44^{2}ft	4	114	$7^{5\frac{1}{4}}$	9^6	9^9	8^{11}	NoguezA^5	14000	62	ⒻSchon116	HisBoy'sPia	10
10Jun76 ^{5}Hol	1	:47^{1}1:13 1:39^{4}sl	10	112	$5^{5\frac{1}{2}}$	3^1	1^h	1^3	NoguezA^4	12500	67	WoolJacket112	DesertSailor	10
26May76 ^{5}Hol	1	:45^{4}1:10^{4}1:36^{4}ft	9	115	10^{15}	9^{11}	9^{15}	7^{16}	PincyLJr^2	18000	66	ⒻSave aLittle116	NshuaTryst	10
5May76 ^{2}Hol	1	:47^{1}1:11^{4}1:37^{2}ft	$9\frac{1}{2}$	116	6^6	$7^{5\frac{1}{4}}$	5^6	4^6	ToroF^8	20000	73	ⒻCpriciousDrm121	Sve aLtle	10
21Apr76 ^{3}Hol	$1\frac{1}{16}$	:47^{3}1:12^{3}1:44^{4}ft	8-5	▲116	$4^{4\frac{1}{2}}$	4^2	2^4	$2^{4\frac{1}{2}}$	ShokrW^5	c16000	66	ⒻMajinai116	WoolJacket	6
8Apr76 ^{4}SA	$6\frac{1}{2}$ f	:22^3 :46 1:17^{4}gd	$5\frac{1}{2}$	114	7^5	$5^{3\frac{1}{2}}$	3^2	1^h	HlyS^{10}	M20000	84	ⒻWoolJacket114	NowSean	10
18Mar76 ^{3}SA	6 f	:22^1 :46 1:11^{2}ft	$7\frac{1}{2}$	117	10^{10}	$7^{6\frac{3}{4}}$	4^5	2^8	MenaF^2	M20000	74	ⒻChquitaTryst117	WoolJackt	11
22Dec75 ^{3}BM	6 f	:22^4 :46^{2}1:11^{3}gd	30	117	$7^{5\frac{1}{2}}$	$5^{5\frac{1}{2}}$	$5^{2\frac{1}{2}}$	$4^{5\frac{3}{4}}$	CaballroR^4	Mdn	76	ⒻAllWekEnd 117	PortalesIsle	12

July 6 Hol 4f ft :49h **June 6 Hol 3 ft :38h** **June 1 Hol 4f ft :48⅖h**

FIFTH RACE
Hol
July 11, 1976

$1\frac{1}{16}$ MILES (Turf). (1:39⅘). CLAIMING. Purse $11,000. 3-year-olds and upward. Fillies and mares. 3-year-olds, 112 lbs.; older, 122 lbs Non-winners of two races at one mile or over since April 8 allowed 2 lbs; of such a race since then, 4 lbs.; of a race since then, 6 lbs. Claiming price $16,000. 1 lb. allowed for each $1,000 to $13,000. (Claiming and starter races for $12,500 or less not considered.) Winners prefered.

Value to winner, $6,050; second, $2,200; third, $1,650; fourth, $825; fifth, $275. Mutuel Pool, $209,123. Exacta Pool, $497,210.

Last Raced	Horses	Eqt A	Wt	PP	St	¼	½	¾	Str	Fin	Jockeys	Owners	Odds to $1
27Jun76 ^{1}Hol^4	Why More Worry	b5	116	9	12	$7^{\frac{1}{2}}$	4^h	1^1	1^3	1^2	WShoemaker	M Ritt	2.10
27Jun76 ^{1}Hol^7	Never Let Go	b4	116	11	11	12	$10^{\frac{1}{2}}$	7^h	4^1	2^2	FToro	H T Sheridan	10.30
27Jun76 ^{1}Hol^3	April's Hope	b4	114	8	10	10^1	$9^{\frac{1}{2}}$	6^1	3^h	3no	SHawley	Riplyn K Stable	4.50
27Jun76 ^{1}Hol^1	Dallas Miss	5	120	12	5	8^1	$7^{\frac{1}{2}}$	$5^{\frac{1}{2}}$	$2^{\frac{1}{2}}$	4^2	OVergara	Daverick Stable	2.50
27Jun76 ^{1}Hol^5	Wool Jacket	3	113	10	9	$5^{\frac{1}{2}}$	6^h	2^h	$6^{\frac{1}{2}}$	5^1	FMena	J Morjoseph	8.30
4Jly76 ^{2}Hol^6	Society Kid	6	116	7	4	4^2	$5^{1\frac{1}{2}}$	$3^{\frac{1}{2}}$	5^1	6^1	RRosales	R F May	19.70
11Jun76 ^{3}Hol^5	Miss Elite	4	110	6	8	$9^{1\frac{1}{2}}$	8^1	8^2	7^2	$7^{1\frac{1}{2}}$	RMGonz'l'z^5	N B Hunt	26.80
29Apr76 ^{5}Hol^8	One Chicken Inn	4	114	4	7	$6^{\frac{1}{2}}$	11^2	$9^{3\frac{1}{2}}$	8^1	8^3	MCastaneda	Mrs R Sahm	39.00
20Jun76 ^{1}Hol^5	Lady Nephilim	5	110	1	2	$2^{\frac{1}{2}}$	$1^{\frac{1}{2}}$	$4^{\frac{1}{2}}$	9^4	9^5	VCalvaJr^5	Royal Hawaiian Stable	61.30
3Jun76 ^{9}Hol^4	Shirley's Wish	b4	113	2	6	11^1	12	11^5	$10^{\frac{1}{2}}$	10no	RCespedes	Hickory Mill Farm	46.10
4Jly76 ^{2}Hol^5	Sand Storm	5	116	5	3	$3^{2\frac{1}{2}}$	$3^{\frac{1}{2}}$	10^h	11^{12}	11^{25}	DGM'Hargue	Benford-Smith	16.50
3Jun76 ^{8}Hol^8	Glitter	4	116	3	1	$1^{\frac{1}{2}}$	2^1	12	12	12	JGuzman	P Lerner	68.60

OFF AT 4:06 PDT. START GOOD. WON DRIVING. Time, :23, :47⅘, 1:12⅗, 1:37⅖, 1:44. Track firm.

$2 Mutuel Prices

9-WHY MORE WORRY	6.20	4.40	3.20
11-NEVER LET GO		8.40	5.40
8-APRIL'S HOPE			3.80

$5 EXACTA (9-11) PAID $188.00

Dk. b. or br. m, by Time Tested—Wave of Joy, by Johns Joy. Trainer, R. Frankel. Bred by W. M. Wickham (Ky.).
WHY MORE WORRY was bumped at the start, rallied wide and drew out in the stretch. NEVER LET GO was steadied at the start, took up behind a wall of horses at the quarter-pole, then when clear, closed to the end. APRIL'S HOPE broke slowly, maneuvered for room and improved her positioin in the drive. DALLAS MISS lost ground and tired after a mild bid. MISS ELITE raced blocked midway and could make little impact. LADY NEPHILIM broke alertly to share the lead along the rail and faltered. GLITTER lost her action.

If you give a careful reading to the chart and compare it with Wool Jacket's July 11 running line, you will discover several missing facts:

1. Specific eligibility conditions for the race ($16,000–$13,000 claiming, and so on).
2. Fractional times for each quarter-mile split (p.p.'s show two splits).
3. Position at the start of the race (missing from the p.p.'s).
4. Position at first quarter-mile split (missing from p.p.'s).
5. Blinkers or no blinkers (available in Eastern-edition p.p.'s).
6. Exact age, weight, odds, jockey, owner, running pattern, and finishing position for entire field (weight and margins of top three finishers available in Eastern-edition p.p.'s).
7. Index date, track, and race number of most recent start by each member of the field.
8. Purse value of the race (missing from p.p.'s).

NOTE: In result charts the margins at each call refer to the horse's margin in front of the *next* horse. In past performance profiles the margins indicate lengths behind the *leader*.

Ordinarily, trackman Jay Woodward includes a comment for each and every prominent horse in the field. For no apparent reason, no remark appears for Wool Jacket, a horse that seemed to make a giant move entering the stretch, only to fall back out of contention in the drive to the wire. Woodward is, however, one of the top chart callers in the country. He, Jack Wilson (New York), Dick Carroll (Detroit), and Bill Phillips (part-time chart caller, full-time columnist) are the four most precise chart callers I have ever had the pleasure of reading. The only unreliable track-man I have ever read has retired and died. May he rest in peace. As for result charts, we have just scratched the surface. With a little research and a few investigative tools, we can use the added information to obtain even more substantial clues, clues that can increase our understanding of the horse, the track, and the nature of the game itself.

4.
The Bias of
the Racing Surface

Suppose someone walked up to you and said he knew a roulette wheel in a Las Vegas casino that was rigged in the player's favor. The wheel paid the customary 32–1 odds for a correct number but seldom stopped on any number higher than 20. I am sure you would have trouble believing it.

With a few important variations, that is precisely what I am about to tell you about the majority of racetracks in America. *Some numbers rarely win.*

At Pimlico racecourse in Baltimore, Maryland, where the first turn is less than a stone's throw from the starting gate in $1\frac{1}{16}$-mile races, horses with sprint speed and inside post positions have a ready-made shot at saving ground and a clear-cut winning edge. Conversely, horses forced to break from post positions nine, ten, eleven, or twelve in such races have to be far superior and perfectly ridden to remain in contention. And there are many racetracks in America with a bias like that. Aqueduct in New York ($1\frac{1}{8}$ miles on the main track, $1\frac{1}{16}$ miles on the new inner dirt track) is a well-known example. But the Fair Grounds in New Orleans and Churchill Downs in Louisville are rarely considered in a similar light.

Most players approach two-turn races at these two racetracks with an eye toward the fast-closing distance-type runner. It's hard to think otherwise while the two longest stretch runs in American racing are in full view. (Each is over 1,300 feet.) But these are two extremely elongated racetracks, with radically sharp turns. And the starting gate is frequently positioned so close to the first bend that the race is over before the stretch comes into play. A player who knows that about the Fair Grounds and Churchill may not pick the winner of every two-turn race, but very often he will be able to plot the way a race is likely to be run. In addition, he will catch many well-meant speed types outrunning their apparent distance limitations.

And there are other kinds of biases worth knowing

about. At Keystone racetrack in Pennsylvania, Garden State Park in New Jersey, and all other racetracks open for business during cold-weather months, extra layers of topsoil are frequently mixed with antifreeze agents to keep the racing surface from turning into a sheet of ice. The effort is usually successful, but not always; sometimes the rail is like a paved highway, and sometimes it's a slushy path to a quick and certain defeat.

No doubt it would be superfluous to spell out the impact such aberrant track conditions have on horse performance, so I won't. But I will say that a handicapper will probably think about throwing away his *Racing Form* if he doesn't take note of them. Indeed, if there is one pervasive influence on the handicapping experience, track bias comes very close to filling the bill. While it isn't fair to say that all races are won and lost because of the influence of a biased racing strip, the player can hardly hope to make consistently accurate predictions without weighing its significance. For instance, take Saratoga, the beautiful track in upstate New York that annually runs a twenty-four-day August meet.

A decade ago Saratoga had a soft racing surface that was biased in the extreme toward stretch runners and outer post positions. This may have contributed to a considerable extent to the track's reputation as a "graveyard for favorites." Confronted with a typical Saratoga race, most players were naturally impressed with recent winners shipping up from Aqueduct, a track that still tends to get pasteboard hard and front-running fast during July. At Saratoga very few of these horses were able to duplicate their prior good form, and race after race went to horses with the best late kick. In the 1960s observant horseplayers could eliminate a lot of short-priced, front-running horses at Saratoga; they can't do that anymore.

In 1974 a new, faster racing strip was installed, and it has turned Saratoga into a front runner's paradise. Now the player has to respect Aqueduct form; the two tracks are nearly identical. Track biases exist, but they are not necessarily the same from year to year.

When Calder racetrack (Florida) was going through its growing pains with the only artificial racing surface in American Thoroughbred racing, a horse capable of running half a mile on the lead in 46 seconds and change, which is not especially fast time at most racetracks, was a horse in fantastic shape. He couldn't win very many races at Calder —the track was powerfully tilted toward stretch-running speed—but when and if the stable was able to keep such a speedball fit enough to get a crack at Hialeah or Gulfstream Park, it was fat city.

Today the Calder-to-Gulfstream angle still works because Gulfstream has the kind of racing surface that speed horses dream about. At the same time, a fit front runner at Calder is no longer an automatic throwout. Times change, people change, and so do track biases.

But track biases do exist. Every racetrack has its peculiarities. Some are small in circumference, some have pasteboard-hard running surfaces, some card races that place a premium on early speed or post position. And nothing can help to change or create a bias as effectively as a shift in weather conditions. A sudden rainstorm on an otherwise normal racetrack is odds on to force a premium on early speed. On the other hand, a few days of rain, a sudden frost, or extreme heat can have totally unpredictable effects. It's wise to hold onto your money during such drastic changes in weather—unless, of course, you are able to see what is happening firsthand.

Out at the track, any racetrack, it is relatively easy to spot a track bias if you:

Watch the turns.
Observe the running patterns. Are horses able to make up

ground going to the outside or is the rail the only place
to be?

Watch the break from the gate. Are horses in certain post
positions always a bit late getting into the hunt?

Watch the run to the first turn (especially in route races).
Are horses able to settle into contending positions from
outer post positions without undue effort?

And watch the top jockeys. Do they consistently steer their
horses to one part of the track over another? (Frankly,
I'm not at all sure I should mention jockeys in this con-
text, because all but a handful seem unable to recognize
a bias until they have lost a bunch of races because of
it. Of course, there are exceptions; and if you happen to
be at a track where Sandy Hawley, Jorge Velasquez,
Angel Cordero Jr., Willie Passmore, Mike Venezia, or
Vince Bracciale Jr. are riding, watch them. They will
spot a favorable path on the racing strip in two or three
runs of the course.)

If you are unable to attend races regularly or are
planning an assault on a new track, the only way to spot a
bias is through careful reading of the result charts. But even
if your on-track observations have detected a bias—it's hard
not to notice the presence of one when six races in a row are
won wire to wire—you will need to refer to the charts to
note those horses that were stuck on the outside, blocked, left
at the gate, or handed the race on a silver platter.

A horse stuck on the rail on a dead rail day will have a
ready-made excuse. A speed horse that cruised to a front-
running victory because it drew into a favorable post may
not be as good as it seems. By way of example I am including trackman Jack Wilson's comments and the charts for
the first four main-track races run at Saratoga on August
21, 1976. If the player had reviewed charts from preceding
days, the front-running accent would have been hard to
miss. (During a rainy spell earlier in the meet, speed held

up, but the inside was a bog.) On August 18, 19, and 20 the inside part of the racetrack was faster than the outside. The charts for August 21 indicate that the tendency toward inside speed was overpowering.

FIRST RACE Sar August 21, 1976 — **6 FURLONGS. (1:08). MAIDENS. CLAIMING. Purse $7,500. Fillies. 2-year-olds. Weight, 119 lbs. Claiming price, $20,000; 2 lbs. allowed for each $1,000 to $18,000. Value to winner $4,500; second, $1,650; third, $900; fourth, $450. Mutuel Pool, $93,694. Off-track betting, $82,077.**

Last Raced	Horse	Eqt	A	Wt	PP	St	¼	½	Str	Fin	Jockeys	Owners	Odds to $1
13 Aug76 ^{1}Sar^{3}	By by Chicken	b	2	115	8	1	$1\frac{1}{2}$	2^{3}	1^{h}	1^{h}	JVelasquez	Harbor View Farm	1.70
13 Aug76 ^{1}Sar^{9}	Sun Bank	b	2	119	5	2	2^{h}	1^{h}	2^{2}	$2^{2\frac{1}{4}}$	MVenezia	B Rose	b-4.30
13 Aug76 ^{1}Sar^{8}	Mean Katrine	b	2	115	1	3	5^{2}	$5\frac{1}{2}$	4^{2}	$3\frac{3}{4}$	ASantiago	Robdarich Stable	7.50
	Peach Flambeau		2	117	4	5	4^{h}	$4^{1\frac{1}{2}}$	$3\frac{1}{2}$	$4^{1\frac{3}{4}}$	DMcHargue	J W LaCroix	a-7.40
	I Gogo	b	2	112	6	9	6^{h}	$6\frac{1}{2}$	6^{1}	$5^{2\frac{1}{2}}$	KWhitley^{7}	Brookfield Farm	18.50
13 Aug76 ^{9}Sar^{6}	Good Party		2	115	3	4	3^{2}	$3\frac{1}{2}$	$5\frac{1}{2}$	6no	EMaple	N A Martini	12.50
25 Jly 76 ^{2}Del^{5}	Tootwright	b	2	119	2	10	$7\frac{1}{2}$	7^{3}	7^{4}	7^{5}	PDay†	D Sturgill	3.00
	North Ribot		2	115	7	8	8^{2}	8^{1}	$8\frac{1}{2}$	8^{h}	MPerrotta	Betty Rose	b-4.30
27 Jun76 ^{9}Bel^{8}	Hot Dogger	b	2	117	9	6	9^{1}	$9\frac{1}{2}$	$9^{1\frac{1}{2}}$	$9\frac{1}{2}$	TWallis	Judith McClung	21.20
13 Aug76 ^{9}Sar^{4}	Behavingaise	b	2	117	10	7	10	10	10	10	RTurcotte	J W LaCroix	a-7.40

†Seven pounds apprentice allowance waived.
b-Coupled, Sun Bank and North Ribot; a-Peach Flambeau and Behavingaise.
OFF AT 1:30 EDT. Start good. Won driving. Time, :22⅘, :46⅗, 1:12⅗. Track fast.

Official Program Numbers↘

$2 Mutuel Prices:			
7-BY BY CHICKEN	5.40	3.40	2.80
2-SUN BANK (b-Entry)		4.60	3.40
3-MEAN KATRINE			3.60

B. f, by The Pruner—Chicken Little, by Olympia. Trainer, Lazaro S. Barrera. Bred by Carl L. Broughton (Fla.).

BY BY CHICKEN saved ground while vying for the lead with SUN BANK and prevailed in a stiff drive. The latter raced outside BY BY CHICKEN while dueling for command and narrowly missed. MEAN KATRINE finished evenly while saving ground. PEACH FLAMBEAU rallied approaching midstretch but hung. I GOGO failed to seriously menace while racing wide. GOOD PARTY tired from her early efforts. TOOTWRIGHT, off slowly, failed to be a serious factor. NORTH RIBOT was always outrun. BEHAVINGAISE showed nothing.

Claiming Prices (in order finish)—$18000, 20000, 18000, 19000, 20000, 18000, 20000, 18000, 19000, 19000.
Scratched—Lots of Flair.

SECOND RACE Sar August 21, 1976 — **1⅛ MILES. (1:47). CLAIMING. Purse $8,500. 3-year-olds and upward. 3-year-olds, 117 lbs.; older, 122 lbs. Non-winners of a race at a mile and a furlong or over since Aug. 1 allowed 3 lbs.; of such a race since July 15, 5 lbs. Claiming price, $12,500; 2 lbs. allowed for each $1,000 to $10,500. (Races when entered to be claimed for $8,500 or less not considered.)**
Value to winner $5,100; second, $1,870; third, $1,020; fourth, $510. Mutuel Pool, $131,999. Off-track betting, $95,870.

Last Raced	Horse	Eqt	A	Wt	PP	St	¼	½	¾	Str	Fin	Jockeys	Owners	Odds to $1
7 Aug76 ^{1}Sar^{6}	Tingle King	b	4	114	1	3	$2\frac{1}{2}$	3^{4}	$1^{1\frac{1}{2}}$	1^{5}	1^{6}	RTurcotte	Vendome Stable	5.40
7 Aug76 ^{1}Sar^{4}	O'Rei		7	113	4	5	4^{h}	4^{h}	4^{4}	3^{3}	2^{4}	TWallis	Mrs L I Miller	3.40
13 Aug76 ^{3}Sar^{1}	Mycerinus	b	5	122	8	7	7	7	6^{2}	4^{7}	3no	MVenezia	Audley Farm Stable	3.40
7 Aug76 ^{2}Sar^{7}	Good and Bold		5	117	5	2	3^{4}	$2\frac{1}{2}$	2^{3}	$2\frac{1}{2}$	$4^{9\frac{1}{2}}$	EMaple	S Sommer	4.00
18 Aug76 ^{7}Sar^{8}	Slaw		3	107	7	4	6^{2}	$6\frac{1}{2}$	7	5^{2}	5^{8}	RD'g'diceJr^{5}†	Betty Anne King	26.40
7 Aug76 ^{1}Sar^{9}	Gene's Legacy	b	4	106	6	6	5^{1}	5^{6}	$5^{1\frac{1}{2}}$	6^{1}	$6^{6\frac{1}{2}}$	KWhitley^{7}	Beau-G Stable	10.40
13 Aug76 ^{3}Sar^{2}	Mister Breezy		4	113	3	1	$1^{1\frac{1}{2}}$	$1\frac{1}{2}$	$3^{1\frac{1}{2}}$	7	7	JCruguet‡	M M Garren	2.50

†Two pounds apprentice allowance waived. ‡Five pounds apprentice allowance waived.
OFF AT 2:05 EDT. Start good. Won handily. Time, :23⅗, :47, 1:11⅕, 1:36⅘, 1:50⅖. Track fast.

$2 Mutuel Prices:			
2-TINGLE KING	12.80	5.80	4.20
3-O'REI II.		5.20	4.00
7-MYCERINUS			3.40

B. c, by Bold Legend—Miss Tingle, by Avant Garde. Trainer, Flint S. Schulhofer. Bred by D. Shaer (Md.).

TINGLE KING raced forwardly into the backstretch, took over while saving ground into the far turn and drew away while being mildly encouraged. O'REI II., never far back, finished well to be second best without menacing the winner. MYCERINUS, void of early foot, passed tired horses. GOOD AND BOLD, a factor to the stretch, tired. MISTER BREEZY stopped badly after showing speed to the far turn.

Overweight—Tingle King, 1.
Claiming Prices (in order of finish)—$10500, 10500, 12500, 12500, 12500, 10500, 10500.
Scratched—Campaigner.

Daily Double (7-2) Paid $56.60; Double Pool, $303,256; OTB Pool, $515,166.

I must confess that I was not at Saratoga on August 21, 1976. I was home writing this book. In fact, I missed the entire Saratoga meeting, which is something I'd rather not do again. Saratoga is a special place, a racetrack where the trees outnumber the people, where the best of racing is on display for twenty-four glorious summer days. Oh, it gets hot in Saratoga Springs. Very hot. But with a track bias like the one you just got a peek at, with races and bets like the one you are about to contemplate, a good player will tell time by the coming of the Saratoga season. Frankly, I've enjoyed the experience of writing this book—I might even do another. But I'll be damned if I ever do one during August again.

6th Saratoga

AUGUST 21, 1976

1¼ MILES SARATOGA — Start / Finish

1¼ MILES. (2:01). 107th running TRAVERS. SCALE WEIGHTS. $100,000 added. 3-year-olds. Weight, 126 lbs. By subscription of $200 each, which shall accompany the nomination; $500 to start, with $100,000 added. The added money and all fees to be divided: 60% to the winner, 22% to second, 12% to third, and 6% to fourth. The winner shall have his name inscribed on the Man o' War Cup and a gold plated replica will be presented to the owner. Trophies will also be presented to the winning trainer and jockey. Closed with 22 nominations.

McKenzie Bridge 126

B. c (1973), by Le Fabuleux—Nanticious, by Nantallah.
Breeder, Carver Stable (Ky.). 1976.. 9 2 1 1 $82,566
Owner, Mrs. Douglas Carver. Trainer, J. S. Dunn. 1975.. 4 1 1 0 $9,626

11 Aug76	^{8}Sar		1⅛	:46^{1}1:10^{3}1:48^{4}gd	3	114	10^{17}	$9^{6\frac{3}{4}}$	$4^{2\frac{1}{2}}$	4^3	McHeDM^6	AlwS 88	FatherHogan114	DanceSpell	10
27 Jun76	^{8}Hol		1¼	:45^{2}1:09^{3}1:59^{1}ft	5¾	114	9^{12}	$6^{6\frac{1}{2}}$	5^6	$5^{9\frac{1}{4}}$	McHeDG^5	AlwS 86	MajsticLight114	CrystlWatr	9
5 Jun76	^{7}Bel		1½	:47 1:11^{1}2:29 ft	6½	126	9^{22}	7^{12}	$3^{7\frac{1}{2}}$	2^{nk}	McHgeD^2	ScwS 75	BoldForbes126	McKzeBrdge	10
24 May76	^{7}Bel		1$\frac{1}{16}$	:46^{2}1:10^{4}1:42^{3}ft	3	113	$7^{7\frac{1}{2}}$	6^6	$5^{1\frac{1}{4}}$	$1^{2\frac{1}{4}}$	VasquezJ^7	Alw 89	McKnzieBridge113	FthrHgn	7
2 May76	^{6}Hol	Ⓣ	1$\frac{1}{16}$	:47^{1}1:12^{4}1:42^{4}fm	3-2	118	5^5	$2^{1\frac{1}{2}}$	$5^{4\frac{1}{2}}$	$5^{3\frac{3}{4}}$	ShoakerW^6	Alw 81	Delta Junction 121	Lean To	6
17 Apr76	^{8}Hol		1⅛	:46 1:09^{3}1:48^{2}ft	152	122	9^{13}	7^8	$6^{6\frac{1}{2}}$	$4^{4\frac{1}{2}}$	AlvarezF^9	SpwS 85	CrystalWater122	Life'sHope	11
28 Mar76	^{8}SA		1⅛	:46 1:10^{1}1:48 ft	16	120	8^{13}	9^9	9^{15}	9^{21}	HawleyS^6	SpwS 71	An Act 120	Double Discount	9
17 Mar76	^{8}SA		1⅛	:47^{1}1:11^{4}1:48^{4}ft	3-2	▲118	8^{12}	$6^{3\frac{1}{2}}$	5^5	$3^{6\frac{3}{4}}$	ShakerW^3	SpwS 81	June's Blazer 118	Pindoro	8
24 Jan76	^{6}SA		1$\frac{1}{16}$	:45^{4}1:10^{4}1:43 ft	3½	114	4^{10}	4^1	2^h	1^4	ShoakerW^7	Alw 87	McKenzieBrdge114	Spoonwd	7
2 Nov75	^{8}SA		1$\frac{1}{16}$	:46^{1}1:10^{4}1:43^{3}ft	21	118	8^8	$8^{6\frac{1}{2}}$	6^7	$5^{6\frac{3}{4}}$	OlivresF^7	SpwS 77	Telly'sPop118	Imcrnishprnce	8
25 Oct75	^{6}SA		6½ f	:21^4 :44^{4}1:16^{1}ft	4½	118	7^{10}	4^5	$4^{2\frac{1}{2}}$	$2^{4\frac{3}{4}}$	ToroF^1	Alw 87	PntedWgn115	McKnzieBdge	7

Aug 19 Sar 4f ft :48⅗b **Aug 10 Sar 4f sy :50⅕b** **Aug 5 Sar 4f ft :49b**

Quiet Little Table 126

Gr. g (1973), by Mr. Leader—Grey Table, by Grey Sovereign.
Breeder, Meadowhill (Ky.). 1976 9 5 1 2 $104,781
Owner, Meadowhill. Trainer, P. G. Johnson. 1975 1 1 0 0 $5.400

11 Aug76	^{8}Sar		1⅛	:46^{1}1:10^{3}1:48^{4}gd	2½	▲123	$5^{7\frac{1}{2}}$	3^1	$6^{3\frac{1}{4}}$	$6^{8\frac{3}{4}}$	MapleE^8	AlwS 82	FatherHogan114	DanceSpell	10
10 Jly 76	^{8}Aqu		1⅛	:46^{4}1:36^{1}1:49 ft	2½	▲111	2^h	$1^{\frac{1}{2}}$	1^5	$1^{2\frac{1}{2}}$	MapleE^7	HcpS 90	Quiet Lttle Tble 111	Sir Lstr	8
30 Jun76	^{8}Aqu		1	:45^{1}1:08^{4}1:34^{1}ft	2	114	3^2	$5^{1\frac{3}{4}}$	3^2	$3^{1\frac{1}{2}}$	TurctteR^1	AlwS 93	Dance Spell 114	Zen	6
5 Jun76	^{8}Bel		1$\frac{1}{16}$	:45^{2}1:10 1:42^{1}ft	4¼	119	$1^{\frac{1}{2}}$	$1^{\frac{1}{2}}$	1^4	$1^{2\frac{3}{4}}$	MapleE^4	Alw 91	QuietLittleTable119	KirbyLe	7
26 May76	^{6}Bel		1⅛	:46 1:10^{3}1:49^{1}ft	3¾	112	2^4	$2^{1\frac{1}{2}}$	1^h	1^{nk}	MapleE^4	Alw 81	QuietLittleTable112	Chrlstn	5
17 May76	^{5}Bel		1	:45^{3}1:09^{4}1:35^{1}ft	4-5	▲115	$2^{2\frac{1}{2}}$	$2^{1\frac{1}{2}}$	$1^{1\frac{1}{2}}$	1^3	MapleE^5	Alw 92	QuietLittleTble115	RdAnchr	6
10 May76	^{6}Bel		1$\frac{1}{16}$	:46 1:10 1:42^{3}ft	6	111	$2^{\frac{1}{2}}$	1^h	$2^{\frac{1}{2}}$	2^2	MapleE^8	Alw 87	Sawbones110	QuietLttleTble	8
20 Apr76	^{8}Aqu		6 f	:22^2 :45^{1}1:10^{1}ft	1	▲110	4^2	4^5	3^4	$1^{1\frac{3}{4}}$	MapleE^4	Alw 92	QuietLittleTble110	Balancer	7
10 Apr76	^{5}Aqu		6 f	:22^3 :46^{1}1:10^{4}ft	3½	▲117	4^4	4^4	$4^{4\frac{1}{2}}$	$3^{3\frac{1}{4}}$	MapleE^5	Alw 86	Bonge 117	Distinctively	9
5 Oct75	^{5}Bel		6 f	:23 :46^{3}1:11^{4}ft	2	122	$3^{\frac{1}{2}}$	2^h	$1^{\frac{1}{2}}$	1^2	CstedaM^2	Mdn 83	QuietLittleTable122	PvtThts	9

Aug 18 Sar 6f ft 1:12⅖h **Aug 5 Sar 1⅛m ft 1:53⅗b** **July 26 Bel 6f ft 1:14⅕h**

Majestic Light 126

B. c (1973), by Majestic Prince—Irradiate, by Ribot.
Breeder, O. M. Phipps (Ky.). 1976 13 6 1 3 $229,123
Owner, Ogden M. Phipps. Trainer, John Russell. 1975 7 1 0 2 $8,400

7 Aug76	^{8}Mth		1⅛	:46 1:10 1:47 ft	5¼	122	7^{12}	5^4	$1^{\frac{1}{2}}$	1^6	HawleyS^3	InvH 105	MajesticLight122	Appssnato	10
18 Jly 76	^{8}Hol	Ⓣ	1⅛	:48 1:12 1:48^{1}fm	2	▲121	$7^{8\frac{1}{2}}$	6^4	$2^{\frac{1}{2}}$	1^1	HawleyS^5	HcpS 95	MajesticLight121	L'Heureux	10
4 Jly 76	^{6}AP	Ⓣ	1⅛	:48^{1}1:12^{2}1:49^{1}fm	2½	121	10^9	$8^{5\frac{1}{2}}$	$3^{5\frac{1}{2}}$	$2^{1\frac{1}{2}}$	CrdoAJr^1	HcpS 89	Ffth Mrine 121	Mjstic Lght	11
27 Jun76	^{8}Hol		1¼	:45^{2}1:09^{3}1:59^{1}ft	20	114	7^{10}	5^4	$3^{1\frac{1}{2}}$	$1^{3\frac{1}{4}}$	HawleyS^7	AlwS 95	MajesticLght114	CrystlWatr	9
5 Jun76	^{7}Bel		1½	:47 1:11^{1}2:29 ft	14	126	6^{16}	$5^{9\frac{1}{2}}$	4^{12}	4^9	VelasqzJ^6	ScwS 66	BoldForbes126	McKzeBrdge	10
15 May76	^{8}GS	Ⓣ	1$\frac{1}{16}$	1:43^{1}fm	6¾	117	9^{15}	$7^{9\frac{1}{2}}$	$5^{1\frac{3}{4}}$	$1^{\frac{1}{2}}$	BarreraC^9	HcpS 89	Majestic Light 117	Chati	12
5 May76	^{8}GS	Ⓣ	1	1:39^{3}fm	2½	115	$7^{5\frac{1}{2}}$	6^4	$4^{1\frac{1}{2}}$	$1^{3\frac{1}{2}}$	BarreraC^7	Alw 75	MajsticLight115	NobleAdml	8
16 Apr76	^{5}Aqu		1	:46^{1}1:10^{2}1:36 ft	27	117	8^9	7^{10}	7^{10}	6^9	BaezaB^6	Alw 77	BestLaidPlns119	Practitionr	8
11 Mar76	^{8}Aqu		1	:46^{4}1:12 1:37^{1}sy	5	113	$2^{\frac{1}{2}}$	$2^{1\frac{1}{2}}$	$3^{3\frac{1}{2}}$	$5^{8\frac{1}{4}}$	CrdroAJr^2	Alw 72	Be-A-Son 113	Cabriolet II.	6
28 Feb76	^{6}Aqu		1	:48^{2}1:13^{3}1:39^{1}ft	7-5	▲117	3^1	2^h	1^h	$1^{1\frac{1}{2}}$	CordroAJr^6	Alw 70	MajesticLight117	Resilient	6
20 Feb76	^{8}Aqu		1	:46^{3}1:11^{3}1:37^{2}ft	6-5	▲119	6^8	4^6	4^4	$3^{1\frac{1}{4}}$	CordroAJr^3	Alw 78	Kupper 115	Distinctively	8

Aug 17 Sar 7f ft 1:26b

Honest Pleasure 126 Dk. b. or br. c (1973), by What a Pleasure—Tularia, by Tulyar.
Breeder, Waldemar Farms, Inc. (Fla.). 1976 8 4 2 1 $229,172
Owner, B. R. Firestone. Trainer, LeRoy Jolley. 1975 8 6 2 0 $370,227

7 Aug76 8Mth	1⅛ :46 1:10 1:47 ft	1	*126	2½	1½	2½	36	PerretC4	InvH 99	MajesticLight122	Appssnato	10
27 Jly 76 8Mth	1 1/16 :46 1:10 1:41¹ft	1-10	*115	1½	1½	2h	2½	BaezaB1	Alw 97	PeppyAddy119	HonestPlsure	6
15 May76 8Pim	1 3/16 :45 1:09 1:55 ft	4-5	*126	2²	2²	4²	57¼	BaezaB6	ScwS 87	Elocutionist126	Play theRed	6
1 May76 8CD	1¼ :45⁴1:10²2:01³ft	2-5	*126	2⁵	2½	2½	2¹	BaezaB5	ScwS 88	BoldForbes126	HonestPlesre	9
22 Apr76 7Kee	1⅛ :48 1:12³1:49²ft	1-10	*121	1⁴	1⁵	1²	1½	BaezaB2	SpwS 90	HontPlease121	CertnRoman	7
3 Apr76 9GP	1⅛ :46⁴1:10³1:47⁴ft	1-20	*122	1³	1³	1³	1³	BaezaB3	AlwS 95	HonestPlsre122	GrtContrctr	6
28 Feb76 9Hia	1⅛ :45⁴1:09 1:46⁴ft	1-3	*122	1²	1⁸	1⁸	1¹¹	BaezaB7	ScwS 98	HonestPleasure122	IncaRoca	8
11 Feb76 Hia	7 f :23 :45²1:22²ft		122	1¹	1⁴	1¹⁰	1¹⁴	BaezaB4	SpwS 93	HonestPlease122	ParcForiln	4

Exhibition race; no wagering.

1 Nov75 8Lrl	1 1/16 :45⁴1:10³1:42⁴ft	1-5	*122	1¹	1³	1½	1¾	BaezaB3	ScwS 99	HonestPlasure122	Whtsyrple	7
18 Oct75 8Bel	1 :45 1:10¹1:36²sy	6-5	*122	1½	1½	1⁵	1⁷	BaezaB9	ScwS 86	HonestPleasre122	DnceSpell	14
8 Oct75 8Bel	7 f :22⁴ :45²1:22³ft	2¾	121	1³	1⁴	1⁵	1⁸	BaezaB7	AlwS 89	HnestPlsre121	Whtsyrplsure	7

Aug 19 Sar 4f ft :46⅕h Aug 14 Sar 7f ft 1:25h

Romeo 126 B. c (1973), by T. V. Lark—Gallizzie, by Tiger Wander.
Breeder, P. Madden (Ky.). 1976 17 3 2 3 $53,760
Ownre, Mary Lou Cashman. Trainer, Paul Adwell.

7 Aug76 7AP	Ⓣ 1 1/16 :47⁴1:12⁴1:44¹fm	9	114	12¹⁰	7⁴½	7¹⁰	8¹¹	GavdiaW2	HcpS 77	Effervescing113	Rule theRge	13
29 Jly 76 9AP	1 1/16 :47¹1:11²1:42¹sy	6-5	*115	4¹	2¹	1½	1¾	GavidiaW6	Alw 101	Romeo 115	Auberge	7
17 Jly 76 6AP	Ⓣ 1 1/16 :48¹1:12¹1:43⁴fm	2¼	115	4⁵½	2¹	3¹½	4³¼	GavidiaW7	Alw 87	NatvePraise117	Fightmaster	9
4 Jly 76 6AP	Ⓣ 1⅛ :48¹1:12²1:49¹fm	12e	111	3⁴	3²	6⁸	6⁹½	SnyderL9	HcpS 81	Ffth Mrine 121	Mjstic Lght	11
27 Jun76 8Hol	1¼ :45²1:09³1:59¹ft	8¾	115	3⁷	4³½	4⁵½	4⁹¼	PincyLJr8	AlwS 86	MajesticLight114	Crystl Wtr	9
13 Jun76 8Hol	1⅛ :46³1:10²1:47²ft	31	115	6⁸	5³	3²	2²	VergraO7	HcpS 93	L'Heureux 119	Romeo	7
23 May76 5Hol	Ⓣ 1 1/16 :46⁴1:11²1:42³fm	7¼	118	7⁴	4¹½	2½	1no	VergaraO7	Alw 86	Romeo 118	Electric Flag	12
8 May76 2Hol	Ⓣ 1 1/16 :48³1:12³1:43¹fm	2	*120	4³	3²	4²	4³½	McHgeDG9	Alw 79	PrinceBoynton115	GasEnrgy	9
25 Apr76 9Hol	Ⓣ 1 1/16 :47²1:11⁴1:42⁴fm	9	120	6⁴½	5³	5³	3⁴½	VergaraO5	Alw 80	Today n'Tmrrw117	HdnWrld	10
17 Apr76 5Hol	Ⓣ 1 1/16 :47³1:11³1:43 fm	7½	120	4²	5²½	3³	3⁵½	VergaraO9	Alw 78	DeltaJnctn120	Tody n'Tmrw	12

Aug 18 Sar 5f ft 1:00h July 28 AP 3f ft :37b July 24 AP 6f ft 1:15⅘b

El Portugues * 126 Ch. c (1973), by Gallant Romeo—Miss Swoon, by Swoon's Son.
Breeder, Copelan & Thornbury (Ky.). 1976..20 2 6 2 $66,593
Owner, E. Ubarri. Trainer, Lazaro S. Barrera. 1975.. 1 M 0 0 $152

11 Aug76 8Sar	1⅛ :46¹1:10³1:48⁴gd	4¾	114	6¹¹	5²	3½	3³	CrdoAJr7	AlwS 88	FatherHogan114	DanceSpell	10
31 Jly 76 8Aqu	Ⓣ 1⅛ :47²1:12¹1:49²fm	8	112	3⁸½	5¹⁰	5⁹½	6⁹¼	VelasqzJ5	HcpS	Mcdred 117	Dream 'n BeLky	7
17 Jly 76 8Pim	1⅛ :46³1:10⁴1:48⁴ft	7¼e	110	7⁶	5⁸	5³¾	4³¾	VelezRI4	HcpS 89	AmericanTradr109	OnTheSly	7
4 Jly 76 6AP	Ⓣ 1⅛ :48¹1:12²1:49¹fm	15	114	7⁶¾	7⁴½	9¹¹	9¹⁰	GvidiaW10	HcpS 81	Ffth Mrine 121	Mjstic Lght	11
27 Jun76 10Tdn	1⅛ :46 1:10³1:49⁴ft	5½e	112	5³¼	3½	3¹	4³	VelezRI14	AlwS 88	Return of a Native115	Cojak	14
14 Jun76 8Bel	1 1/16 :47 1:11³1:43⁴ft	3-5	*110	5²¼	3³	3³	2³¾	CordroAJr1	Alw 79	Brown Cat 117	El Portugues	6
23 May76 8Bel	1 :45³1:10¹1:36 ft	8-5	*116	6⁴¾	5³	5¹¾	2½†	CrdroAJr6	AlwS 87	Sir Lister114	El Portugues	9

†Disqualified and placed third.

8 May76 8Bel	1 :45³1:10 1:35 ft	8¼	126	6⁷	5⁴	2²	2½	CrdroAJr2	ScwS 92	Sonkisser 126	El Portugues	6
1 May76 6Aqu	1 :45 1:09 1:34³sy	5½	110	5³¼	4⁵½	3⁸	2⁸½	AmyJ7	Alw 84	Cinteelo 104	El Portugues	7
24 Apr76 6Aqu	1 :45²1:09 1:35 ft	9½	113	5⁸½	5⁷½	5⁶½	5⁴¾	VelasquzJ3	Alw 86	NewCllection112	Cplet'sSng	7

June 24 Tdn 5f ft 1:02b

Legendaire 126 Ch. c (1973), by Le Fabuleux—Native Guide, by Raise a Native.
Breeder, W. P. Little (Ky.). 1976.. 8 2 1 0 $15,157
Owner, Silk Willoughby Farm. Trainer, J. P. Conway. 1975.. 4 1 0 0 $5,400

11 Aug76 8Sar	1⅛ :46¹1:10³1:48⁴gd	19	114	9¹⁶	10⁸¾	9⁸¾	7¹⁰	TurctteR4	AlwS 81	FatherHogan114	DanceSpell	10
31 Jly 76 6Aqu	Ⓣ 1⅛ :47²1:12 1:50 fm	11	112	3³	1h	6⁶¼	6³¾	TurctteR1	HcpS	FabledMonrch114	Effrvscing	8
10 Jly 76 8Aqu	1½ :46⁴1:36¹1:49 ft	9	112	6⁷½	7¹¹	7¹⁶	7¹⁵	VasquzJ4	HcpS 75	Quiet Lttle Tble 111	Sir Lstr	8
26 Jun76 8Bel	1 1/16 :46²1:11 1:42 ft	6	113	7⁴½	3¹	1¹	1²¾	VasquezJ2	Alw 92	Legendaire113	RedAnchor	7
13 Apr76 7Kee	1 1/16 :47¹1:11¹1:43¹ft	7	113	6³¾	6⁹	6¹²	6²⁰	BrumfldD5	Alw 70	No Link 121	Inca Roca	6
24 Mar76 8GP	Ⓣ a 1 1:39 fm	6	116	8⁹½	6³½	5³¾	4⁴†	MarquzC5	Alw 82	Hall ofRean114	Fightmaster	10

†Placed third through disqualification.

6 Mar76 6GP	1 1/16 :47²1:12¹1:43⁴ft	2¼	*122	4⁵	3³	2½	1¾	RuaneJ5	Alw 82	Legendaire122	ArchieBmish	11
20 Feb76 7Hia	7 f :22⁴ :46¹1:24 ft	62	115	10⁹	6⁶	3¹½	2nk	MapleE3	Alw 85	Sonkisser 122	Legendaire	11
21 Nov75 7Aqu	1 :44⁴1:08⁴1:34⁴sy	11	122	9¹⁸	9³⁰	9³²	9⁴⁰	CastandaK5	Alw 52	Cinteelo 117	Play the Red	9

Aug 17 Sar 1 ft 1:43b Aug 10 Sar 3f sy :36b Aug 7 Sar 5f ft 1:07b

Dance Spell 126 B. c (1973), by Northern Dancer—Obeah, by Cyane.
Breeder, Christiana Stables (Ky.). 1976.. 7 3 1 1 $72,702
Owner, Christiana Stables. Trainer, J. W. Maloney. 1975..10 2 6 1 $93,846

11 Aug76 8Sar	1⅛ :46¹1:10³1:48⁴gd	3½e	121	2⁵	1¹	1h	2¹	VasquzJ5	AlwS 90	FatherHogan114	DanceSpell	10
10 Jly 76 8Aqu	1½ :46⁴1:36¹1:49 ft	3½	117	3¹	2½	3⁵	3²¾	CrdoAJr8	HcpS 87	Quiet Lttle Tble 111	Sir Lstr	8
30 Jun76 8Aqu	1 :45¹1:08⁴1:34¹ft	3¼e	114	1½	1¹	1²	1¹¼	CdroAJr3	AlwS 95	Dance Spell 114	Zen	6
12 Jun76 6Bel	6 f :22³ :45³1:09³ft	2¾	112	2¹½	3²	6⁸	6¹¹	CruguetJ3	Alw 83	QueenCityLd115	VlidAppeal	6
8 May76 8Bel	1 :45³1:10 1:35 ft	1	*126	2½	2½	4⁴	4⁹	CruguetJ3	ScwS 84	Sonkisser 126	El Portugues	6
21 Apr76 6Aqu	7 f :22⁴ :45⁴1:22 ft	2¼	110	2¹½	2¹½	1¹½	1²¾	CruguetJ1	Alw 91	DanceSpll 110	GabeBnzur	7
31 Mar76 7Aqu	7 f :23 :45⁴1:22³ft	8-5	*111	3¹½	1h	1h	1½	CruguetJ3	Alw 88	DanceSpel 111	Kohoutek	7
29 Nov75 8Aqu	1⅛ :46³1:10⁴1:49¹ft	9-5	*113	3⁵	3¹½	2²½	2½	CrugutJ10	AlwS 88	Hang Ten 116	Dance Spell	12
19 Nov75 8Aqu	6 f :22¹ :45¹1:09⁴ft	2½	115	2¹½	2h	2²½	2²¼	CruguetJ3	AlwS 92	LordHenribee117	DanceSpell	6
1 Nov75 8Lrl	1 1/16 :45⁴1:10³1:42⁴ft	7½	122	3¹½	3³½	3³½	3⁶	CruguetJ7	SpwS 93	HonestPlsre122	Whatsyrplse	7

Aug 20 Sar 3f ft :36b Aug 17 Sar 5f ft :58⅗h Aug 8 Sar 5f sy 1:02⅕b

While it's not necessary to handicap this prestigious stakes race in depth to select Honest Pleasure as a front-running stickout, I am also including (below) the chart of the Monmouth Invitational, the race Majestic Light won over Honest Pleasure by six lengths. The Trackman's comments clearly show that Honest Pleasure was regaining his early season form.

Leroy Jolley wisely stopped on Honest Pleasure after the Preakness debacle (May 15) and was patiently reestablishing the horse's speed and staying power. The recent workouts indicate further progress.

Majestic Light is a slow-breaking, fast-closing three-year-old that appreciates true distance racing. Trainer John Russell has done an excellent job, and there is very little doubt that Majestic Light is fit enough or good enough to win. Thus, a good performance, despite the bias, is possible; however, it's not likely. Much depends on whether Majestic Light can get clear sailing on the rail for an uninterrupted rally. Unfortunately, he will need an unusual degree of co-operation from the rest of the field to get that kind of running room. Finally, he will still have to run faster than Honest Pleasure, who is on the improve and likely to have the rail and the lead for the entire race!

Quiet Little Table, a well-managed speed horse, would have a fine winning chance in any good field. But with Honest Pleasure in the race, Quiet Little Table has virtually no chance at all. It is further doubtful that he has enough speed to stop Honest Pleasure from getting a clear lead over the field in the run to the first turn. That's important for two reasons: (1) most front-running types tend to race better when they are able to relax in front of the pack; (2) everything in Honest Pleasure's record says he is a horse that improves dramatically when he is able to make the lead without undue stress.

Dance Spell has generally good form and cannot be completely eliminated.

The shipper Romeo is a stretch runner that has never beaten a good field.

EIGHTH RACE
Mth
August 7, 1976

1⅛ MILES. (1:48). Ninth running MONMOUTH INVITATIONAL HANDICAP. Purse $100,000. 3-year-olds. by invitation only, with no nomination or starting fees. The winner to receive $65,000, with $20,000 to second; $10,000 to third; and $5,000 to fourth. A representative field of those weighted will be invited to participate. The Monmouth Park Jockey Club reserves the right to reassign weight to any horse after the release of the weights. Owner of the winner to receive a trophy.

Value to winner $65,000; second, $20,000; third, $10,000; fourth, $5,000. Mutuel Pool, $349,197.

Last Raced	Horse	EqtA	Wt	PP	St	¼	½	¾	Str	Fin	Jockeys	Owners	Odds to $1
18 Jly 76 8Hol1	Majestic Light	3	122	3	2	72	72	51½	1½	16	SHawley	O M Phipps	5.30
31 Jly 76 8Aqu5	Appassionato	3	113	7	9	91½	92	92	51½	2no	RHernandez	F A Luro	27.10
27 Jly 76 8Mth2	Honest Pleasure	3	126	4	1	22	24	11½	22½	3½	CPerrtt	B R Firestone	1.10
17 Jly 76 8Pim3	Zen	3	118	6	7	6h	51½	4½	33	42½	JVasquez	Pen-Y-Bryn Farm	3.10
25 Jly 76 8Del1	On The Sly	3	115	2	8	87	86	86	42	51½	GMcCarron	Balmak Stable	6.00
31 Jly 76 8Aqu2	Dream 'N Be Lucky	3	114	5	10	10	10	10	75	66	MSolomone	G A Zimmerman	33.00
17 Jly 76 8Mth6	Wardlaw	b3	115	1	3	3h	32½	32	6h	74	JTejeira	D Lasater	39.30
27 Jly 76 7Mth1	Best Bee	b3	113	10	6	51½	61½	7½	84	86	RWilson	Dixiana	65.10
31 Jly 76 7Aks2	Joachim	b3	117	8	5	42½	41	62	9h	9h	SMaple	E Pratt-J C Van Berg	18.90
17 Jly 76 8Pim1	American Trader	b3	114	9	4	13	11½	2h	10	10	AAgnello	Mrs B Cohen	19.60

OFF AT 5:57 EDT. Start good. Won driving. Time, :22⅗, :46, 1:10, 1:34⅗, 1:47 (new track record). Track fast.

B. c, by Majestic Prince—Irradiate, by Ribot. Trainer, J. W. Russell. Bred by O. M. Phipps (Ky.).

$2 Mutuel Prices:				
	3–MAJESTIC LIGHT	12.60	6.80	4.20
	7–APPASIONATO		19.40	6.20
	4–HONEST PLEASURE			2.80

MAJESTIC LIGHT, taken in hand after the start, angled to the outside leaving the clubhouse turn, remained outside when roused under a flurry of right-handed whipping at the far turn, brushed lightly with ZEN on the stretch turn but continued strongly to gain the lead in the upper stretch, swerved out when struck left-handed at the eighth-pole but continued to draw off with authority and was under only mild encouragement in the final seventy yards. APPASSIONATO, outrun for three-quatrers, rallied gamely outside the leaders when roused for the drive but could not threaten the winner. HONEST PLEASURE, reserved off the early pace outside AMERICAN TRADER, moved willingly to the lead when asked at the far turn, resisted the winner gamely in the stretch but hung in the closing yards. ZEN rallied just inside MAJESTIC LIGHT at the far turn, brushed with that one but finished with good courage. ON THE SLY did not reach contention with a mild closing rally. JOACHIM and AMERICAN TRADER were finished after three-quarters.

Overweight—Dream 'N Be Lucky, 1 pound.

In summary, what we have here is a fit front-running racehorse of obvious quality getting a track he should absolutely relish. The betting crowd made the wrong favorite.

SIXTH RACE
Sar
August 21, 1976

1¼ MILES. (2:01). 107th running TRAVERS. SCALE WEIGHTS. $100,000 added. 3-year-olds. Weight, 126 lbs. By subscription of $200 each, which shall accompany the nomination; $500 to start, with $100,000 added. The added money and all fees to be divided: 60% to the winner, 22% to second, 12% to third, and 6% to fourth. The winner shall have his name inscribed on the Man o' War Cup and a gold plated replica will be presented to the owner. Trophies will also be presented to the winning trainer and jockey. Closed with 22 nominations.

Value of race $108,400. Value to winner $65,040; second, $23,848; third, $13,008; fourth, $6,504. Mutuel Pool, $328,104. Off-track betting, $342,517.

Last Raced	Horse	EqtA	Wt	PP	¼	½	¾	1	Str	Fin	Jockeys	Owners	Odds to $1
7 Aug76 8Mth3	Honest Pleasure	3	126	4	12	16	14	12	13	14	CPerret	B R Firestone	2.10
7 Aug76 7AP8	Romeo	b3	126	5	51½	51½	51	41	2h	21½	BBaeza	Mary L Cashman	49.30
11 Aug76 8Sar2	Dance Spell	3	126	8	41	41	31½	3½	31	33	JCruguet	Christiana Stable	14.70
11 Aug76 8Sar6	Quiet Little Table	3	126	2	31	31½	21	21½	42	4nk	EMaple	Meadowhill	12.50
11 Aug76 6Sar3	El Portugues	b3	126	6	21	2h	41½	5½	5½	51½	JVelasquez	E Ubarri	23.60
11 Aug76 8Sar4	McKenzie Bridge	3	126	1	8	7½	73	712	724	6¾	DMcHargue	Mrs D Carter	4.60
7 Aug76 8Mth1	Majestic Light	3	126	3	7½	6½	62	61½	6½	730	SHawley	O M Phipps	1.00
11 Aug76 8Sar7	Legendaire	b3	126	7	6h	8	8	8	8	8	RTurcotte	Silk Willoughby Fm	64.40

As a footnote to the Travers result chart, you might be interested to know that Dance Spell—the colt that moved outside to launch his bid against the Saratoga bias—came back to win the Jerome Mile in his next start, paying $17.60. That price was inflated by Dance Spell's number-one post position, generally interpreted by most Belmont fans as an unfavorable post. I can well understand that interpretation because the rail is usually dead at Belmont during the fall meeting. Nevertheless, it is my experience with track biases that logic still prevails in such conditions.

A dead rail only eliminates horses that race on the dead rail.

A front runner breaking from post one should be automatically downgraded if not eliminated under such conditions.

A stretch runner breaking from post one may have to give up a length or two at the start. That of course is frequently reason enough to eliminate many stretch runners.

Horses like Dance Spell—those that have tractable speed, speed that frequently permits maneuverability—may yet get trapped along the rail if the jockey is not alert. That's a smaller risk factor, but it cannot be overlooked. Several issues must be balanced against that risk:

How superior is the horse breaking from post one?
How many horses figure to break with him?

How good is the jockey?

Have most of the riders been breaking toward the outside in order to avoid the rail, thus leaving post one with room to maneuver?

What kind of odds are available for the risk?

of encouraging answers to these
qu first and last questions, would
su

EIGHTH red and seventh running JEROME HANDICAP. $100,000
Be iption of $100 each, which shall accompany the nomina-
Septemb'r 0,000 added. The added money and fees to be divided:
cond, 12% to third and 6% to fourth. Trophies will be
Value of race $ er, trainer and jockey. Closed with 30 nominations.
Mutuel Pool, $5 24,420; third, $13,320; fourth, $6,660.

Last Raceu		¾	Str	Fin	Jockeys	Owners	Odds to $1
2¹ Aug76 ⁶Sar³		1¹	1¹½	1³¾	RHernandez	Christiana Stable	7.80
30 Aug76 ⁶Bel³		3¹½	3¹½	2ⁿᵒ	PDay	Strapro Stable	3.00
26 Aug76 ⁸Sar¹		2ʰ	2¹	3²	JImparato	Tartan Stable	30.60
19 Aug/6 ⁸Mth³		5ʰ	4½	4ⁿᵏ	DMontoya	Buckland Farm	61.90
17 Jly 76 ⁸Rkm⁶		4½	5½	5ʰ	MSolomone	Harbor View Farm	31.50
21 Aug76 ⁶Sar⁴		6¹	6¼	6³	EMaple	Meadowhill	7.20
18 Aug76 ⁶Sar¹		3¹½	7¹	7¾	HGustines	Greentree Stable	5.20
18 Aug76 ⁸Mth²		1½	9¹	8ʰ	BBaeza	H I Snyder	3.10
30 Aug76 ⁶Bel²		2	8½	9½	ACorderoJr	Gedney Farms	6.30
11 Aug76 ⁸Sar¹		10	10	10	MVenezia	Sea Spray Farms	8.00
Uncoupled for		LANE.					

OFF AT 5:53½ E , :46⅗, 1:10⅗, 1:35. Track fast.
$2 Mutu 17.60 7.60 4.60
.... 6.00 3.60
.... 9.00

B. c, by Norther es W. Maloney. Bred by Christiana Stable (Ky.).
DANCE SPELL, when ready while racing well out in the track
approaching the stre ....ng while continuing wide. SOY NUMERO UNO,
reserved behind the ...u while racing wide nearing the stretch, lugged in slightly
approaching the final , ...u was just up for the place. A foul claim against SOY NUMERO UNO by the
rider of FULL OUT, for alleged interference through the stretch, was not allowed. CLEAN BILL, off slowly,
rushed through along the rail to take over before going a quarter, remained a factor to midstretch and
weakened. FULL OUT, never far back, remained a factor into the stretch but lacked a late response while
drifting out. LIFE'S HOPE made a mild bid along the inside leaving the turn but hung. QUIET LITTLE TABLE
tired from his early efforts. SAWBONES, outrun early, was sent up between horses leaving the far turn but
failed to be a serious factor. SONKISSER, steadied along while in close quarters between horses approaching
the end of the backstretch, lacked a further response. KIRBY LANE failed to seriously menace while racing
very wide. FATHER HOGAN showed nothing.
Scratched—Fighting Bill.

Dance Spell's next start was in Forego's Woodward Stakes on September 18. Honest Pleasure was also in the field, making his first start since the Travers. Honest Pleasure drew the rail, Dance Spell the extreme outside post in a ten-horse field. There was really no betting issue involved. Forego was a stickout with a tempting 1–1 price, considering his tendency to go off at 1–2. But there is just no margin for profit or error playing horses at those odds.

Because of the post position draw, the second-best horse looked convincingly like Dance Spell; the third choice depended on how much post one would actually cost Honest Pleasure. As the chart below indicates, the Woodward was no less formful than the other two races we have examined in this series of Saratoga-Belmont stakes races.

EIGHTH RACE
Bel
Sept'ber 18, 1976

1⅛ MILES (chute). (1:45⅖). Twenty-third running WOODWARD HANDICAP. $150,000 added. 3-year-olds and upward. By subscription of $100 each, which shall accompany the nomination; $500 to pass the entry box, $1,500 to start, with $150,000 added. The added money and all fees to be divided 60% to the winner, 22% to second, 12% to third and 6% to fourth. Mrs. William Woodward has donated a trophy to be presented to the owner of the winner and trophies will also be presented to the winning trainer and jockey. Closed with 27 nominations.

Value of race, $173,200. Value to winner $103,920; second, $38,104; thirds, $15,588 each. Mutuel Pool, $550,396.

Last Raced	Horse	EqtAWt	PP	St	¼	½	¾	Str	Fin	Jockeys	Owners	Odds to $1
21 Aug76 ^{8}Mth^{3}	Forego	6 135	2	10	7^{h}	7^{h}	7^{2}	4^{3}	$1^{1\frac{1}{4}}$	WShoemaker	Lazy F Ranch	1.10
6 Sep76 ^{8}Del^{4}	Dance Spell	3 115	10	1	6^{4}	$5^{1\frac{1}{2}}$	$2^{\frac{1}{2}}$	1^{h}	$2^{2\frac{3}{4}}$	RHernandez	Christiana Stable	7.10
21 Aug76 ^{6}Sar^{1}	DH Honest Pleasure	3 121	1	2	1^{1}	$1^{1\frac{1}{2}}$	1^{1}	3^{2}	3	CPerret	B R Firestone	2.10
14 Sep76 ^{4}Bel^{1}	DH Stumping	b6 109	4	7	5^{1}	6^{2}	5^{1}	5^{7}	$3^{\frac{1}{2}}$	JAmy	Hobeau Farm	27.80
6 Sep76 ^{8}Bel^{2}	Soy Numero Uno	3 112	5	4	3^{1}	$3^{\frac{1}{2}}$	3^{2}	$2^{\frac{1}{2}}$	$5^{8\frac{1}{4}}$	EMaple	Strapro Stable	11.20
21 Aug76 ^{8}Mth^{1}	Hatchet Man	b5 114	3	9	10	10	$8^{\frac{1}{2}}$	7^{1}	6no	HGustines	Greentree Stable	11.30
21 Aug76 ^{8}Mth^{8}	El Pitirre	4 112	7	5	9^{4}	$9^{\frac{1}{2}}$	9^{h}	$6^{\frac{1}{2}}$	7^{3}	ASantiago	E Ubarri	29.20
6 Sep76 ^{8}Del^{4}	Dancing Gun	b4 112	8	2	$2^{1\frac{1}{2}}$	2^{h}	6^{h}	$8^{\frac{1}{2}}$	8^{h}	JVelasquez	Gedney Farms	37.30
6 Sep76 ^{8}Bel^{8}	Sonkisser	3 117	6	8	$4^{\frac{1}{2}}$	$4^{\frac{1}{2}}$	4^{2}	$9^{1\frac{1}{2}}$	9^{nk}	BBaeza	H I Snyder	37.40
7 Sep76 ^{8}Bel^{8}	Right Mind	5 114	9	6	8^{h}	8^{5}	10	10	10	RTurcotte	Deronjo Stable	70.90

DH Dead–heat.

OFF AT 5:45 EDT. Start good. Won ridden out. Time, :23, :45⅗, 1:09⅕, 1:33⅘, 1:45⅘. Track fast.

$2 Mutuel Prices:			
2–FOREGO	**4.20**	**3.00**	**2.20**
11–DANCE SPELL		**5.40**	**3.00**
1–HONEST PLEASURE (Dead-heat)			**2.20**
4–STUMPING (Dead-heat)			**2.80**

B. g, by Forli—Lady Golconda, by Hasty Road. Trainer, Frank Y. Whitley, Jr. Bred by Lazy F. Ranch (Ky.).
FOREGO, unhurried after breaking slowly, was steadied along while racing along the inside to the turn, eased out for room approaching the three-eighths pole, moved fast while continuing wide after entering the stretch, caught DANCE SPELL inside the final sixteenth and drew clear under good handling. DANCE SPELL, eased back after breaking in front, moved fast to make his bid while racing well out in the track leaving the turn, took over from SOY NUMERO UNO with a furlong remaining but wasn't able to withstand the winner while besting the others. HONEST PLEASURE sprinted to the front along the inside soon after the start, made the pace while racing well out from the rail, held on well to midstretch and finished on even terms with STUMPING while weakening. STUMPING, never far back, finished with good energy. SOY NUMERO UNO, reserved behind the early leaders, moved through along the inside to gain a narrow advantage nearing the stretch, remained prominent to the final furlong and gave way. HATCHET MAN was always outrun. EL PITIRRE was never close. DANCING GUN was finished soon after going five furlongs. SONKISSER gave way after racing forwardly for six furlongs. RIGHT MIND was always outrun.

Track bias is one of the fundamental realities of racing. There really is a logic to the race, a surprisingly consistent stream of logic. But it can rarely be appreciated without understanding the role of the racetrack itself as it influences the flow of the action from start to finish.

A SAMPLE RACE. The Schuylerville Stakes, July 29, 1974. Opening day at Saratoga. Five of the first six races were main-track sprints and all were won wire to wire. Not one horse made a move on the outside all day and no horse was passed in the stretch. The logical front runner in this race paid $22.40. I'll give you one guess. The winner will be revealed in Chapter 12.

7th SARATOGA **JULY 29, 1974**

6 FURLONGS. (1:08) Fifty-seventh running SCHUYLERVILLE (1st Division).

My Compliments **116** B. f (1972), by Delta Judge—Granny's Pride, by Roman.
Breeder, R. L. Reineman (Ky.). 1974 3 2 1 0 $11,580
Owner, R. L. Reineman. Trainer, W. C. Freeman.

Jly 20-74[3]Mth	5½ f	1:05⅕	ft	9-5	▲119	4^{2}	2½	1h	$1^{2\frac{3}{4}}$	RuaneJ[5]	Alw	91	Ⓕ MyComplim'ts119 Q Up Myst'ryM'd	6
Jly 6-74[3]Aqu	5½ f	1:05	ft	6-5	▲117	1½	1^{3}	1^{3}	1^{2}	VeneziaM[6]	Mdn	88	Ⓕ MyC'mpliments117 Aware Q'n'sTurf	7
Jun25-74[3]Aqu	5½ f	1:05	ft	15	117	$6^{3\frac{3}{4}}$	$6^{3\frac{1}{4}}$	3½	2no	VeneziaM[8]	Mdn	88	Ⓕ LadyP'tia117 MyC'plim'ts M'lyB'ne	10

July 27 Sar 4f ft :49⅗b July 17 Aqu 4f ft :47⅗h July 13 Aqu 4f ft :51b

Our Dancing Girl **116** B. f (1972), by Solo Landing—Amber Dancer, by Native Dancer.
Breeder, Elcee-H Stable (Fla.). 1974 5 1 1 2 $11,793
Owner, Elcee-H Stable. Trainer, J. Rigione.

Jly 10-74[8]Aqu	5½ f	1:02⅘	ft	11	115	3^{1}	3^{9}	3^{14}	3^{21}	HoleM[3]	AlwS	78	Ⓕ Ruff'n118 L'gh'gB'dge OurD'c'gGirl	4
Jly 1-74[7]Mth	5½ f	1:06	ft	7¾	117	1^{4}	1h	2^{1}	3^{3}	GallitanoG[6]	Alw	84	PropMan118 Prev'ler OurDanc'gGirl	7
Jun15-74[3]Bel	5½ f	1:06	ft	3¾	116	1^{4}	1^{5}	1^{6}	$1^{4\frac{1}{2}}$	HoleM[4]	Mdn	85	Ⓕ O'rD'c'gG'l 116 Tricks Bl'de ofR's's	10
Jun 7-74[3]Bel	5½ f	1:05⅗	ft	3¼	116	1^{2}	1^{2}	$1^{1\frac{1}{2}}$	2^{1}	HoleM[2]	M40000	86	Ⓕ Curlique116 OurD'c'gGirl SwiftImp	10
May30-74[3]Bel	5½ f	1:06	ft	4½	114	3^{1}	1^{1}	$2^{1\frac{1}{2}}$	$4^{7\frac{1}{2}}$	HoleM[3]	M35000	77	Ⓕ CurtainCall 116 M'snM'se Cl's'gM't	8

July 24 Bel 5f ft :59⅘h July 8 Bel 4f ft :47⅖h June 29 Bel 4f ft :48⅗b

La Bourresque **116** Dk. b. or br. f (1972), by Victoria Park—Nearanna, by Nearctic.
Breeder, J. L. Levesque (Can.). 1974 6 1 2 2 $7,164
Owner, J. L. Levesque. Trainer, J. Starr.

Jly 14-74[6]WO	6 f	1:11⅖	ft	8e	119	5^{4}	$5^{5\frac{1}{2}}$	$5^{4\frac{3}{4}}$	2no	TurcotteN[1]	Alw	86	R'son'bleWin119 LaB'r'sque Dap'rS'dy	12
Jly 6-74[6]WO	6 f	1:11⅗	ft	15	112	3nk	1h	2½	$3^{2\frac{1}{2}}$	D'tfashH[4]	HcpS	83	Ⓕ Deepstar112 M'dowsw't LaB'r'sque	8
Jun27-74[6]WO	6 f	1:13⅗	sl	9½	116	5	$^{2}5^{3\frac{1}{4}}$	5^{6}	$5^{9\frac{3}{4}}$	RogersC[4]	InvH	65	P'sleyPal 117 H'pe forS'Shine Petrus	7
Jun 8-74[4]WO	5½ f	1:04⅗	ft	1	▲119	3½	3^{2}	$3^{3\frac{1}{2}}$	3^{9}	RogersC[6]	Alw	87	Ⓕ Kn'tlyPr's119 M'd'sw't LaB'r'sque	6

Some Swinger **116** Ch. f (1972), by Tirreno—Batting a Thousand, by Hitting Away.
Breeder, H. T. Mangurian, Jr. (Ky.). 1972 4 2 0 1 $6,475
Owner, H. T. Magurian, Jr. Trainer, T. F. Root, Sr.

Jly 8-74[6]Crc	6 f	1:13⅗	ft	4-5	▲118	4¾	$4^{1\frac{3}{4}}$	2½	1^{4}	GuerinE[1]	Alw	85	Ⓕ SomeSw'g'r118 B'PrineR'se Whirl It	8
Jun29-74[9]Crc	5 f	1:00⅘	ft	17	118	$8^{5\frac{3}{4}}$	$8^{3\frac{1}{2}}$	5^{3}	$3^{1\frac{1}{2}}$	GuerinE[5]	HcpS	89	Ⓕ MyM'mN'h113 W'd a.L'l'g S'eS'g'r	12
Jun17-74[2]Crc	5½ f	1:07⅘	ft	9	118	3nk	$1^{1\frac{1}{2}}$	1^{4}	1^{3}	Gr'nst'nB[3]	Mdn	91	Ⓕ S'eS'g'r118 Fl'daN'dles H'K andEye	10
Jun 5-74[2]Crc	5½ f	1:07⅘	sy	18	118	9^{10}	9^{11}	9^{16}	9^{13}	StLeonG[3]	Mdn	78	Ⓕ SoloRoyal 118 Sm'l theRoses OldH'n	9

July 25 Bel 4f sy :46hg July 21 Bel 6f ft 1:16b July 17 Bel 3f ft :37b

Secret's Out

119 **Lt. ch. f (1972), by Royal Saxon—Secret Verdict, by Clandestine.**
Breeder, Mrs. M. W. Schott (Fla.). 1974 4 3 0 0 $24,603

Owner, Marcia Schott. Trainer, J. E. Picou.

Jun19-74^{8}Mth	5½ f 1.04	ft	6	119	2^{1}	$7^{4\frac{3}{4}}$	$6^{9\frac{3}{4}}$	$5^{9\frac{1}{4}}$	B'mf'ldD^{2}	AlwS 88	(F)F'rWind 115 Copernica Fant'ticMiss	7
May26-74^{9}Suf	5 f 1:00⅘	sm	3-5	▲121	1½	1^{2}	$1^{3\frac{1}{2}}$	$1^{3\frac{1}{4}}$	W'dh'eR^{9}	HcpS 85	Secret'sOut121 Inchiq'lah Wh't aT'k't	9
Apr24-74^{7}Kee	4½ f :53⅕	ft	1	▲119	2	1^{3}	1^{1}	$1^{4\frac{1}{2}}$	B'f'ldD^{1}	AlwS 89	(F)S'cr't'sOut119 Fl'lPrinc's Ain'tE'sy	8
Mar15-74^{3}Hia	3 f :33⅖	sy	2¼	▲117	3		1^{1}	$1^{3\frac{1}{4}}$	W'dh'seR^{1}	Mdn 95	(F)S'cr't'sO't117 Ebbtide W'tATrink't	14

July 17 Bel 6f ft 1:12⅘h **July 11 Bel 6f ft 1:13h** **June 29 4f ft :48⅘b**

Precious Elaine

112 **Dk. b. or br. f (1972), by Tom Fool or Advocator—Imgoinaway, by On-and-On. Br., Mrs. J. R. Pancoast (Fla.)** 1974 3 M 1 0 $1,980

(Formerly named Idontlikehim).

Owner, A. J. Brodsky. Trainer, J. P. Conway.

Jly 15-74^{3}Aqu	6 f 1:13	ft	10	117	$1^{1\frac{1}{2}}$	$1^{1\frac{1}{2}}$	1½	$2^{1\frac{3}{4}}$	S'nt'goA^{1}	Mdn 76	(F)GoldB'x117 Pr'ciousEl'ne G'rd nQu'd	11
Jun12-74^{8}Bel	5½ f 1:03	ft	18	112	6^{4}	6^{11}	6^{23}	6^{30}	Cast'daM^{5}	AlwS 70	(F)Ruffian 117 Copernica Jan Verzal	6
May22-74^{3}Bel	5½ f 1:03	ft	4½	116	2^{3}	3^{9}	7^{21}	9^{34}	Cast'daM^{1}	Mdn 66	(F)Ruffian 116 Suzest Garden Quad	10

July 24 Bel 4f ft :49b **July 10 Bel 5f ft 1:00⅕h** **July 5 Bel 3f ft :36⅘b**

But Exclusive

116 **Ch. f (1972), by Exclusive Native—Royal Bit, by Alcibiades II.**
Breeder, L. Combs II. (Ky.). 1974 3 1 2 0 $9,470

Owner, W. A. Levin. Trainer, D. A. Imperio.

Jly 12-74^{4}Aqu	5½ f 1:05⅖	ft	3	118	$6^{5\frac{1}{2}}$	$4^{7\frac{1}{2}}$	3^{6}	2^{4}	VeneziaM^{1}	Alw 82	(F)Sc't'shM'l'dy118 B'tExcl've C's'nlvy	8
Jun22-74^{3}Bel	5½ f 1:05⅕	ft	3-2	▲116	$6^{4\frac{1}{4}}$	2^{2}	2½	1^{h}	VeneziaM^{5}	Mdn 89	(F)ButExclu'vei16 Aw're Sc't'shM'l'dy	9
Jun10-74^{4}Bel	5½ f 1:05⅕	ft	7¾	116	$5^{7\frac{1}{2}}$	4^{6}	4^{5}	$2^{3\frac{1}{2}}$	Ven'ziaM^{1}	Mdn 85	(F)FrchR'le116 B'tExcl've M'lyB'l'tine	10

July 26 Bel 4f ft :48⅕h **July 19 Bel 4f ft :47⅖hg** **July 11 Bel trt 3f ft :35⅖h**

5.
The Money Tree

Trainer Glenn C. Smith will never make the Hall of Fame at Saratoga. But I doubt seriously that he cares.

Mr. Smith, never more than a part-time claiming-horse trainer with few horses and no following, did quite well during the winter meets at Bowie a decade ago. He also helped to teach a particular struggling student of handicapping an important lesson: You can't really understand this game without taking the role of the trainer into account.

It was February 1, 1963, and I had just had a miserable afternoon at Bowie, a zero-for-nine afternoon, and I was not enjoying the four-hour bus ride back to New Jersey one bit. My handicapping had been awful, but the fellow in the back of the bus who had done considerably better was bent on giving me a headache. He was succeeding more than I cared to admit. In exasperation, I opened up the *Racing Form*—half to punish myself, half to get out of his range. What I saw is what you see below—Trojan Seth, the wire-to-wire winner of the sixth race. A 3–1 stickout trained by Mr. Smith.

Trojan Seth * **112** B. h (1958), by Trojan Monarch—Cedquest, by Alquest.
Breeder C B. Caldwell.

Owner, G. C Smith. Trainer, G. C Smith. $7.500

1962	8	4	0	4	$10.422
1961	13	2	3	1	$7,240

Apr27-62^{7}Lrl	7 f 1:24⅖ft	5	114•	1^{2}	1½	2^{2}	3^{2}	AddesaE^{5}	10000	88	Cycount103 C'ch a'dF'r109 Troj'nSeth	6
Apr18-62^{6}Lrl	6 f 1:12⅘ft	3¼	114•	1½	2½	2h	3¾	AddesaE^{5}	10000	90	Klinkh'se116 C'h andF'r108 Tr'j'nSeth	10
Apr 7-62^{6}Lrl	6 f 1:11⅕sy	3	114•	2h	2½	2½	3^{2}¼	AddesaE^{1}	12000	97	Adorette115 Polyn'nB'ly115 Tr'nSeth	7
Mar28-62^{7}Bow	6 f 1:11 ft	6-5	112‡	1^{5}	1^{6}	1^{6}	1^{5}	AddesaE^{1}	Alw	96	Tr'j'nS'th112 S'r andC'm107 En'shS'le	6
Mar17-62^{7}Bow	6 f 1:11⅘ft	3-2e	113	1h	2½	2^{1}	3^{4}†	McKeeC^{2}	Alw	88	Yeuxdoux115 Adorette119 TrojanSeth	7
†Dead heat.												
Mar 5-62^{7}Bow	5½ f 1:05⅖ft	2½	▲117‡	1^{2}	1½	1h	1no	AddesaE^{2}	9000	92	TrojanSeth 117 Dollmaker 117 OleKel	6
Feb20-62^{7}Bow	6 f 1:14⅖m	2¾	▲113‡	1^{3}	1^{1}½	1h	1¾	AddesaE^{6}	8000	79	Trojan Seth 113 Dollmaker 112 Ji-Jo	6
Feb14-62^{7}Bow	6 f 1:14 sy	6-5	▲108‡	1^{1}½	1^{4}	1^{1}	1^{2}½	AddesaE^{2}	7000	81	TrojanSeth108 Dalsax1*4 Tourdan	8
Dec13-61^{6}P.m	6 f 1:13 m	12	107‡	2^{1}	2^{2}	4^{3}½	5^{6}	AddesaE^{5}	9000	79	Ano rArt114 Giewith116 Barb'raLeeG.	7

Jan 30 Bow 1m ft 1:45⅖b

According to all the rules of traditional handicapping theory, Trojan Seth should have been a throwout on the grounds of physical condition. The colt had not been out on the track for a race in over nine months. The workout, a single slow mile just two days before the race, could hardly have sharpened the colt's speed. And as the race shaped up, it was not an easy spot.

There were four recent winnners shipping in from the South and two confirmed $8,500 horses dropping down in class. Now, when it was too late, the bottom two races in Trojan Seth's chart barked out their message.

Instantly, it was clear that Trojan Seth was not a horse that needed to be raced into shape. Was Smith, I wondered, the kind of man who made a habit of such doings?

The answer, along with the cure for my headache, came later that night when I compared the past performance records of all Smith's starters from the previous winter. Nine horses. Thirty-two starts. Ten total victories. An excellent 30 percent win record. But there was more, much more. I checked back over the prior year just to be sure.

There was no doubt about it; this little-known trainer brought considerable skill to his craft. Smith had a pattern. An amazing 60 percent win record with first-time starters and absentees, only one of which was a post-time favorite. But the most astounding part of the pattern was the long, slow workout that accompanied six out of his seven absentee winners. All were sprinters, all showed early speed in their past performances, and all but one scored after several months of inactivity.

The lone exception raced in a route, finished out of the money, and then came back five days later to score in a sprint at 16–1. Mr. Smith was a horseplayer's dream. A veritable money tree. He trained all his horses back on the farm, away from the prying eyes of the clockers and the competition. And the long, slow workout was just the final touch of a well-thought-out training regimen.

Each year Smith invaded Bowie with a stableful of razor-sharp claimers, got the money, went back to the farm, and smiled a lot.

I was smiling too. By meeting's end Smith won nine more races to lead the Bowie trainers. His overall win record was an excellent 30 percent. But he was five for nine with the pattern, and I was four for eight. But the moral of the story is not complete without sharing one additional detail.

One of the nonpattern horses that won for Mr. Smith was a cheap but useful three-year-old named Cedar Key. Smith lost him via the claim box for $5,000, took him back for $6,500, and then lost him again at the end of the meeting for $6,500 to Don McCoy, the same trainer who had taken him away from Smith the first time.

McCoy wanted this colt as badly as Smith, but for a very different reason. McCoy's New York client owned a bakery shop with the identical name—the Cedar Key Bakery. Of such motives are champions made.

Over the next two years, while Smith was breaking his back to win $100,000 in purses with his band of hobbled platers, Cedar Key was winning nearly $200,000 in turf stakes coast to coast. That may be one reason Mr. Smith will never make the Hall of Fame at Saratoga. For what it's worth, he has my vote.

6.
Coaching Counts

There are many successful trainers like Glenn C. Smith. Every racetrack has its aces, and each horseman brings to his craft one or more special skills (or winning strategies) that separate him from the rest of the crowd.

Some are small-time operators, patient men who spend months getting cheap, sore-legged horses fit enough to deliver one or two sharp efforts. Others travel the racing circuit first class, commanding large armies of horses on several fronts. And there are a few—throwbacks to the days when racing was truly the sport of kings—who deal only with the best-bred racing stock money can buy.

Because of these vastly different economic situations, because different trainers have rather personal methods, preferences, and skills, there is no single, simplistic formula that can be applied to a reading of physical condition. Although we all tend to forget it from time to time, the Thoroughbred racehorse is an athlete in the purest sense of the word. And to a far greater degree than most people think, the trainer is its coach.

From dawn until well after dusk, 365 days a year, the trainer must watch over the feed tub, consult the veterinarian, study the *Racing Form,* plan the workout schedule, saddle the horses, watch the day's races, make travel arrangements, supervise the stable help, reassure the owners, select the class, distance, jockey, equipment, and date of the race. The horse is a wonderfully fast, woefully fragile creature, and it takes considerable skill, timing, and patience to keep it in competition. (It also costs the owner about $7,500 a year per horse.)

"I can usually tell when a horse is a race away from losing its form," said Allen Jerkens, master horseman and the best coach a thoroughbred athlete could posssibly want. No other trainer in racing is more dangerous with recently acquired stock and no other trainer is more in touch with the subtle day-to-day changes of the horses in his barn.

"There are many signs," explained Jerkens. "Every horse has his own habits. You get to know them pretty well. The ankle doesn't respond as quickly, or the hair on the coat begins to lose its sheen, or he leaves some feed in the tub. You've got to look them over very carefully. Any change makes an impression." Later, Jenkens added, "If you want to save a horse for future racing, the time to stop on him is *before* he stops on you."

A handicapper who happens to be a reporter can learn a lot touring the backstretch.

"A great many good horses are abused at an early stage in their careers," said articulate John Russell, the versatile horseman in charge of the blue-blooded Phipps Stable, a man with a strong winning history with lightly raced horses stretching out in distance, stakes-class three-year-olds, turf routers, and shippers.

Russell amplified his point. "It's a complex dilemma. First, you have to get a two-year-old to develop a little confidence, train him hard enough to be fit so he gets some benefit out of his racing. Second, the money is out of this world for a good two-year-old; and when you've got one, you have to decide how much potential the horse has to remain sound, how far you think he will want to run, and how much you can afford to push him.

"Frankly," Russell added, "I'm not opposed to breaking a horse's maiden in a first or second start—an early win is a magnificent confidence builder, the best in fact—but I'm more concerned with having a horse reach its natural peak in the spring or summer of its three-year-old season."

Not all trainers can afford the luxury of long-range planning. Where cheap horses are concerned, most goals begin and end with the here and now. Nevertheless, at each racetrack there are a few claiming-horse trainers who seem to have more patience and a better sense of timing than many stakes-class horsemen. One such trainer is Richard E.

Dutrow, who has been ripping up Maryland racing since he graduated from Charles Town minor-class racing in West Virginia a few years ago. Another is King Leatherbury, who for fifteen years has been no less a force on the same circuit. Between them, Leatherbury and Dutrow win approximately 350 of the 1,800 races run in Maryland each season. In a very real sense they are at war with each other, but they conduct their operations in the spirit of détente.

Very rarely do they claim from each other. Very rarely do they compare notes or share insights or anything else. But they respect each other's talent and they learn from each other by competing tooth and nail throughout the long Maryland season.

Dutrow used to have difficulty stretching horses out in distance. Leatherbury is an ace at that. Leatherbury used to win most of his races with horses dropping in class. Dutrow likes to push his horses up the class ladder. Today each trainer has incorporated a few of his rival's methods. Leatherbury still has an astounding 60 percent win record with dropdowns coming back after thirty or more days' rest. But he wins more often with repeaters stepping up in class than he used to. Dutrow still wins one race in every four attempts, a record only the top twenty or thirty trainers in America can claim, but he now wins them at any distance with all types of horses.

"I'm not a claiming-horse trainer," Dutrow said to a bleary-eyed reporter one morning. "At least I'm not anymore. Right now I'm training two-year-olds, stakes horses, turf horses, and as many allowance-class runners as I have claimers." What Dutrow didn't say was that most of the allowance horses in his care started out as claimers before he solved their problems and moved them up in class.

King Leatherbury has more than a few allowance runners in his barn too, but it is still the cheap, sore-legged horse that brings out the man's best work. "When you're dealing with cheap horses, you have to be part horseman, part businessman," he explained. "You have to have the patience to wait on a horse; you can't be too aggressive, too forceful, but you can't waste a whole lot of time either. Once the horse begins to respond, you can't be thinking about next year or next week; you've got to put it in a race where it can win . . . dropping it down a notch or two in class is like taking out insurance."

"I agree," said Johnny Campo, the ebullient, oft-quoted, New York-born and -based horseman who decided he wanted to become a trainer the day he saw a Hopalong Cassidy movie in his youth. Campo is the closest thing to a Damon Runyon character on the New York backstretch, and the Belmont Stakes "Alibi Breakfast" would not be the same without him. Almost unnoticed, or perhaps partially obscured by his deceivingly clownish reputation, Campo is one of the most effective trainers of two-year-old fillies in the country, and he has nearly as much skill with allowance-class routers on the main track and with claimers of every age and sex. While Campo is not the most patient trainer of a promising three-year-old, he has trained two juvenile champions—Protagonist and Talking Picture—and has been among the top five trainers in New York since the day he took out a trainer's licence in 1970.

"I can't tell you how interesting it is to be a trainer," Campo said in a serious moment. But that didn't stop him from trying. By the third sentence he was in high form.

"Every horse is different. Some need a long-drawn-out program to get them to do anything; others will kick down the barn to get in a race or a work every three days. But don't get me wrong," he added, "I'm no genius or anything. I don't do nothing special. I just work hard, harder than most, especially on the legs. I learned a lot about legs from working for Eddie Neloy when he had all those top two-year-olds for Wheatley in the sixties. Don't let anybody tell you that top horses don't have leg problems. All horses have leg problems. That's one thing at least that all horses have in common. Fact is," he continued, "the biggest leg problem I've ever seen was on the best horse I've ever had—Protagonist—and not getting him to the Derby was my biggest disappointment so far. He would've won it. I know he would've won it. But I'll get another chance; I've got some pretty good two-year-olds in my barn right now. But what was that question you asked, something about claimers?"

"Yes, claimers, Johnny—what about claimers? Do you like to drop them in class as often as King Leatherbury?"

"Well, it works both ways," Campo responded. "A drop in class has to help most horses. That's just plain common sense. But sometimes I'll drop a horse in class because I'm praying somebody'll take the stiff off my hands. I'm sure Leatherbury does the same thing. It's like poker. Sometimes you've got to bluff and sometimes you're laying there waiting with the best hand at the table."

Phil Johnson, a first-rate public stable trainer who wins most of his races with two-year-old maidens, first-time starters, fillies, turf specialists, and high-priced claimers, had more to say on this subject: "As a rule, I'm very suspicious about dropdowns. There are few bargains and too many bargain hunters. I much prefer to take a horse that has come to life and is being stepped up a notch or two in company. You can always drop it back a bit later, but a sound, improving horse is where the money is."

Anthony Doyle, who trained the rugged Avatar to a victory in the 1975 Belmont Stakes via a series of demanding workouts at various distances, had some poignant insights into the trainer's dilemma a few hours before his greatest victory. "If you see a horse show some speed when you didn't train it hard enough to expect it, that's the time to think you might have something special," said the Irish-born Doyle, a West Coast–based horseman whose winners at every class level usually telegraph their potential via improved workouts. "But," he added, fully aware that Avatar was going to put up or shut up later in the day, "if you do train a horse hard and draw a blank, the horse is telling you something. Maybe you've made a mistake; maybe blinkers would help or a change of scenery or a switch in distance. Maybe you pushed too hard, or not hard enough. Sometimes you have to guess, sometimes the jockey will give you a clue, and sometimes the answer comes in the middle of the night."

In the middle of the night Charles Town ace Wade Johnson is usually just returning from the track. "By the time I get to work with a horse," said Johnson, "it's had maybe ten, twenty, or thirty starts, four or five different trainers, a couple of major injuries, a lot of medication, and everything has been tried already. But every horse has its hole card and every horse—even a sore-legged, eight-year-old, $1,500 claimer—can be treated with patience and respect.

"When I claim a horse like that, I'm betting my time and money that I can straighten it out fast."

Leroy Jolley, controversial, talented, and every bit as articulate as John Russell, was not talking much during Honest Pleasure's troubles in the 1976 Triple Crown chase. But in a calmer period the previous summer he offered several insights into the pressures faced by the trainer of a million-dollar horse. "If you're shooting for a major race like the Derby or the Travers or the Jockey Club Gold Cup, you can't start thinking about it two weeks beforehand," said the trainer of Foolish Pleasure, Honest Pleasure, and Optimistic Gal.

Jolley continued: "You have to know your horse and know what you are trying to do. Every workout, each race, must have a purpose. Good horses tend to be precocious workers and you have to let them test their limits; get them tired and move them out in distance or up in company step by step. The biggest problem," Jolley said with emphasis, "is not getting them fit but *keeping* them fit. One unlucky break or bad step can ruin a month's worth of training or even end a horse's career. I suppose I've been pretty lucky so far, but I've also been very careful."

"I don't know about the Derby. I've never had a horse good enough to think about it," said Ida Mae Parrish, a Midwestern-based horsewoman who annually demolished the Massachusetts fair circuit (40 percent winners) over a ten-year period. "But to get a stableful of cheap claimers ready to win, you have to freshen them up, give them a lot of long, slow gallops, a decent work or a prep race, and crack down hard at the first sign of improvement. If you get too cute or wait too long to put them in a sensible spot, you'll never pay the feed bills, much less win a race."

According to the American Racing Manual and other authoritative sources, there are approximately 7,000 licensed trainers in North America.

More than a thousand failed to win a single race in 1974, 1975, or 1976.

A thousand more failed to win as few as ten races, and another thousand failed to win twenty.

Looking at this picture from the opposite perspective, the top 400 trainers have won approximately 25 percent of all the purse money distributed in each of the past three calendar years. Barely more than 100 were good enough to win one race in every five attempts.

For his own protection alone, the player should know which trainers have winning skill, what that skill is, and which ones can't train their way out of a paper bag.

7.
The Trainer's Window

In the hands of one trainer, a horse with good recent form might be an excellent wager; in the care of another, the horse might be ready to fall apart at the seams.

In the hands of an ace, a horse stepping up sharply in company or stretching out in distance might well be expected to handle the task; in the care of a lesser talent, such a maneuver might only be an experiment or an unnecessary risk.

Naturally, the vast majority of trainers like to bet to overcome their financial difficulties or to take advantage of their skill; but the player is misled if he thinks they are any better at handicapping than they are at their chosen craft. The horse may have a fine turn of speed or suddenly show signs of life; but if the trainer is impatient, sloppy, or incompetent, he will find a way to lose control of the horse and blow the best of opportunities.

Maybe the horse is crying for a route race on the turf, or perhaps he needs a better jockey or a change in equipment or a shorter resting period between starts. Maybe the horse has been too ambitiously placed too often or has left his race on the training track. You'd be amazed how many horses are mismanaged in that fashion.

The positive and negative impact of the trainer on horse performance is all too rarely taken into account by the average horseplayer, who at best glances at the leading trainers' list and automatically assumes universal competence.

But the mistake is easily corrected, and it is great fun.

After all, the past performance profile is not only a summation of horse performance but a window through which the talents, habits, and strategies of the trainer can be seen.

For example, by comparing the past performance records of a dozen or so winners (and losers) trained by Frank Whiteley Jr., the player will know for a certainty that every last horse this man (and his son David) send to the post is a dangerous contender.

There are no frills, no tricks, no wild experiments.

A sprinter is kept sprinting, a stakes horse is given a balanced, well-spaced campaign, and a first-time starter is well prepared and well meant.

Mistakes are made; but they are seldom repeated. Experiments are tried; but if they do not produce improvement or satisfactory results, the horse is promptly returned to familiar conditions.

You can learn a lot about good horsemanship by looking through the Whiteleys' window.

Forego **137** B. g (1970) by Ferli—Lady Golconda by Hasty Road. Breeder. Lazy F Ranch (Ky.). 1976 7 5 1 1 $321,481; 1975 9 6 1 1 $429.521

Owner, Lazy F Ranch. Trainer, Frank Y. Whiteley. Jr.

18 Sep76 ^{8}Bel	1 1/8	:45^{3}1:09^{1}1:45^{4}ft	1	▴135	76	76 1/2	42 1/2	11 1/4	ShmkrW^{2}	HcpS	98	Forego 135	Dance Spell	10
21 Aug76 ^{8}Mth	1 1/4	:47^{2}1:11^{2}2:00^{3}ft	3-5	▴136	33	22	21	31	VasquzJ^{7}	HcpS	98	HatchetMan112	IntrepidHro	8
24 Jly 76 ^{8}Aqu	1 1/4	:46^{4}1:11^{1}2:01^{1}ft	2-3	▴134	68 1/2	21 1/2	2h	12	CustinsH^{4}	HcpS	90	Forego 134	Lord Rebeau	8
5 Jly 76 ^{8}Aqu	1 3/16	:47^{4}1:11^{2}1:55^{2}ft	2-5	▴134	32 1/2	21 1/2	31 1/2	2no	GustinsH^{2}	HcpS	85	Foolish Pleasure 125	Forego	4
13 Jun76 ^{8}Bel	1 1/8	:47^{2}1:11^{2}1:48^{3}ft	4-5	▴132	42 1/2	32	1h	12 3/4	VsquezJ^{1}	HcpS	84	Forego 132	El Pitirre	5
31 May76 ^{8}Bel	1	:45^{3}1:09^{2}1:34^{4}ft	1	▴130	54 1/2	44	41 1/2	1h	GustinsH^{4}	HcpS	94	Forego 130	Master Derby	6
20 May76 ^{8}Bel	7 f	:23^{4} :46^{4}1:22 ft	1-3	▴126	41 1/2	3 1/2	1h	11 1/4	GustinesH^{2}	Alw	92	Forego 126	Wishing Stone	4

Oct 1 Bel 4f sy :46h Sept 27 Bel 1f ft 1:43⅕b Sept 25 Bel 5f ft 1:05b

Sarsar **117** Ch. f (1972), by Damascus—Durga, by Tatan. Breeder, A. B. Hancock, Jr. (Ky.). 1974 0 M 0 0 (——)

Owner, W. H. Perry. Trainer, D. A. Whiteley.

July 15 Bel 5f ft :58h July 9 Bel 4f ft :49bg July 4 Bel 4f ft :47⅕h

Arabian Law **108** Dk. b. or br. c (1973), by Damascus—Lagides by Lacaduv. Breeder, Mrs. Martha F. Gerry (Ky.). 1976 7 3 3 1 $46,735; 1975 3 M 1 0 $3,060

Owner, Lazy F Ranch. Trainer, D. A. Whiteley.

18Jly 76 ^{8}Aqu	6 f	:22^{1} :45^{1}1:10^{3}ft	6-5	▴112	78	68 3/4	64	1nk	VasqezJ^{3}	HcpS	90	ArabianLaw112	FullOut	7
8Jly 76 ^{8}Aqu	6 f	:22^{2} :45^{1}1:09^{2}ft	8-5	113	63 3/4	62 1/4	2 1/2	2nk	VasquezJ^{1}	Alw	96	SoyNumeroUno111	ArabanLw	6
6Jun76 ^{7}Bel	6 f	:22^{4} :46^{1}1:10^{1}ft	3-5	▴115	64 1/2	62	11	12 3/4	VasquezJ^{7}	Alw	91	ArabianLaw115	TaxBracket	8
20May76 ^{7}Bel	6 f	:22^{3} :45^{3}1:09^{4}ft	3-2	▴114	96 3/4	64	43 1/4	2no	VasquezJ^{4}	Alw	93	KaiserFluff106	ArabianLaw	10
10May76 ^{4}Bel	6 f	:22^{4} :46 1:10^{1}ft	6-5	▴114	64 1/2	33	12	16 1/4	VasqezJ^{11}	Mdn	91	ArabianLaw114	ThirdWorld	12
15Apr76 ^{4}Aqu	1	:44^{3}1:09 1:36 ft	6-5	▴113	58	59	45 1/2	31 1/2	VasquezJ^{1}	Mdn	84	RedAnchor112	Gaytense	10
29Mar76 ^{1}Aqu	6 f	:23^{1} :47 1:10^{4}ft	8	113	83 3/4	53	31 1/2	2 1/2	VasqezJ^{11}	Mdn	88	Arachnoid114	ArabianLaw	12
21Sep75 ^{4}Bel	1	:47^{4}1:12^{4}1:37^{4}m	4 1/4	122	63 3/4	67 1/2	414	419	GustinesH^{4}	Mdn	60	ArtAboveAll 122	RoyalMssion	10

July 15 Bel 4f ft :47h July 5 Bel 4f ft :46⅘h June 30 Bel 4f sl :47⅕h

Revidere **118** Ch. f (1973), by Reviewer—Quillesian, by Princequillo. Breeder, Claiborne Farm (Ky.). 1976 7 7 0 0 $181,018

Owner, W. H. Perry. Trainer, David A. Whiteley.

4 Sep76 ^{8}Bel	1 1/8	:46^{3}1:10^{1}1:47^{4}ft	3-5	▴124	23	23	22	11 1/2	CrdoAJr^{1}	HcpS	88	(F)Revidere124	PcificPrincss	5
5 Jly 76 ^{8}Mth	1 1/8	:48 1:12^{2}1:50^{3}ft	3-5	▴121	21	1 1/2	2h	1h	VasqezJ^{7}	AlwS	87	Reidere 121	Javabine	8
26 Jun76 ^{7}Bel	1 1/2	:48^{2}1:13^{3}2:28^{2}ft	2 1/2	121	2 1/2	1 1/2	2h	1 1/2	VasquzJ^{5}	ScwS	78	(F)Revidere121	OptimisticGal	10
12 Jun76 ^{8}Key	1 1/16	:47^{4}1:12^{2}1:44 ft	3-5	▴118	1h	1h	11 1/2	14	VasqezJ^{3}	AlwS	84	(F)Revidere 118	Critical Miss	8
11 May76 ^{7}Bel	1 1/16	:46 1:10^{4}1:43^{1}ft	6-5	114	2 1/2	1h	12	13	VasquezJ^{7}	Alw	86	(F)Revidere114	Cohabitation	7
22 Apr76 ^{7}Aqu	1	:46 1:10^{3}1:35^{1}ft	6-5	▴114	2 1/2	12	11 1/2	12 3/4	VasquezJ^{7}	Alw	90	(F)Revidere 114	Perl	7
5 Apr76 ^{3}Aqu	7 f	:23^{2} :47^{1}1:25 ft	1-2	▴112	21	2 1/2	11 1/2	17 1/2	VasquezJ^{8}	Mdn	76	(F)Revidere 112	How Pleasing	8

Sept 24 Bel 3f ft :35b Sept 20 Bel 6f ft 1:12⅕h Sept 16 Bel 5f ft 1:02⅕b

NOTE: *Honorable Miss' past performance profile is on page 126.*

If you were to perform a similar study on Jack Van Berg, probably the busiest and best trainer in the Midwest, you would also find unmistakable patterns staring you in the face.

Like Whiteley, Van Berg gives stakes horses consistent, thoroughly professional management. But with claimers and modest-class allowance stock, Van Berg operates with an arsenal of maneuvers that produces one winner in every four attempts and a nation-leading total of 350–400 victories per year. It is astounding, perhaps, but Van Berg's three most productive winning patterns account for almost half his total victories and would have produced a flat bet profit over the past ten years.

Along with Dave Vance, who handles a division of the far-flung Lasater Stable, Dick Dutrow (Maryland), Bobby Frankel and the father-son team of F. W. and Gary Jones (California), Ned Allard (New England), Richard Hazelton (Illinois), H. N. Steck (New Jersey), C. P. Sanborn (Florida), W. J. Danner (Ohio), Wade Johnson (West Virginia), Dewey Smith (Louisiana), Laz Barrera, Frank Laboccetta and Joe Trovato (New York), and several other fine horsemen, Van Berg is deadly with repeaters going up in class as well as with recent claims. On the other hand, a Van Berg winner attempting a repeat victory at the same class level or lower is usually a poor risk (approximately one win for every eight attempts). The same is true for most of the other horsemen who tend to win going up the ladder.

Obviously, it takes considerable horsemanship to know that a horse is fit enough and fast enough to beat better competition. And it takes no less skill to spot genuine value in another man's horse. It costs money to claim a horse. Not Monopoly money—*real* money: $5,000, $10,000, $20,000 and up. If a trainer at your favorite track seems particularly skillful with recent claims, it would be worthwhile to pull out a few past performance profiles and compare them. Possibly he likes to give his recent claims a few weeks off, or else break them in with an easy race. Some trainers prefer to wait out the thirty-day "jail" period which most states require. (After a claim, the trainer is forced to race the horse at a price at least 25 percent higher for a period of thirty days.) Perhaps you will conclude that there is no apparent pattern. Don't believe it. That is rarely the case. You're probably not looking at the right clues. For example, the third and most significant Van Berg pattern has nothing to do with past performance records as they appear in the *Daily Racing Form*. It merely has to do with where he is!

To a far greater extent than any horseman I have ever seen, Jack Van Berg is prone to go on incredible winning binges, seemingly at will. In amazing Ripley-like fashion, these streaks invariably coincide with his travel itinerary.

Van Berg has many horses under his wing and operates at two or three tracks simultaneously, often leading the trainers' standings at each racetrack. But if he is not on the grounds to personally supervise the training regimen of his stock, only his recent claims and repeaters win more than their share of races. If he is on the grounds, however, and has indicated control over the situation by winning two races back to back or three out of five, the odds say he'll win fifteen more before he saddles thirty or thirty-five to the post. Sometimes such a streak will last a month or more; sometimes it will be the only clue a player will get.

During the 1974, 1975, and 1976 racing seasons, I'm familiar with at least twenty-five such explosions at a dozen different racetracks. The only dependable form pattern I've detected is the extraordinary reliability of his repeaters stepping up in company. Actually, there is no theory of handicapping or insight into the conditioning process that will explain some of his wins. But don't say I didn't warn you.

Can you imagine the kind of bet Lucky Principio was when he came back April 2 to attempt a repeat victory in the middle of a Van Berg streak?

Lucky Principio **112** Dk. b. or br. g (1972), by Sir Ivor—Spar Officer, by Round Table.
Breeder, Carver Stable (Ky.).
Owner. P J. Luckino. Trainer, J. Van Berg.

1976	4	2	0	0	$19,500
1975	7	3	2	0	$14,744

2 Apr76	8OP	6 f	:214	:4511:093ft	14	115	68¾	66¼	52½	1no	WhitedDE1	Alw	97	LckyPrncpo115		ChnceLndng		7
27 Mar76	5OP	6 f	:213	:4511:11 ft	11	119	63¼	52¾	2h	1no	WhitdDE1	25000	90	LuckyPrincipio119		King'sCre		12
19 Mar76	7OP	6 f	:214	:4441:11 ft	28	110	610	68½	66	73½	MiceliM4	33000	86	JustAWondr112		MilingoEstr		8
28 Feb76	7Hia	6 f	:22	:45 1:094ft	14	117	63½	63½	85¾	108¾	FieslmnJ4	25000	85	LoveReality115		LucayanBrze		10
29 Nov75	9HP	6½ f	:232	:4911:23 sy	3½	110	1½	2h	33	49½	JonesK5	HcpS	56	Ske theAnvl 118		Dr'sEnjyDs		6
22 Nov75	3HP	6½ f	:232	:48 1:202go	2	*119	11	1½	16	110	JonesK4	Alw	79	LckyPrincipio119		I CanHcktt		8
13 Nov75	7HP	6 f	:243	:4931:16 ft	1-2	*119	21½	11	14	15	JonesK6	Alw	72	LkyPrincipio119		BelmrLanes		7
7 Nov75	8HP	4 f	:224	:474ft	1	*114	5	33	22	1no	JonesK5	Alw	86	LkyPrincpio114		Whps aDaisy		10
1 Apr75	4OP	6 f	:214	:4511:112ft	3½	113	75¾	55½	51¼	22½	LivelyJ4	Mdn	85	BeauMatt113		LckyPrincipio		11
26 Mar75	4OP	6 f	:221	:4531:111ft	1	*113	2h	2h	41	44½	StrassRO1	Mdn	84	Galley Ho 113		Beau Matt		12

April 9 HP 4f ft :49⅗b   March 10 HP 4f gd :53b

Winding River (below) was a Van Berg claim on March 27. There was no streak going at Sportsman's Park on April 8, but there was a repeater pattern. Thirteen to one is mind bending. In today's race Winding River remains at the same $8,500 class level. I hope there is something else worth playing in this race because Winding River is going to be the favorite. He may win, but Van Berg knows this horse is not as sharp as he looks. Otherwise he would step him up in class again.

Winding River * **116** Dk. b. or br. h (1971). by Crafty Admiral—Santa's Creek, by River War.
Breeder, S. Cohn (Md.).
Owner, J. Van Berg. Trainer, J. Van Berg. **$8,500**

1976	7	2	0	2	$8,640
1975	14	0	5	3	$9,383

8 Apr76	9Spt	1	:4841:1511:411ft	13	115	33	2h	11	12¼	TurctteRL5	8500	74	WindgRivr115		Sctch andSda		10
27 Mar76	6FG	1 1/16	:4741:1311:463ft	3¼	114	67	36	22½	1nk	GuajdoA2	c8500	82	WindingRiver114		FowlLuck		8
21 Mar76	7FG	6 f	:22 :4541:11 ft	19	112	87¼	77	54¾	55¾	GuajrdoA5	8000	84	Kerry Debby 104		Timoteo		8
10 Mar76	7FG	6 f	:222 :4621:114ft	15	114	75¾	65	33½	54½	GuajrdoA3	8000	81	Bandwagon114		NationalNote		8
18 Feb76	9FG	140	:4641:1221:403ft	7¼	113	56½	34½	43½	39	PowerJ10	c6250	81	Sctch andSda113		CurusKitn		10
7 Feb76	3FG	1 1/16	:4821:1411:46 ft	3½	113	41¾	1h	21	34½	DayP8	6500	80	Tumizon 116		Tipo Ke'		8
31 Jan76	5FG	6 f	:222 :4621:12 ft	4¼	115	85½	911	917	910	TrosclrAJ9	7500	75	SpanishState117		FuelPrince		9
14 Sep75	6LaD	6 f	:23 :4611:122ft	8¼	116	67	57½	35½	51¾	DupasR3	13000	101	Peerless Prince 120		Truxton		9
6 Sep75	7LaD	7 f	:234 :4741:272sl	2¼	*116	67	67½	611	59½	FrominM2	1500	89	Amberope118		WindingRiver		6
30 Aug75	6LaD	6 f	:231 :4731:134ft	2	116	48	49	37	27¼	FrominM5	16000	88	Bill'sCmet116		Run to theWe		8

April 16 Spt 5f ft 1:03b   April 5 Kee 5f ft 1:02b

The following horse is one of eight stakes winners trained by Jack Van Berg during the first six months of 1976. Looks like Frank Whiteley's work, doesn't it? Obviously, the man knows how to read a condition book and is not afraid to go hunting.

Summertime Promise 119 B. f (1972), by Nijinsky II.—Prides Promise, by Crozier.
Breeder, P. Mellon (Va.).

Owner, K. Opstein. Trainer, J. Van Berg.

| | | | | | | | | | | | | 1976 | 9 | 3 | 5 | 1 $139,250 |
| | | | | | | | | | | | | 1975 | 8 | 2 | 1 | 2 $65,300 |

7Jly 76 8AP	Ⓣ 1 :47³1:114¹:38 fm1-2 ▲122	1½	14	14	1¹	SnyderL7	Alw 85 Ⓕ SmrtmePmise122 Ksaptmus 7
19May76 8Hol	Ⓣ 1₁⁶ :472¹:113¹:414fm 2¾ ▲119	2¹	2½	2h	3²	LivelyJ7	HcpS 88 Ⓕ MiaAmore116 Bastonerall. 7
8May76 8Haw	Ⓣ 1 :49²1:142¹:404sf 4-5 ▲120	12½	1h	13	13	LivelyJ3	HcpS 67 Ⓕ SmrtimePmise120 MiniGift 10
17Apr76 8Pim	Ⓣ 1₁⁶ :47³1:112¹:42¹fm 3¼ 117	1h	1h	1h	2nk	MHeDG9	HcpS 100 Ⓕ Dese duVl 119 SmtmePmse 9
31Mar76 8OP	1⁷⁰ :46²1:112¹:40³ft 2 119	2¹	2½	12	1nk	McHeDG2	HcpS 93 Ⓕ SumertmePrmise119 Baygo 9
29Feb76 8SA	1 :48²1:123¹:492ft 17 114	1¹	3¹	2h	2no	McHgeDG5	InvH 85 Ⓕ FscntgGrl 115 SmrtmePmse 8
14Feb76 9Hia	Ⓣ 1½ 1:48²hd 3½ 114	2½	21½	2¹	2½	McHgeD1	HcpS 91 Ⓕ YsDrMggy116 SmrtmePmse 14
4Feb76 9Hia	Ⓣ 1₁⁶ 1:414fm 4¾ 115	1²	11½	12	2no	McHeD12	HcpS 89 Ⓕ Redndcy117 SrmtimePrmse 12

No streak, no claim, no repeat, no step-up in class. No play.

Nowata Pride 117 Gr. c (1973), by Thermos—Swing Time Too, by Leisure Time.
Breeder, C. E. Stewart (Okla.).

Owner, Mrs. J. Potrykus. Trainer, J. Van Berg.

| | | | | | | | | | | ($12.500) | 1976 | 2 | 1 | 0 | 0 | $6,400 |
| | | | | | | | | | | | 1975 | 3 | 1 | 1 | 0 | $3,768 |

11 Mar76 1OP	6 f :22¹ :46²1:13 ft	2 ▲122	4²	3²	42½	51¾	MapleS7	15000 78 Two Rivers 115 Quen Boy 12
24 Feb76 1OP	6 f :21⁴ :46 1:113ft	12 116	1½	11	13½	1½	MapleS1	15000 87 NwataPride116 RunForClem 12
22 Nov75 10HP	6½ f :23² :474¹:222gd	4½ 113	12⁶	11¹	11⁶	22⁴12²³	StraussR8	HcpS 46 Alastair 122 Tidoc 12
11 Nov75 1HP	6 f :25 :49¹1:16¹ft 3-5 ▲120	11	12	13	15	StraussR1	Mdn 71 NowataPre120 NationlArmr 8
29 Oct75 1HP	4 f :23³ :48³ft	3¾ 120	4	44½	47½	2⁵	StraussR7	Mdn 77 SenatrKiddoo120 NowtaPde 10

Feb 8 OP 4f ft :49⅗b

Van Berg isn't the only trainer who goes on winning streaks. All good trainers tend to get hot from time to time. It's important to be able to detect such patterns in the making.

Sometimes a trainer will point for a particular meeting, à la Glenn C. Smith or Ida Mae Parrish. Sometimes he must sacrifice a month or two of racing to get ready.

When Frank Martin, a hard man to pin down, went to California for the 1974–1975 winter racing season, he obviously had Aqueduct on his mind. Martin won only two races in fifty-odd starts at Santa Anita, but he returned to New York with a barnful of tigers. Three weeks into his 1975 Aqueduct winter invasion Martin had nineteen winners; eight weeks later he had fifty. An astute player in California or New York, who was willing to look through Frank Martin's window might well have gotten the message by the third racing day.

Just as the best trainers tend to get hot, they also suffer occasional losing streaks. Fortunately, the player can often spot such losing patterns in the making.

Has the trainer abandoned a successful pattern or strategy? Perhaps he has had to push his horses very hard of late in pursuit of extra victories. Maybe horses and trainer need a rest. Or maybe the horseman is trying to shake off the effects of tough recent defeats or a disastrous break. A few years ago John Parisella, a fine horseman, lost most of his horses by fire. Even when he got new stock it took him a full year to get back into a winning groove. And there are some trainers who don't need a disaster to bring out their worst.

Del Carroll, Reggie Cornell, and John Gaver Sr. are three interesting cases in point. For many years Carroll has been a prominent trainer with a decent overall record. His fillies have won many allowance-class sprints in New Jersey, Kentucky, Delaware, and Florida. He is also a consistent winner on the turf course and does quite well with lightly raced two- and three-year-olds in maiden races. But he has a hole in his game. A big hole.

When Bee Bee Bee upset the Preakness field in 1972, leaving Key to the Mint and Riva Ridge in his wake, the sloppy track helped, but the race was no fluke. Carroll had a very fast horse on his hands. In 1970 Carroll got Bushido ready to score a well-deserved and quite predictable upset in the prestigious John B. Campbell Handicap; Bushido looked very impressive that day. In 1974 Carroll had Better Arbitor and Eastern Lord, two genuinely fast three-year-olds in a year that sorely lacked quality. With all these horses, Carroll changed strategies, pointed for silly races, worked his horses too fast and too often, missed numerous opportunities, and won very few races.

I'll consider a Carroll-trained longshot in a stakes event; but once the form of his horse is exposed, I expect it to deteriorate as fast as he developed it. No trainer can lose control of a good horse and expect it to run to its potential.

Although Carroll has squandered opportunities several times, I doubt any trainer has lost control more often than Reggie Cornell. After gaining a noteworthy reputation in 1958 as the man behind the incredible Silky Sullivan (would you believe Silky once won a 6½-furlong race at Santa Anita after breaking *forty-seven lengths* behind his field!), Cornell won some and lost some during the next twelve years without stirring up much fuss. In the early 1970s, however, he was given the top training post at fabled Calumet Farm, once the nation's premier racing stable. It turned out to be a disastrous relationship.

Calumet had been in decline for much of the 1960s but began a strong comeback under Henry Forrest in 1968 with Forward Pass and other promising horses. Cornell inherited a stable on the rebound, a stable that was destined to provide him with more top-class racing prospects during the next few years than most trainers get to work with in a lifetime: horses like Gleaming, Bold and Able, Eastern Fleet, Prince Turian, Turn to Turia, and the freakishly fast Raise a Cup. All these horses won at least one stakes race very impressively to signal championship potential, and at least half a dozen more showed similar ability in their first or second starts. Every spring Calumet seemed loaded for bear. But by

August Cornell had very few sound horses to work with; most, it seems to me, were kept out of races that were all too obviously theirs to win and instead were pushed to the breaking point on the training track. In my opinion, there is no trainer in all of racing who asks so much of his horses in the morning and gets so little for the effort in the afternoon. With first-timers and absentees Cornell, who was fired by Calumet in early 1976, still remains a 20 percent winner. But two or three races and a dozen workouts later the player can begin marking the calendar for the day when he will read of the horse's sudden departure from competition.

John Gaver Sr., who is always dangerous with a first-time starter and has some outstanding victories to his credit, is nevertheless another trainer who tends to put excessive pressure on his horses in the morning. After years of watching him handle the Greentree Stable stock, I am three-quarters convinced the man thinks each horse is or should be Tom Fool, the rugged handicap star Gaver developed in the early 1950s. Some horses need that kind of intense training regimen to get into shape; a few even require it throughout their careers. Most, however, will buckle under the punishment and either sulk or break down. Frankly, my mind boggles at the number of races a patient trainer like Frank Whiteley Jr. or Elliott Burch would have won with some of the horses trained by Carroll, Cornell, and Gaver, horses that flashed signs of brilliance and horses that you and I will never hear about. The player has to be on his guard with trainers like that. The horses they train are liable to run off form or lose races they should win.

Give Burch a promising two-year-old and you may see an early win, but it is doubtful you'll see the true ability of the horse until it turns three on New Year's Day. Like Charles Whittingham, king of West Coast stakes competition, Burch trains horses to run far and to last from one season to the next.

Fast workouts? Definitely. But each workout is designed to complement the horse's progress in actual races—to advance it toward a longer distance, sharpen its speed, or just keep it within range of Burch's control between important engagements. Once top form has been achieved, Burch will decrease the frequency, the speed, or the distance of the workouts (or all three) in direct proportion to the horse's actual racing opportunities. With that kind of sensible management, Elliott Burch frequently gets two, three, or four wins in a row out of his best-grade stock. And he is just as liable to do that with a good grass horse as he is with a three-year-old colt or filly. The player who knows that about Burch's training skill can string along for a very profitable ride.

Glowing Tribute

121 B. † (1973), by Graustark—Admiring, by Hail to Reason.
Breeder, P. Mellon (Va.).

| | 1976 | 9 | 5 | 1 | 1 | $91,825 |
| | 1975 | 5 | 1 | 1 | 1 | $8,460 |

Owner, Rokeby Stable. Trainer, E. Burch.

6 Aug76 ⁸Sar	ⓣ 1¹⁄₁₆ :46 1:10¹¹:41¹¹fm 6-5 ▲113	2¹¹⁄₂	2¹	1ʰ	1²	DayP⁸	HcpO 91 ⒻGlowgTrbte113 Assmblyn 10
17 Jly 76 ⁶Aqu	ⓣ 1¹⁄₄ :49 1:13 1:49¹gd 3¹⁄₄ 110	1ʰ	2ʰ	1¹⁄₂	1¹⁄₂	DayP⁴	HcpS ⒻGlwngTribute110 Bubbling 6
10 Jly 76 ⁷Aqu	ⓣ 1 :47²1:12¹¹:36¹fm 4-5 ▲111	1¹	11¹⁄₂	14	12³⁄₄	DayP⁴	Alw ⒻGlwngTrbute111 StdntLdr 8
31 May76 ⁶Bel	ⓣ 1¹⁄₁₆ :46²1:10¹¹:41¹fm 10 112	1²	11¹⁄₂	13	15	DayP,	Alw 94 ⒻGlowngTrbte112 StdntLdr 9
4 May76 ⁷Bel	6 f :22⁴ :45³1:11 ft 11 111	86¹⁄₂	98¹⁄₂	75³⁄₄	33	GustinesH⁸	Alw 84 ⒻFurling 113 Desert Boots 10
9 Apr76 ⁷Aqu	6 f :23 :46²1:114ft 4¹⁄₂ 121	52³⁄₄	35¹⁄₂	47	45	GustinesH⁵	Alw 79 ⒫In theOffing114 DesertBts 6
29 Mar76 ⁶Aqu	7 f :23 :46¹1:234ft 3 121	55	54¹⁄₂	43	44¹⁄₄	VasquezJ⁶	Alw 78 ⒻFrlssQueen118 In theOffng 9
5 Mar76 ⁶Hia	6 f :22¹ :46 1:112ft 4³⁄₄ 116	55	33¹⁄₂	11	15	GustinesH⁹	Alw 86 ⒻGlowingTrbte116 PlsntTne 10
21 Feb76 ⁵Hia	6 f :22¹ :46¹1:12¹ft 5³⁄₄ 116	3³⁄₄	4³⁄₄	2ʰ	21	GustinesH²	Alw 81 ⒻSecretGss111 GlwingTrbte 9
4 Nov75 ⁶Bel	7 f :23 :464¹1:243ft 7³⁄₄ 113	1³	11¹⁄₂	43¹⁄₂	79¹⁄₄	MontoyaD⁵	Alw 70 ⒻZookalu 116 Dalton Road 8
10 Oct75 ³Bel	7 f :22³ :45²1:244ft 1 ▲121	1ʰ	2³	53¹⁄₂	6⁹	MontoyaD⁶	Alw 69 ⒻDancer'sVixen121 FstSaw 7

Aug 3 Sar 4f ft :48b | | **July 7 Bel 5f ft 1:01b** | | **July 2 Bel 6f ft 1:13b**

Here are the past performances of Arts and Letters as they appeared in early 1969. The workout line shows that Burch was beginning to crank this horse up for major improvement. He got it. Ten months later Arts and Letters was voted Horse of the Year over one of the best crops of three-year-olds I've ever seen.

Arts and Letters **113** Ch. c (1966), by Ribot—All Beautiful, by Battlefield.
Breeder, P. Mellon (Va.).

Owner, Rokeby Stable. Trainer, E. Burch.

										1969 1 0 0 1	$550
										1968 6 2 1 0	$18,898
Jan25-69 6Hia	7 f 1:22⅗ft	3½	119	54½	45	36	36	CruguetJ4	Alw 89	AckAck117 Dist'ctive119 A'ts a'dL't'rs	9
Nov 2-68 8Lrl	1 1/16 1:44 ft	2¾	122	42½	22	32	41¼	Vel'q'zJ7	ScwS 96	King Emperor 122 Dike 122 Mr. Leader	8
Oct15-68 6Bel	1 1:36⅖ft	9-5	▲122	2½	12	13	12½	Vel'squezJ9	Alw 92	A'ts a'dL'rs122 Hyd't122 K'g of t'eC'e	9
Sep25-68 5Bel	7 f 1:24⅕ft	3	▲122	63	33	1h	13½	Velasq'zJ9	Mdn 86	A'ts a'dL't'rs122 H'd'l'g't122 W'c'tH'ls	12
Sep18-68 1Bel	6 f 1:11⅕ft	3¾	122	33	21½	2½	23	Vel'quezJ2	Mdn 86	K'g of t'e S'a122 A's a'd L's122 El'tW'k	14
Sep11-68 4Aqu	6 f 1:12⅖sy	2	▲122	57½	56	45½	44¾	TurcotteR6	Mdn 76	Royal Tom 122 Full of Gin 119 Izaak	12
Aug 9-68 5Sar	5½ f 1:04⅘ft	5	122	3½	21	33½	47	PincayLJr1	Mdn 86	DixieGus122 Ch'nHarb'r122 B'uBr'm'l	12

Feb 14 Hia 3f ft :35h Feb 11 Hia 5f ft :59h Feb 8 Hia 1m ft 1:37h

Some trainers are very strong or weak in one type of racing situation, and the player should know that too.

When Anthony Basile saddles a first-time starter in Kentucky during the spring, the results say 60 percent wins or seconds.

When Lou Rondinello puts a first-timer on the track, anytime, anywhere, a 96 percent losing record says throw the horse out.

Mackenzie Miller, an ace with fast-working two-year-olds, is even better than that with grass-racing stock of all ages. Miller has few peers on the turf, and his win record with newcomers to the infield is better than 40 percent. Again, there is no theory of handicapping that will explain Miller's uncanny success on the turf with horses that look like Student Leader and Fun Forever. But knowledge of the man's special talent can surely help us evaluate their chances when we see them.

Student Leader **115** Dk. b. or br. f (1973), by Personality—Class Is Out, by Outing Class.
Breeder, K. Frazheim II. (Ky.).

Owner, K. Franzheim II. Trainer, M. Miller.

										1976 3 1 0 0	$6,600
										1975 3 1 0 1	$6,480
16 May76 6Bel	Ⓣ 1 :4531:0931:36 fm	5	111	41¾	34½	22	11½	VelsquezJ6	Alw 91	StudentLeadr111 PrmsdOne	9
3 May76 4Bel	6 f :224 :4631:111ft	8¼	114	812	810	87	64½	VelsquezJ1	Alw 81	ⒻDesiree 114 Light Frost	8
24 Apr76 5Aqu	6 f :222 :4521:11 ft	6	114	54¼	66½	711	814	VelsquezJ1	Alw 74	ⒻFurling 118 Swim	8
9 Nov75 3Aqu	7 f :234 :4721:251ft	6-5	▲1195	2½	1h	1h	11¾	VelasquzJ3	Mdn 75	ⒻStudentLeadr119 InteOfg	7
29 Oct75 1Bel	6 f :23 :4641:113ft	5	119	88½	76½	45	34¾	VelasquzJ7	Mdn 79	ⒻSweetBernice119 InteOfg	12
13 Oct75 4Bel	6 f :224 :4631:112ft	3	121	917	1012	611	612	VelasqzJ12	Mdn 73	ⒻZooKaly 121 Bite the Dust	12

May 27 Bel trt 5f ft 1:02⅖b May 22 Bel trt 4f ft :49h May 13 Bel trt 3f ft :36⅘b

Fun Forever **117** B. f (1973), by Never Bend—Fairway Fun, by Prince John.
Br., L. Combs II. & Wm. Floyd (Ky.).

Owner, W. Floyd. Trainer, Mac Miller.

										1976 7 1 1 2	$10,960
20 Aug76 2Sar	Ⓣ 1 1/16 :4631:1141:422fm	4½	117	21½	11½	13	17¾	VelasqzJ4	Mdn 85	ⒻFunFrvr117 Two fr theShw	11
11 Aug76 6Sar	1⅛ :4711:1211:504gd	3-2	▲117	33	23	413	421	VelsqezJ2	Mdn 60	ⒻTable Hopper 110 Bashful	8
26 Jly 76 5Aqu	6 f :222 :4541:12 ft	6½	116	65½	44	25	22¾	MartnsG12	Mdn 80	ⒻIronPromise116 FunForver	12
29 May76 2Bel	1 1/16 :4621:1141:444ft	7	1105	2½	32	717	922	MartensG9	Mdn 56	ⒻLaughingKys115 TbleHppr	9
12 May76 9Bel	1 1/16 :48 1:1231:443ft	8-5	▲114	4nk	31½	67	714	VelsqezJ3	Mdn 62	ⒻDonaMaya114 TbleHopper	10
30 Apr76 4Aqu	6 f :221 :4531:11 ft	1	▲114	65½	56	37½	34½	VelasqzJ4	Mdn 83	ⒻSisterJulie112 MissPrism	8
19 Apr76 2Aqu	6 f :22 :45 1:104ft	2e	▲112	44½	46	53½	32½	VelquezJ2	Mdn 87	ⒻShnghaiMry114 Qn'sGmbt	10

Aug 17 Sar tc 3f fm :36⅖h Aug 10 Sar 3f sy :34⅘h Aug 7 Sar trt 4f ft :48⅕h

J. M. Bollero, Joe Pierce, and T. J. Kelly are other trainers who do exceptionally well in grass races, especially in allowance and stakes company. There are, in fact, too many successful turf trainers for me to list, for grass racing has become very popular in recent seasons. Which introduces a digression of sorts.

There is a book on the market, a well-intentioned generally informative book, that tells all the secrets of turf race handicapping. Or so the ads claim. It sells for twenty bucks.

The only problem with this book (ignoring the $20 price) is that it may be five years too late. Turf racing is no longer a one-dimensional game for students of breeding who happen to have a smattering of knowledge about trainers or class. Yes, you can pick winners on the turf by knowing something about bloodlines—some breeds do show a natural affinity for grass racing (see Chapter 13). Yes, you can also pick winners on the turf by paying attention to trainers like Mackenzie Miller and J. M. Bollero. But you should know a great deal about class, track bias, and condition as well.

Turf racing is extremely competitive now. Whereas formerly three-quarters of the horses entered in any grass race could be easily eliminated on the basis of wrong blood or poor turf form, today the majority of grass races include many horses that are well suited to the conditions. To successfully handicap turf races in the late 1970s you need no fewer tools and skills than you do for any other kind of race. End of digression.

Of all the 7,000 trainers in North America, there is one man who seems to be in a class by himself. He is an incredible talent named Allen Jerkens.

In the early 1960s Jerkens revved up a sprint-type named Beau Purple to take the measure of the mighty Kelso, not once, but three times.

Later in the decade he took Handsome Boy, another

sprinter, and developed him into a winner of four straight $100,000 route races.

During that period he was the leading trainer in New York. More wins, more money won, more stakes, highest win percentage. But no trainer has ever had the kind of year that Jerkens had in 1973.

In the early spring Jerkens cranked up a $25,000 claiming filly named Poker Knight to win an allowance sprint. The result was a surprise, for Jerkens had not trained the filly for speed. Building her stamina through long, slow training gallops, he had hoped to stretch her out in distance at a later date. By virtue of her surprising victory, Jerkens realized that Poker Knight was going to be a much better horse than he had thought.

On April 3 Jerkens entered her in another allowance sprint. Another win. He then stepped up his program, working her a mile in modest time four days later—a work too slow to make the clocker's tab. April 10, another sprint race, this time against the fastest three-year-old filly in the country—the undefeated Windy's Daughter.

"I was more curious to see what she would do than thinking she would win," said Jerkens later that summer. What she did was come within a length of beating Windy's Daughter, closing ground in the stretch.

Two weeks later Jerkens was convinced that Poker Knight could beat any filly in the country at a mile or more. In successive races the ex-claimer proved him right, beating Numbered Account and Summer Guest, the two top fillies in America.

A few months later Jerkens was at it again. Onion to beat Secretariat, paying $13.60; although I've made larger wagers, this was the most painful, most professional bet I have ever made.

Onion came into the Whitney Stakes on the first Saturday in August 1973 with a superior sprint race win over the track on the first Tuesday. The great Secretariat came into the same race with subpar workouts, a signal that had tipped off his subpar performance in the Wood Memorial at Aqueduct in April. Onion was the speed of the field, a four-year-old getting a weight concession from a three-year-old. (That's a big edge, bigger than most people know; see page 126.)

Secretariat drew the rail, which was as dead as I had ever seen it at Saratoga. The few horses that had made moves hugging the rail on the far turn during the preceding week of racing were all eligible to improve dramatically in their next starts.

In all my handicapping experiences I have rarely encountered a situation that was more ripe for an upset. But I was torn and I was angry. Secretariat was the most compelling horse I had ever seen. Every race he ran was different, each more dynamic than the one before. I was emotionally involved with this horse. I rooted for him just like I root for other superior athletic talents—not only the ones that hit the home runs, leap higher than anyone else, or shoot the eyes out of the basket, but the ones that step into another dimension of performance when nothing less than that will get the job done. Damascus, Dr. Fager, Kelso, Majestic Prince, and Canonero II had shown me that kind of talent a few times each. Secretariat did it better than any of them, and he did it repeatedly: in his debut, in his second start, in the Sanford Stakes, in the Hopeful Stakes, in each of the Triple Crown races (and later in the Man O' War Stakes on the grass). I was angry because I was spoiled. I did not want to see him at anything less than his best.

Cold logic said the race was even up. Onion and Jerkens versus a potentially subpar Secretariat and Lucien Laurin. No other result seemed possible. But the tote board said Onion.

Actually Secretariat put in a fine race, gaining three

lengths along the deepest part of the track on the final turn. At the top of the stretch it looked like he was going to drive past Onion and win by daylight. My schizophrenia was showing. I forgot about my bet and screamed for him to do it. But he never uncorked his explosive move. Onion stayed in the middle of the track the whole trip and pulled away in the final five strides. I cashed all my tickets save one.

But Jerkens was hardly through. Days later he bought Prove Out, who had been an allowance-class sprinter for the better part of three seasons. Under Jerkens the horse needed but three weeks to begin a new career as the biggest giant killer of them all.

On the next-to-last day at Saratoga, Jerkens cut him loose to defeat Forego in a seven-furlong allowance race, posting a new track record.

Two weeks later Prove Out tied the Belmont Park track mark for $1\frac{1}{16}$ miles. Two weeks after that he was at Bowie, facing the improving True Knight, a bona-fide handicap horse. I was there too, and of course I bet Prove Out even though he went to post at 8–5 odds. By now I was as mesmerized as everyone else. At the top of the stretch Prove Out was in front and beginning to tire when he bounced off the inner rail. There went some of my Onion money.

One week later I decided to skip a Secretariat race for the first time in his career. It was the Woodward Stakes, and Prove Out put in a superior performance, one of the top ten races of the past twenty years. Secretariat ran just a bit below his exceptional Kentucky Derby form and got his head handed to him. Jerkens again. Incredible.

For an encore, Prove Out showed he was no fluke by beating the other half of the Meadow Stable's team, Riva Ridge, in the two-mile Jockey Club Gold Cup.

In day-to-day racing at Aqueduct, Belmont, and Saratoga, Jerkens is a 25 percent winning trainer overall, but he does have a pattern that produces better than 40 percent winners.

What does Allen Jerkens do with an improving horse? Move it up in company as soon as possible. Or stretch it out in distance or put it on the turf course.

How does one spot a ready-set-go Jerkens runner? Very fast recent trials or a sharp race within the past seven days.

Arcadio II. * **114** Dk. b. or br. h (1971), by Granadero II.—Aretina, by Bell Hop.
Breeder, Haras La Companaia (Chile). 1976 6 2 1 2 $17,508
Owner, Hobeau Farm. Trainer, H. Allen Jerkens. 1975 21 3 4 3 $2,448

24 Aug76	^{8}Sar	Ⓣ 1$\frac{1}{16}$	:46^{1}1:11^{1}1:41^{4}fm	4½	115	$4^{4\frac{1}{4}}$	$4^{1\frac{1}{2}}$	2½	1no	HerndezR^4	Alw	88	Arcadio II. 115	Blue Times	7
17 Aug76	^{5}Sar	6 f	:22^3 :45^{3}1:10^{1}ft	17	115	2^1	$2^{1\frac{1}{2}}$	$3^{2\frac{1}{2}}$	$3^{2\frac{1}{2}}$	RolonJ^4	37500	86	JacksnSqre117	BldandStrmy	8
18 Apr76	^{6}ClH	Ⓣ a 1¼	2:02^{2}fm	3½e	132	Chilie			10	UlloaP	Stk		Jadar 132	Poccardi	10
7 Apr76	^{4}HCh	a 6½ f	1:19 ft	7½	134	Chile			3^3	UlloaP	Stk		Piche 134	Venezuela	10
21 Mar76	^{7}Val	Ⓣa 1$\frac{3}{16}$	1:55^{4}fm	4½	106	Chile			2½	GnzlzF	HcpS		Royal Fun 110	Arcadio II.	13
4 Jan76	^{7}CiH	Ⓣa 1$\frac{1}{16}$	1:41^{3}fm	1	▲121	Chile			$1^{1\frac{1}{4}}$	RiveraC	Hcp		Arcadio II. 121	Espionaje	8
25 Dec75	^{7}ClH	Ⓣ a 1	1:34^{2}fm	3	106	Chile			2^2	GnklezL	Hcp		Retraido 132	Arcadio II.	9
14 Dec75	^{5}ClH	Ⓣ a 1¼	2:01^{4}fm	†	134	Chile			$1^{2\frac{1}{2}}$	UlloaP	Hcp		Arcadio II. 134	Mesurado	5

†No Pari-mutuel wagering.

Aug 22 Sar 3f f :36b **Aug 12 Sar 3f ft :37⅖b** **Aug 4 Sar 4f ft :47⅕hg**

Tell Me All **121** B. f (1973), by Cyane--Lead Me On, by Native Dancer.
Breeder, Mooring Stable (Md.). 1976 8 5 1 0 $57,355
Owner, Hobeau Farm. Trainer, H. A. Jerkens. 1975 1 M 1 0 $1,760

5 May76	^{8}Bel	7 f	:22^3 :45^{3}1:23^{1}ft	6¾	113	3^2	2^1	2^h	1½	RuaneJ^4	AlwS	86	ⒻTellMeAll 113	DrlyPrcious	5
26 Apr76	^{4}Aqu	1	:46^{3}1:10^{3}1:35 ft	3-2	▲109	$1^{1\frac{1}{2}}$	1^2	1^7	1^{11}	RuaneJ^1	Alw	91	ⒻTellMeAll 109	BusySaxon	5
12 Apr76	^{5}Aqu	6 f	:23^4 :47^{2}1:11^{2}ft	4-5	▲109	1^h	1^h	1^1	$1^{2\frac{1}{2}}$	RuaneJ^1	Alw	86	ⒻTellMeAll 109	FnnyPculiar	6
3 Mar76	^{9}Hia	1⅛	:46^{1}1:10^{2}1:49^{3}ft	20	114	1^1	$3^{5\frac{1}{2}}$	7^{14}	8^{19}	RuaneJ^8	AlwS	65	ⒻT.V.Vixen116	AnneCmpbll	10
18 Feb76	^{9}Hia	7 f	:23 :46 1:23^{1}ft	4	112	$5^{1\frac{1}{2}}$	$7^{5\frac{3}{4}}$	6^6	$6^{7\frac{3}{4}}$	RuaneJ^6	AlwS	81	T.V.Vixen11	FortyNineSnsts	11
7 Feb76	^{6}Hia	7 f	:23^4 :47 1:24^{2}ft	2-3	▲116^5	3½	1^h	1^1	1^1	VelezRI^8	Alw	83	ⒻTellMeAll 116	Cohabitatn	10
24 Jan76	^{6}Hia	7 f	:23 :45^{4}1:23^{2}ft	7-5	▲109^5	3^2	2^3	1^1	1^4	VelezRI^3	Alw	88	ⒻTell Me All 109	Polipeg	12
16 Jan76	^{3}Hia	6 f	:21^4 :45^{1}1:10^{2}sy	9-5	▲121	$2^{1\frac{1}{2}}$	$2^{1\frac{1}{2}}$	2½	2^1	BaezaB^8	Mdn	90	ⒻMisukaw 121	Tell Me All	11
24 Sep75	^{3}Bel	6 f	:22^3 :46^{3}1:11^{2}sy	3¾	121	$6^{3\frac{3}{4}}$	$3^{1\frac{1}{2}}$	2^4	$2^{7\frac{3}{4}}$	SthRC^9	M45000	77	ⒻXalapaSnrse121	TellMeAll	10

May 21 Bel 3f ft :34⅕h **May 18 Bel 6f ft 1:12⅘h** **May 4 Bel 3f ft :34⅕h**

Clean 'Em Up **112** Dk. b. or br. c (1973), by Handsome Boy—Mopkins, by Bolero.
Breeder, Hobeau Farm (Fla.). 1976 4 1 1 0 $7,380
Owner, Hobeau Farm. Trainer, H. Allen Jerkens.

19 May76	^{5}Bel	6 f	:22^4 :46^{1}1:10^{1}sy	3	114	4¾	1^h	2^h	1^3	MapleE^7	Mdn	91	Clean 'EmUp114	ThirdWorld	8
15 May76	^{3}Bel	7 f	:22^4 :45^{4}1:24^{2}ft	7-5	▲114	2^h	1^h	1^4	2¾	GustinesH^6	Mdn	79	Azirae 114	Clean 'Em Up	8
26 Jan76	^{4}Hia	6 f	:22 :45 1:11 ft	9-5	▲122	6^5	4^5	$4^{3\frac{1}{2}}$	$5^{6\frac{3}{4}}$	GustinesH^6	Mdn	81	LittleFishrmn122	DancgThf	11
19 Jan76	^{4}Hia	6 f	:22^2 :45^{3}1:11^{3}ft	3¾	122	$7^{3\frac{1}{4}}$	$9^{9\frac{1}{4}}$	6^9	$7^{6\frac{3}{4}}$	GustinesH^3	Mdn	78	GaitorRatn122	Knight ofLve	12

May 31 Bel 7f ft 1:24⅕h **May 26 Bel 1m ft 1:39⅘h** **May 25 Bel trt 5f ft 1:02⅕h**

How can a player uncover the special winning abilities of new trainers operating at any racetrack, or simply formulate intelligent judgments about the present form of any horse entered in any race at any track? A single past performance profile may well answer all the fundamental questions. The trick is to recognize the implications of the evidence. The examples in the next chapter may help to crystallize this point.

8.
"What's He Doing in Today's Race?"

The horse has had ten starts; his last race was a strong performance; the trainer is somebody we have never heard of, or somebody who wins a few races now and then but we don't know how he wins them. How do we decide whether the horse is going to improve, run the same race, or fail to make an impression? What clues in the past performances will help us rate this horse in this field today?

The answer is all the clues we can get—the result charts, the workout listings, and the past performance records of other horses trained by this man or woman. If we had occasion to do that kind of research before we came out to the track, we would be able to make a confident assessment.

In a single past performance profile there are important clues about the fitness of the horse, its class, distance capabilities, and soundness. And in fact about the trainer too.

---

6 FURLONGS—MAIDEN SPECIAL WEIGHT, HIALEAH, FEBRUARY 18, 1976

Nancy's Robert 122 B. c (1972), by Subpet—Sonodra, by Midpassage.
Breedtr, H. E. Robinson (Fla.).   1976   2 M 0 1 $600
Owner, H. E. Robinson. Trainer, G. Zateslo.   1975   5 M 0 0 $165

3 Feb76	2Hia	6 f :22³ :46 1:10³ft	71	117⁵	2h	6⁵	5⁴	34½	DruryMA⁴	Mdn 86 OldFrankfrt122	DbleMerger 10
27 Jan76	3Hia	7 f :23 :46 1:23¹ft	51	122	10¹²	9¹⁵10¹⁵10¹⁶			BrussrdR⁹	Mdn 73 SunnyClime122	DoubleTudor 12
10 Oct75	1Mth	6 f :22³ :45⁴1:10⁴ft	36	111⁷	3¹	52¾	54¾	65½	DruryMA¹	Mdn 81 BalTalk118	SparklingSuccs 7
27 Aug75	5Mth	17⁰ :47 1:13¹1:44²ft	13	115	4²	43½	57½	61⁵	ThornbgB⁵	Mdn 81 Doc Rofus 115	West End 8
20 Aug75	3Mth	6 f :22¹ :46¹1:12¹gd	42	117	76½	73¾	58¼	58¼	ThornbgB⁸	Mdn 71 HigherMarks 117	WestEnd 9
13 Aug75	3Mth	6 f :22¹ :45²1:11²ft	37	117	41½	56½	51²	71⁴	MacBthD¹	Mdn 69 RoyalPower117	IrishOuting 8
Feb 14 GP 5f ft 1:01⅗h			Jan 25 GP 3f ft :37b						Jan 16 GP 6f sy 1:15⅗b		

Notice the August 1975 races and the six-week gap until Nancy's Robert was able to get back on the track.

The October 10 race was an encouraging effort; but there was no follow-up race to take advantage of the horse's slight but real improvement. Obviously, this sparsely raced colt has had his physical problems.

On January 27, 1976, Nancy's Robert returned to competition but did very little, running in back of the pack.

Without checking the result chart for the race, we

might consider the possibility that there was interference at the start. In any case, this bad trip didn't put Nancy's Robert out of commission again. In fact, his trainer put him back on the track for another race the following week and gave him a five-furlong workout just four days before today's race.

The February 3 race was a marked improvement, the best race of Nancy's Robert's interrupted career. The workout that followed was also good. A positive sign of health, a touch of speed, and a logical move toward better condition.

The evidence says that trainer Zateslo has done a fine job straightening this horse out, and there is every likelihood that Nancy's Robert is on the verge of reaching his peak. We don't know what that peak is, we don't know how long he will be able to hold it, and we don't know whether he will reach it today. But we do know that he is already competitive at this class level and distance, and we have a right to think he's going to run a stronger race, his best to date. Our optimism for this horse's winning chances would be tempered by other strong contenders, but this is a typical maiden race—only two other horses in the field look like they can run. One has had fourteen previous maiden races and three seconds. The other is a well-bred first-time starter that has been training well enough to be dangerous. Nancy's Robert, who should have been a 9–5 favorite, paid $12 to win. The first-timer ran second, beaten by four lengths.

6½ FURLONGS—$8,500 CLAIMING, HAZEL PARK, NOVEMBER 15, 1975

Toolin Around **117** B. g (1968), by Tooley—Saragino by Cosmic Bomb.
Breeder, A. J. Algeri (Ky.). 1975 14 2 3 1 $11,073
Owner, Standen Stable. Trainer, A. Blundell. $8.500 1974 4 1 0 1 $8.000

8 Nov75 5HP	4 f :224 :474ft	4	1175	6	76½	76¾	77½	GarciaJR7	Alw	78	WinsomeWine119	RightPckt	7
1 Nov75 5HP	6½ f :223 :4711:204ft	4	1125	2½	1½	13	31	GarciaJR4	10000	76	Fast Left 112	I Can Hackett	7
18 Oct75 4HP	6½ f :223 :4721:20 gd	9-5	▲1125	44½	32	1h	24	GrciaJR3	10000	77	OwnPower119	ToolinAround	6
11 Oct75 5HP	6½ f :224 :4631:184ft	3¾	1125	54¼	1½	13	2¾	GrciaJR5	10000	86	Bandwagn117	ToolinAround	9
4 Oct75 7HP	4 f :221 :464ft	26	118	5	85¼	75½	71¾	MillerS7	Alw	89	FastTrackMiss115	BoldDggr	9
20 Sep75 6HP	6½ f :23 :4731:211hy	17	117	42	23	24	610	MillerS6	10000	64	LightCharger117	FamsPatrt	8
13 Sep75 7HP	6½ f :224 :4641:192ft	15	117	2h	2½	68½	710	BreenR5	12500	74	Brunate 115	Light Charger	8
30 Aug75 5HP	6½ f :232 :4831:232m	4¾	117	55½	56	713	816	MillerS5	10000	48	LightCharger110	Chest Eqle	3
23 Aug75 5HP	6½ f :232 :4811:21 m	3	120	33	32	23	615	MapleS2	12500	61	WavetheFlag115	LdyRchelle	7
9 Aug75 5HP	6½ f :222 :4621:184ft	4-5	▲•20	53½	54	45	711	MapleS1	15000	76	E'Omer 115	Fast Fun	8

Oct 30 HP 3f ft :38⅖b   Oct 2 HP 3f ft :36⅖h

After two wins and one second no longer appearing in the current past performance profile (see consistency box in upper right corner), Toolin Around was unable to sustain his speed throughout August and September.

Instead of resting this useful gelding, trainer Blundell tried an unusual strategy. If it hadn't worked we might have had reason to think Blundell was off his rocker or at least out of touch with his horse; but the maneuvering did work, so we ought to take a closer look.

On October 4 Blundell ran the already fast-breaking Toolin Around in an ultrashort four-furlong race against some of the fastest-breaking horses on the grounds. The betting public dismissed him at 26–1, and it was right. But one week later Toolin Around was back in top form, the form he maintained without winning in his next two starts at $10,000 claiming.

On November 8, one week before today's race, Blundell repeated the same four-furlong prep race strategy, but this time, unfortunately, the betting public was unaware of the trainer's intentions.

The "go" part of the pattern is today's race, an $8,500 claimer, a slight but important drop in class. This time Toolin Around should (and did) get back on the winning track. Put Mr. Blundell's name down for future reference. He has some unusual methods and was slow to realize the need for a drop in class, but he did use his head with this horse. At $7.60 Toolin Around was a steal.

---

6 FURLONGS—$20,000 ALLOWANCE PURSE, BELMONT PARK, JUNE 7, 1976

Desert Boots **107** B. f (1973), by Ridan—Signal Flag, by Restless Wind.
Breeder, Mrs. Barbara Joslin (Fla.). 1976 . . 7 1 4 1 $16,300
Owner, W. M. Joslin. Trainer, S. DiMauro. 1975 . . 2 1 0 0 $5,940

17 May76	^{7}Bel	6 f	:22 :44^{4}1:10^{3}ft	$7\frac{3}{4}$	106^5	$1^{1\frac{1}{2}}$	$1^{1\frac{1}{2}}$	1^2	$2^{\frac{1}{2}}$	MartinJE^4	Alw 88	ⒻFurling 114	Desert Boots	7
4 May76	^{7}Bel	6 f	:22^4 :45^{3}1:11 ft	$6\frac{1}{2}$	105^5	$1^{\frac{1}{2}}$	1^h	2^h	$2^{1\frac{1}{4}}$	VelezRI^6	Alw 86	ⒻFurling 113	Desert Boots	10
9 Apr76	^{7}Aqu	6 f	:23 :46^{2}1:11^{4}ft	2	▲113^5	1^2	1^4	1^5	2^h	VelezRI^6	Alw 84	ⒻIn theOffing114	DesertBts	6
15 Mar76	^{7}Aqu	6 f	:22^1 :45^{3}1:11^{1}ft	$2\frac{1}{2}$	118	$1^{\frac{1}{2}}$	1^2	1^3	3^2	BaezaB^3	Alw 85	ⒻAncntFbles114	Rsn frTrce	9
3 Mar76	^{8}Aqu	6 f	:22^2 :45^{2}1:10^{1}ft	$4\frac{3}{4}$	114	$1^{\frac{1}{2}}$	2^h	2^4	$7^{8\frac{1}{4}}$	HoleM^4	AlwS 84	ⒻToughElsie116	LightFrost	13
14 Feb76	^{6}Hia	6 f	:21^3 :44^{3}1:11^{2}ft	4-5	▲116	$1^{\frac{1}{2}}$	1^3	1^4	$1^{1\frac{1}{2}}$	BaezaB^5	Alw 86	ⒻDesertBoots116	She'sTrble	8
31 Jan76	^{6}Hia	6 f	:22 :45^{1}1:11^{1}ft	$2\frac{3}{4}$	114	$1^{\frac{1}{2}}$	1^3	$1^{1\frac{1}{2}}$	$2^{2\frac{1}{2}}$	MapleE^8	Alw 84	ⒻDaltonRoad114	DesrtBoots	12
1 Sep75	^{3}Bel	5 f	:22^1 :45^{4}1:1'^{2}ft	3	▲119	$1^{1\frac{1}{2}}$	1^4	1^7	$1^{8\frac{1}{2}}$	BracleVJr^9	Mdn 85	ⒻDesertB'ts119	Sw'tB'rn'e	12

June 3 Bel trt 1m ft 1:46⅖b May 29 Bel trt 1m ft 1:45⅕b May 23 Bel trt 1m ft 1:46⅖b

---

With two champs in the barn (Wajima and Dearly Precious), Steve DiMauro had quite a season in 1975. In 1976 things were not all that bad, but this particular horse must have driven DiMauro crazy.

Desert Boots is a one-dimensional speedball that simply refuses to keep something in reserve for the stretch run. DiMauro is trying to solve her problem through a program of long, slow, stamina-building workouts. The prescription might work and it might not, but it is sensible. In this case it did not work.

Perhaps a route race would get the message across better than the workouts. But there is a chance too that nothing will work. Desert Boots could have congenital wind problems that will always keep her from beating good horses at six furlongs.

In a game like racing we have a right to go our separate ways with a horse like this.

Some may be willing to give DiMauro the benefit of the doubt. I prefer not. Not unless there is a track bias operating in the horse's favor. I want proof that DiMauro has overcome Desert Boots' problem or insurance if he hasn't—insurance of a track bias or proof only a winning race can provide. And I also want a big price.

Although horses with strong early speed are always dangerous and Desert Boots could well win at any time, I'm willing to give her up to the rest of the crowd until she learns to carry her speed to the wire.

Horses that quit in race after race are notorious money burners.

---

6 FURLONGS—$10,500 CLAIMING, BELMONT PARK, SEPTEMBER 1, 1976

Panda Bear **113** B. g (1973), by My Dad George—Gold Threat, by Infidel.
Breeder, Martha Broadbent (Fla.). 1976 7 2 1 1 $12,770
Owner, B. Combs II. Trainer, J. Martin. **$10,500** 1975 3 1 1 1 $5,865

11 Aug76	^{2}Sar	6 f	:22^{2}	:46^{2}	1:11^{2}m	4¼	119	3$^{2\frac{1}{2}}$	3$^{1\frac{1}{2}}$	5$^{2\frac{1}{4}}$	5$^{3\frac{1}{4}}$	BaezaB^{4}	12500	80	Chompchomp 117	I'mProud	7
18 Jly 76	^{2}Aqu	6 f	:22^{4}	:46^{3}	1:12^{2}ft	8-5	▲117	3$^{1\frac{1}{2}}$	3$^{2\frac{1}{2}}$	2^{2}	1^{nk}	BaezaB^{7}	10000	81	PandaBear117	TakeYourBts	7
16 Jun76	^{9}Bel	7 f	:23	:46^{4}	1:25^{2}ft	3	117	2$^{1\frac{1}{2}}$	2$^{1\frac{1}{2}}$	3^{nk}	3$^{6\frac{1}{4}}$	CrdroAJr^{6}	12500	69	Fling 119	Spotted Gem	8
22 May76	^{9}Bel	6 f	:22^{3}	:46	1:11^{3}ft	4½	119	3^{nk}	3$^{\frac{1}{2}}$	4$^{2\frac{1}{4}}$	7$^{6\frac{1}{2}}$	CrdoAJr^{8}	16000	77	Cayman Isle117	Mgie'sPride	11
13 May76	^{2}Bel	6 f	:22^{3}	:46^{2}	1:11^{3}ft	2½	117	1$^{1\frac{1}{2}}$	1$^{1\frac{1}{2}}$	1^{h}	1$^{\frac{1}{2}}$	CdroAJr^{5}	12500	84	PandaBear117	CaymanIsle	9
8 May76	^{4}Bel	6 f	:22^{4}	:46^{1}	1:11^{3}ft	2¼	▲112^{5}	4$^{1\frac{1}{4}}$	4$^{1\frac{1}{4}}$	5^{2}	4^{3}	MrtinJE^{8}	14000	81	HowiesHeat117	TakeYrBoots	8
15 Apr76	^{7}Aqu	6 f	:22^{3}	:46	1:12^{2}ft	2¾	▲117	3^{1}	1^{h}	2^{h}	2$^{1\frac{1}{2}}$	HerndzR^{7}	12500	79	Break theLock115	PndaBear	11
12 Jly 75	^{9}Tdn	5 f	:23^{2}	:48	1:00^{3}ft	2½	114	2^{1}	1^{h}	3^{nk}	3$^{2\frac{1}{4}}$	WeilerD^{3}	AlwS	85	FierceRuffian115	HpyMircle	7
2 Jly 75	^{9}RD	5½ f	:22	:45	1:04^{1}ft	3½	113	2^{h}	2^{1}	3^{nk}	2^{7}	RieraRJr^{3}	AlwS	87	ChanningRoad113	PndaBear	9
21 May75	^{3}CD	5 f	:22^{2}	:47	:59^{4}ft	5½e	122	2$^{\frac{1}{2}}$	1$^{1\frac{1}{2}}$	1$^{\frac{1}{2}}$	1^{h}	RieraRJr^{7}	Mdn	90	Panda Bear 122	Sam's Act	11

Aug 30 Bel trt 3f ft :37b **Aug 24 Sar trt 3f ft :37⅖b** **Aug 19 Sar trt 4f ft :54b**

If you've never encountered a horse trained by Jose Martin before, this one should be enough to convince you of his skill with claimers.

In the spring Panda Bear was a solid $12,000 racehorse. During the summer Martin found out she was able to beat only $10,000 stock.

Up and down the class ladder Panda Bear won two races and $12,770. Each time Martin dropped the horse to her proper level, she delivered an improved effort.

Three workouts on the deeper training track leading up to today's race assure us of Panda Bear's fitness. Today's drop in class tells us Martin is thinking win. If you're thinking the same thing after you get through with the rest of the field, you'll catch a $9 mutuel.

---

6 FURLONGS—$9,500 CLAIMING, BELMONT PARK, SEPTEMBER 1, 1976

Tacky Lady   **116**   Ch. f (1973), by Nail—Lady Cavan, by Cavan.
Breeder, Mrs. W. A. Kelley (Del.).   1976..11   3   1   0 $15,930

Owner, Stu–Al Stable.   Trainer, Frank Laboccetta.   **$9,500**   1975.. 2   1   0   0 $2,280

24 Aug76	3Sar	7 f :23	:46	31:24	4ft	3	116	4^2	2^2	4^2	45$\frac{3}{4}$	VelasqzJ^8	15000 75 ⓟJrry'sMona116 JyeuxNelll. 8
6 Aug76	2Sar	6 f :23^1	:46	41:12	ft	3$\frac{1}{2}$	118	6$^2\frac{1}{2}$	63$\frac{1}{2}$	63$\frac{3}{4}$	65$\frac{1}{2}$	CdroAJr^2	20000 74 ⓟShawi 111 Jerry's Mona 9
15 Jly 76	7Aqu	6 f :22^4	:46	11:11	4ft	2$\frac{1}{2}$	^114	3^2	2$^1\frac{1}{2}$	1h	1no	TurtteR^9	19000 84 ⓟTackyLady114 JoyousPlsre 9
4 Jly 76	1Aqu	7 f :23^2	:46	41:24	ft	3$\frac{1}{2}$	116	2^2	2^1	11$\frac{1}{2}$	12$\frac{3}{4}$	MapleE^{10}	15000 81 ⓟTackyLady116 FineAsWne 10
20 Jun76	1Bel	6 f :22^4	:46	41:11	3ft	2$\frac{1}{2}$	^116	1$\frac{1}{2}$	1$\frac{1}{2}$	1^1	2no	MapleE^1	12500 84 ⓟDela Pet 121 Tacky Lady 7
9 Jun76	3Bel	6 f :22^4	:47	21:24	ft	17	113	3^2	3$^1\frac{1}{2}$	13	13$\frac{1}{2}$	MapleE^2	7500 78 ⓟTackyLady1t3 Encapslate 9
13 May76	1Bel	7 f :23^1	:46	31:26	1ft	5$\frac{1}{2}$	114	4^3	45$\frac{1}{2}$	67$\frac{1}{2}$	81^2	TurcotteR^4	8500 59 ⓟFiredRed111 NeverFlow 12
4 May76	1Bel	6 f :23^2	:47	31:24	ft	3$\frac{1}{2}$	116	7^4	105$\frac{1}{2}$	83$\frac{3}{4}$	67$\frac{3}{4}$	CruguetJ^2	8500 70 ⓟGldnSl 113 StkeUp theBnd 10
20 Apr76	7Aqu	7 f :22^4	:46	1:25	1ft	6	116	117$\frac{1}{2}$	10^1	110^9	106$\frac{1}{4}$	CrguetJ^{11}	15000 68 ⓟHoldingOn116 FineAsWine 12

Aug 19 Sar trt 5f ft 1:03$\frac{3}{5}$b   Aug 2 Sar 3f sy :36b   July 27 Aqu 5f ft 1:02$\frac{3}{5}$b

---

Barely six weeks before today's race Tacky Lady was winning against horses worth twice as much as those she is facing today. Tacky Lady is dropping down sharply in class, and the bettors at the track think she's a mortal lock, a 3–5 betting favorite. If they were willing to question why this horse is being discounted so suddenly they might make her 3–5 to wind up being carted off the track in a hurry-up wagon.

This is what is known in the trade as a negative drop in class. A horse that is deteriorating so fast that the owner and trainer can't wait to get rid of her. The player should not be so hasty; there are some trainers who win races with horses like this, but in this specific case, all the signs are negative.

Tacky Lady's best races came when trainer Laboccetta had confidence in her ability. He successfully stepped her up in company four straight times.

This is the second steep drop in class in two weeks. Instead of resting this horse, trainer Laboccetta can't wait to get rid of her. I don't think his loss of confidence should be taken lightly. Throw the horse out.

---

1 1/16 MILES (turf)—$10,000 CLAIMING, ARLINGTON PARK, SEPTEMBER 20, 1976

Manager Ed **113** B. c (1973), by Dust Commander—Amberly, by Ambiorix.
Breeder, R. E. Lehmann (Ky.). 1976 5 0 1 1 $2,774
Owner, A. J. Wozneski. Trainer, John C. Wozneski. $10,000 1975 12 1 1 2 $4,798

10 Sep76	^{9}AP	Ⓣ 1	$:48^{1}\ 1:14^{2}\ 1:40^{2}$ fm	$3\frac{1}{2}$	114	$9^{9\frac{3}{4}}$	9^{9}	$8^{7\frac{3}{4}}$	8^{6}	FiresE^{9}	11500	67	BlckCrw114	Knck'sOlympus	11
26 Aug76	^{5}AP	$1\frac{1}{16}$	$:48\ 1:12^{2}\ 1:44^{1}$ ft	2	▲114	$3^{5\frac{1}{2}}$	$3^{3\frac{1}{2}}$	$3^{\frac{1}{2}}$	$2^{1\frac{1}{4}}$	StoverD^{1}	11500	90	Lex Legio 112	Manager Ed	7
12 Aug76	^{7}AP	$1\frac{1}{16}$	$:47^{2}\ 1:14^{1}\ 1:43^{4}$ ft	20	112	$5^{8\frac{1}{2}}$	5^{8}	4^{4}	$4^{4\frac{1}{2}}$	StoverD^{2}	13500	88	Sum Chipper 113	Fleet Flit	8
27 Jly 76	^{7}AP	[T] a $1\frac{1}{16}$	$:46^{3}\ 1:14^{1}\ 1:44^{2}$ fm	25	107^{5}	5^{13}	6^{15}	$6^{9\frac{1}{2}}$	$3^{3\frac{3}{4}}$	RdgzDP^{1}	10500		SumChipper114	UnitdKngdm	7
16 Jly 76	^{6}AP	6 f	$:22\ :46\ 1:12^{2}$ ft	29	108^{5}	10^{12}	11^{13}	10^{12}	10^{12}	RdrgzDP^{4}	10000	69	Demon Run 113	Ahga Mag	11
13 Nov75	^{9}Haw	$6\frac{1}{2}$ f	$:22^{2}\ :45^{4}\ 1:18^{1}$ ft	$9\frac{1}{2}$	118	8^{7}	5^{6}	$2^{1\frac{1}{2}}$	2^{nk}	StoverD^{8}	7500	82	Key Sa 117	Manager Ed	10
4 Nov75	^{9}Haw	6 f	$:22^{2}\ :46^{1}\ 1:12$ sy	8	118	9^{10}	7^{9}	7^{11}	$7^{9\frac{3}{4}}$	StovrD^{10}	10000	76	Lil'sTommie117	SumChipper	11
20 Oct75	^{7}Haw	6 f	$:22^{2}\ :45^{3}\ 1:10^{2}$ ft	26	114	6^{7}	6^{12}	6^{14}	6^{20}	CoxR^{1}	Alw	74	Elocutionist 119	Irish Port	6
14 Oct75	^{3}Haw	6 f	$:22^{2}\ :45^{4}\ 1:12^{4}$ ft	13	118	9^{11}	$9^{8\frac{1}{2}}$	$6^{3\frac{1}{4}}$	$4^{4\frac{3}{4}}$	StoverD^{9}	10000	77	Jim James 116	Rich Passion	9
29 Aug75	^{4}AP	$5\frac{1}{2}$ f	$:22^{4}\ :47^{2}\ 1:07^{4}$ sy	6-5	▲122	$4^{1\frac{1}{2}}$	$3^{3\frac{1}{2}}$	2^{1}	1^{nk}	PatsnG^{1}	cM7000	76	Manager Ed 122	Kid Louie	12

Sept 20 AP 4f ft :51⅗b   Aug 19 AP 4f ft :50b   Aug 3 AP 3f ft :36⅘b

---

Following eight months of inactivity and a terrible six-furlong race on July 16, Manager Ed delivered a vastly improved performance on July 27. It was Manager Ed's first try beyond a sprint distance, his first try around two turns, and his first attempt on grass. We have no way of knowing whether trainer John Wozneski knew his horse was fit enough to perform as well as it did, but he had a right to feel proud of his work. I suspect, in fact, that it went to his head.

On August 12 Wozneski stepped Manager Ed up in company and switched him back to the main track. The horse ran its best but had to settle for fourth money after failing to gain ground in the stretch. We can excuse the trainer for trying to upgrade his horse on that occasion, but the result was not very encouraging.

On August 26 Wozneski dropped the horse a notch, keeping him on the main track, at a level slightly higher than the prior good race. Again, Manager Ed raced to the full limit of his apparent talent, only to lose momentum in the final yards. He did finish second, but that loss of ground marked the second straight wasted opportunity, a sign that trainer Wozneski misjudged his horse's class or distance capability.

Two weeks and *no* workouts later Wozneski decided to try Manager Ed on the grass again. While everything in the horse's record indicates the preference for a slightly cheaper race, the most plausible explanation for the horse's lackluster performance is that trainer Wozneski has blown it. Today's $10,000 race on the turf is not likely to help this horse's chances. Wozneski had a fit horse on his hands but overestimated its talent. The evidence says this horse has lost its edge in condition and will need every break possible to earn a piece of the purse.

1¼ MILES—$350,000 PURSE, HOLLYWOOD PARK, JULY 20, 1974

Chris Evert **121** Ch. f (1971), by Swoon's Son—Miss Carmie, by T. V. Lark.
Breeder, Echo Valley Horse Farm (Ky.). 1974 4 3 0 1 $159,789
Owner, C. Rosen. Trainer, J. A. Trovato. 1973 5 4 1 0 $93,012

Jun22-74 8Bel	1 1-2	2:28⅘ft	4-5	▲121	2h	1h	1 1½	1 3½	Vel'q'zJ1	ScwS 76	F ChrisEvert121	F'staLibre	M'dM'll'r	10
Jun 1-74 8Bel	1 1-8	1:48⅗sy	2¾	121	3 2	2 1½	1h	1½	Vel'ezJ14	ScwS 84	F ChrisEvert121	M'dMuller	QuazeQ'lt	14
May11-74 8Aqu	1	1:36 ft	9-5	▲121	2 1	4 3	3 1½	1¾	Vel'q'zJ1	ScwS 87	F ChrisEvert121	ClearC'py	FiestaLibre	9
May 1-74 8Aqu	7 f	1:24⅖ft	2	▲118	7 4¾	6 6¼	6 7½	3 4½	Vel'q'zJ10	AlwS 74	F ClearCopy113	ShyDawn	ChrisEvert	10
Nov14-73 8Aqu	1	1:36⅖ft	4-5	▲121	2h	2h	1 1	1 1¼	Pi'yLJr11	AlwS 85	F ChrisEvert121	Amb'lero	Kh'd'sK'er	11
Nov 3-73 8CD	7 f	1:25⅕ft	6-5	▲116	9 11	9 13	4 3½	1 1¼	Pin'yLJr2	AlwS 81	F ChrisEvert116	B'ndl'r	KissMeD'rlin	13
Oct 6-73 7Bel	1	1:36⅖ft	6¼	121	9 4	3 1½	4 1	2½	Cas'aM11	ScwS 85	F Bundler121	ChrisEvert	I'm a Pl's're	14
Oct 2-73 6Bel	6 f	1:10⅘ft	3	120	5 2½	4 4½	3½	1 2¾	Pinc'yLJr10	Alw 92	F ChrisEv'rt120	Symp'th'tic	F'h'gL'dy	10
Sep14-73 3Bel	6 f	1:11 ft	3½	120	3 1½	3 2	2½	1 1¾	Pin'yLJr10	Mdn 88	F ChrisEvert120	M'dMuller	MamaKali	13

July 18 Hol 4f ft :46⅖h July 14 Hol 1m ft 1:38⅖h July 9 Hol 6f ft 1:15b

---

Here from top to bottom is a well-managed, top-grade racehorse at her seasonal peak. Notice the way trainer Joe Trovato established a solid foundation in 1973 and stretched Chris out in distance with each succeeding start in 1974. A fine piece of work by a man who knows how to get a horse to produce and keep producing.

These were the past performances of Chris Evert prior to her fifty-length "upset" victory over the speedy Miss Musket on July 20, 1974 in one of the richest match races of all time. Although the key to her winning performance was in the workout line, it was not possible to know that without searching for other clues published in that day's edition of the *Form*.

For Saturday stakes races, and especially for championship-caliber events, the *Daily Racing Form*'s reportage is often excellent. For the Kentucky Derby, for instance, Joe Hirsch does an incredible job, logging the daily doings of all the key eligibles for the two months leading up to the race. Every player should take some time to read the news items and columns in the *Daily Racing Form;* there are many useful tidbits and insights that can be gleaned from them.

Deep within the pages of the July 20, 1974, edition of the *Form*, California correspondent Pat Rogerson reported on the fractional times for the latest workouts of both horses. Although he was most impressed with Miss Musket's blazing one-mile training trial in 1:35⅕, the astute player might have noted that Chris' first quarter-mile fraction in her one-mile workout was noticeably faster. On July 17 Miss Musket worked a half-mile in 48 seconds, a relatively slow move compared with Chris' final workout on July 18. "I told Velasquez to break Chris sharply from the starting gate and not to be worried about getting her tired," said Trovato in Rogerson's report. The significance of Trovato's instructions could hardly be lost on the player who knew that 85 percent of all match races have been won wire to wire. The player may not wish to spend his time researching trainer patterns, but he surely can read his *Racing Form* between races at the track.

9.
The Key Race Method

In late October 1972 I was faced with a unique problem. I had just moved to Columbia, Maryland, and was going to conduct a daily five-minute seminar on handicapping over WLMD radio in the Washington-Baltimore area.

Based on my private results, I thought that I could pick 50 percent winners, show a flat bet profit in the thirteen-week test period, and explain handicapping in the process.

The format was simple. I would handicap races at Laurel racetrack and explain the theories behind the best betting opportunities of the day.

There was one catch. I had been to Laurel racetrack only once, on opening day, October 2. And because I had just joined the staff of *Turf and Sport Digest,* I knew I would not be able to go out to the track more than once a week. I had some familiarity with the leading trainers and their patterns, but I didn't know the horses, the track, or very much else about the local conditions. And I only had a week to prepare myself. In desperation, I did further trainer research, studied post positions, pulled out past performance records and workout listings, and studied the result charts as if I were preparing for an examination before the bar.

A brand new racing surface complicated the problem. Wild upsets were taking place every day as the maintenance crew fought to stabilize conditions. Horses with late speed seemed to have a built-in edge during this period, but it was not easy to tell from the past performance records which horses would be able to produce that late speed. I solved the problem by using a simple research tool I had developed a few years earlier, one that investigates the relationship between a race over the track and future winning performance.

Strange as it may seem, almost every stretch-running Laurel winner with a prior race over the track had displayed one major characteristic: a sign of increased speed on the turn in the previous Laurel race. The implications were too powerful to ignore. The turn was the roughest piece of real estate in Maryland. Any horse in good enough shape to make a move on it was a horse worth tabbing for improvement next time out.

Admittedly, as form settled down and the track stabilized, I was forced to handicap races more thoroughly than that. But I got past the first four weeks with 45 percent winners, including some outrageous longshots. And I was on the air to stay.

It is also true that this was a particularly unusual set of conditions, yet the investigative tool has served me well for many purposes, as it might well serve you. Here is how to set it up. Again you will need to work with a set of chronologically dated result charts.

First, with the most recent race on top, check the index date and race number of the winner's last race: see below, 6Aug76 ^{1}AP^{3} Windy City Butch means Windy City Butch last raced in the first race, August 6, and finished third.

THIRD RACE AP August 23, 1976 — **6 FURLONGS. (1:08⅗). MAIDENS. SPECIAL WEIGHTS. Purse $7,000. 2-year-olds. Weight, 119 lbs. Value to winner $4,200; second, $1,400; third, $770; fourth, $420; fifth, $210. Mutuel Pool, $144,583.**

Last Raced	Horse	EqtAWt	PP	St	¼	½	Str	Fin	Jockeys	Owners	Odds to $1
6 Aug76 ^{1}AP^{3}	Windy City Butch	2 119	6	5	7^{1}	$6^{\frac{1}{2}}$	5^{3}	1^{nk}	MGavidia	S Berry C Scott	2.80
	Cornucopian	2 119	5	6	5^{h}	$5^{2\frac{1}{2}}$	4^{h}	$2^{\frac{1}{2}}$	GPatterson	E A Cox Jr	a-1.80
14 Aug76 ^{3}AP^{2}	Hinkston	2 119	3	4	4^{3}	$3^{\frac{1}{2}}$	$1^{\frac{1}{2}}$	3^{5}	EFires	Levitch-Stone	3.30
29 Jly 76 ^{5}AP^{7}	Bask	2 119	9	3	3^{1}	2^{1}	2^{1}	4^{h}	LSnyder	Reineman Stable Inc	a-1.80
	Wellspoken	2 119	7	9	2	9	7^{2}	5^{h}	RBreen	EJmendorf	20.60
1 May76 ^{1}Sun^{4}	Knotty Knave	b2 119	1	7	6^{1}	7^{1}	$6^{1\frac{1}{2}}$	$6^{3\frac{1}{2}}$	JLively	M Ross et al	6.30
6 Aug76 ^{4}AP^{7}	East Union	b2 119	4	2	1^{2}	$6^{2\frac{1}{2}}$	3^{1}	$7^{\frac{1}{2}}$	JPowell	B-G Bromagen	17.20
23 Apr76 3Kee^{7}	Count Tumiga	2 119	8	8	8^{2}	8^{1}	8	8^{2}	RSibille	G'ld'n Ch'nce F'm Inc	36.10
11 Aug76 ^{3}AP^{2}	Debarcation	b2 119	2	1	2^{1}	$4^{1\frac{1}{2}}$	8^{1}	9	JDBailey	S Laser	9.90

Coupled, a-Cornucopian and Bask.

OFF AT 2:53 CDT. Start good. Won driving. Time, :22⅖, :46⅖, :59⅕, 1:11⅘. Track fast.

$2 Mutuel Prices:			
6-WINDY CITY BUTCH	7.60	3.40	2.40
1-CORNUCOPIAN (a-Entry)		3.20	2.40
4-HINKSTON			2.60

Ch. c, by Lurullah—Christy Blue, by Porterhouse. Trainer, Clifford J. Scott. Bred by Estate of Charles Cunningham (Ky.).

WINDY CITY BUTCH was unhurried early, rallied wide leaving the upper stretch to run down CORNUCOPIAN in the final strides. The latter was unhurried early, drove inside the leaders leaving the eighth pole to wrest the lead late in tht drive but was unable to contain the winner approaching the finish. HINKSTON circled rivals coming out of the turn to take the lead a furlong out, faltered late in the drive. BASK moved between horses coming out of the turn, lacked a closing rally. WELLSPOKEN had to steady while in tight quarters leaving the gate, rallied mildly late to pass tiring rivals. KNOTTY KNAVE went evenly. EAST UNION sprinted out o a clear lead in the early running, tired leaving the upper stretch. COUNT TUMIGA was always outrun. DEBARCATION was through after a half.

Scratched—Dravir.

Next, thumb back to the date and race number indicated to see what the winner did in his last race. But whatever he did, *circle his name*. That circle will forever mean that Windy City Butch won his *next* start.

FIRST RACE
AP
August 6, 1976

6 FURLONGS. (1:08⅗). MAIDENS. SPECIAL WEIGHTS. Purse $7,000. 2-year-olds Weight, 119 lbs.
Value to winner $4,200; second, $1,400; third, $770; fourth, $420; fifth, $210.
Mutuel Pool, $64,776.

Last Raced	Horse	EqtAWt	PP	St	¼	½	Str	Fin	Jockeys	Owners	Odds to $1
21 Jly 76 5AP8	Fiddlefish	b2 119	4	2	1h	13½	12½	11¼	APatterson	Mary Lou Cashman	5.00
29 Jly 76 1AP6	Barely Safe	2 119	9	6	5½	3½	21½	22½	RSibille	Golden Chance F'm Inc	8.40
21 Jly 76 5AP2	Windy City Butch	b2 119	8	5	6²½	4h	32½	35	WGavidia	S Berry-C Scott	2.00
	Victory Flag	2 119	6	3	4½	5¹	64	4½	EFires	Elmendorf	14.00
29 Jly 76 1AP5	Gordon Pasha	b2 119	3	1	3³	21	41½	5¾	RLTurcotte	D A Hess	2.70
21 Jly 76 5AP5	Beau Dustin	b2 119	7	7	78	76	5½	61¼	CStone	Mary Zimmerman	16.50
	Selaru	b2 119	2	9	9	8h	7¹½	72	PRubbicco	Bar R J's Stable	22.10
	The Stinger	2 119	5	8	81	9	8²	82½	HArroyo	R F Salmen	15.90
29 Jly 76 5AP2	Coldwater	2 119	1	4	2h	6¼	9	9	RBreen	R Russell	9.00

OFF AT 2:00½ CDT. Start good. Won driving. Time, :22⅗, :46⅖, :58⅘, 1:11⅗. Track good.
Official Program Numbers ↘

$2 Mutuel Prices:

5-FIDDLEFISH	12.00	6.60	4.00
10-BARELY SAFE		7.80	3.80
9-WINDY CITY BUTCH			2.80

Ch. c, by Piko—Noholme's Gal, by Noholme II. Tr., Paul T. Adwell. Bred by Fontainebleau Farm, Inc. (Ky.).
FIDDLEFISH broke alertly to vie for the lead outside two rivals, drew out in the turn and won under a strong hand ride. BARELY SAFE circled rivals coming out of the turn and was gradually getting to the winner. WINDY CITY BUTCH was outrun early, rallied strongly between rivals after a half but was no threat to the top pair. VICTORY FLAG went evenly. GORDON PASHA pressed the early lead while between rivals, faltered leaving the turn. BEAU DUSTIN had no excuses. SELARU and THE STINGER were always outrun. COLDWATER had brief early speed along the rail.
Scratched—Brach's Honey, Promising Dream, Uncle Jett, Restless Rascal.

If you repeat this simple exercise for the most recent fifty or sixty races (you can go back as far as you wish) and if you continue the process every day, you will be adding exceedingly valuable information to dozens of result charts. The data may help you distinguish patterns that are not otherwise detectable.

Maybe you will discover, as I did, that the majority of route race winners at Hazel Park and Latonia racetracks had a prior sprint race for a jumpoff effort. Maybe you will observe that horses shipping from California to New York during the early spring win an astounding percentage of races first crack out of the box. Perhaps you will note that horses coming off the turf course at Delaware Park and other tracks tend to show improved early speed in their next try on the dirt. The possibilities are without limit. Without really trying, you will automatically create the Key Race method, a powerful tool that isolates especially well-run races at every class level.

For example, the three horses circled in the following chart came out of the race to win their very next starts. A Key Race.

FIRST RACE
Aqu
July 15, 1976

1⅛ MILES. (1:47). CLAIMING. Purse $7,500. For 3-year-olds and upward. 3-year-olds, 116 lbs.; older, 122 lbs. Non-winners of a race at a mile and a furlong or over since July 1 allowed 3 lbs.; of such a race since June 15, 5 lbs. Claiming price $8,500; if for less, 2 lbs. allowed for each $250 to $8,000. (Races when entered to be claimed for $7,000 or less not considered.)

Value to winner, $4,500; second, $1,650; third, $900; fourth, $450. Track Mutuel Pool, $106,946. OTB Pool, $87,971.

Last Raced	Horses	Eqt	A	Wt	PP	St	¼	½	¾	Str	Fin	Jockeys	Owners	Odds to $1
25Jun76 6Bel3	Charms Hope	b5		113	1	2	4⁴	4³	4⁷	3½	1ⁿᵏ	MVenezia	J J Stippel	2.50
7Jly 76 1Aqu1	Finney Finster	b4		117	3	7	6⁸	5²	3¹¹½	2ʰ	2¹½	ASantiago	Camijo Stable	5.60
9Jly 76 1Aqu1	Good and Bold			5 110	4	1	1⁴	1⁶	1⁶	1³	3¹³	BDiNicola⁵	Emmarr Stable	3.00
9Jly 76 1Aqu6	Just Like Pa	b3		109	2	4	3½	3¹½	2ʰ	4⁸	4⁹	DMontoya†	Audley Farm Stable	8.50
8Jly 76 1Aqu1	Wave the Flag			6 115	5	6	7	7	7	5⁶	5⁴½	RHernandez	O S Barrera	3.40
1Jly 76 2Aqu1	Jolly Mister	b4		113	6	5	5¹	6⁷	6½	6¹²	6²²	PDay	Stan-Mar Stable	7.30
9Jly 76 3Aqu5	Acosado II.			4 117	7	3	2⁵	2³	5¹	7	7	JVasquez	Bellrose Farm	11.90

†Five pounds apprentice allowance waived.

OFF AT 10:30 PDT. START GOOD. WON DRIVING. Time, :24; :47⅕, 1:12⅗, 1:39⅗, 1:53⅖. Track fast.

$2 Mutuel Prices {

1-CHARMS HOPE	7.00	4.00	2.60
3-FINNEY FINSTER		6.20	3.60
4-GOOD AND BOLD			2.80

B. h, by Abe's Hope—Cold Dead, by Dead Ahead. Trainer, F. J. Horan. Bred by Criterion Farms (Fla.).

CHARMS HOPE, unhurried early, rallied approaching the stretch and outfinished FINNEY FINSTER. The latter, off slowly, advanced steadily to loom a threat near midstretch and continued on with good courage. GOOD AND BOLD tired from his early efforts. JUST LIKE PA rallied leaving the far turn but lacked the needed late response. WAVE THE FLAG was never close. JOLLY MISTER was always outrun. ACOSADO II tired badly.

Charms Hope claimed by M. Garren, trainer G. Puentes; Good and Bold claimed by S. Sommer, trainer F. Martin.
Claiming Prices (in order of finish)—$8000, 8500, 8250, 8250, 8250, 8000, 8500.

Wave the Flag won a $5,000 claimer on July 21. Charms Hope won an allowance race on July 23. Good and Bold won a $10,000–$12,000 claimer on July 31. In addition, Just Like Pa ran fourth on July 29, encountering traffic problems, and won a $9,000 claimer on August 18.

Coincidence might dilute the impact of the added information, but nine out of ten times there is a better explanation. Either this race was superior to the designated class or else it contained an unusually fit group of horses. In either case, that's important information.

Indeed, after Wave the Flag's easy score at $5,000 claiming and Charms Hope's five-length victory in allowance company, the Key Race method would have certainly pointed out the merits of Good and Bold at 9–1 in a six-furlong race on July 31 (note the running line of Good and Bold in the Key Race chart). Observant race watchers and chart readers might similarly have made a strong case for Just Like Pa when he went to the post at 6–1 on August 18.

The Key Race method has many applications, but it is simply sensational in pointing out above-average fields in maiden races and turf events.

Maiden races are a mixed bag. Very few horses entered in such races have established their true class level. Some maidens will turn out to be useful racehorses; others will be little more than walking feed bills. Sooner or later, most often sooner, the best of the maidens wind up in the winner's circle. With deadly precision the Key Race method points out those maiden races that contained the fastest nonwinners on the grounds.

Maybe the winner of a maiden race returns to win a stakes race. Maybe the fifth horse in the maiden race comes back to graduate in its next start. If so, I would begin looking for the second, third, and fourth horses to come out of that maiden race. There could be little question that they had raced against above-average stock. Naturally, I would not suspend the handicapping process. I would still want to know what the rest of the field looked like, whether there was a prevailing track bias, what type it was, what if any trainer patterns were present, and so on. I would, however, surely upgrade the chances of any horse coming out of such a strong field.

Similar logic explains the effectiveness of the Key Race method in classifying turf races. Regardless of a horse's record on dirt, its ability to compete on grass is never established until it has raced on grass. In effect, the horse is a maiden on the turf until it wins on the turf. Again, the Key Race method will isolate the stronger fields.

Every once in a while you will encounter the phenomenon of a result chart with six, seven, or more circled horses —a Key Race in the ultimate sense of the word. My research says this occurs at least once in every 500 races. By the time four horses come out of the same field to win their next starts you should get the message.

The Key Race at Saratoga on August 5, 1972, is my personal favorite. The circles are not included. They aren't necessary. Every last horse provided a winning effort.

EIGHTH RACE
Saratoga
AUGUST 5, 1972

1 $\frac{1}{16}$ MILES.(turf). (1.39 2/5) ALLOWANCES. Purse $15,000. 3-year-olds and upward which have not won three races other than maiden, claiming or starter. Weights, 3-year-olds, 117 lbs. Older, 122 lbs. Non-winners of $7,200 at a mile or over since July 1, allowed 2 lbs. $6,600 at a mile or over since June 17, 4 lbs. $6,000 at a mile or over since May 15, 6 lbs. (Maidens, claiming and starter races not considered in allowances.)

Value of race $15,000, value to winner $9,000, second $3,300, third $1,800, fourth $900. Mutuel pool $128,695, OTB pool $70,388.

Last Raced	Horse	Eqt.A.Wt	PP	St	1/4	1/2	3/4	Str	Fin	Jockey	Odds $1
23Jly72 8Del2	Scrimshaw	4 116	2	2	7^1	7$\frac{1}{2}$	4^1	1^3	1^4	Marquez C H	2.40
20Jly72 6Aqu4	Gay Gambler	3 108	8	8	9$1\frac{1}{2}$	9^5	9^8	8$1\frac{1}{2}$	2$1\frac{1}{2}$	Patterson G	5.60
22Jly72 6Aqu3	Fast Judge	b 3 111	7	7	6^2	6^1	6$\frac{1}{2}$	4^{hd}	3^{hd}	Velasquez J	10.00
28Jly72 6Aqu1	Straight To Paris	3 115	9	3	2$\frac{1}{2}$	2$1\frac{1}{2}$	2$\frac{1}{2}$	2$\frac{1}{2}$	4no	Vasquez J	2.70
25Jly72 9Aqu1	Search the Farm	b 4 116	3	9	8$1\frac{1}{2}$	8$1\frac{1}{2}$	8^1	6^{hd}	5no	Guadalupe J	11.20
23Jly72 8Del3	Chrisaway	4 116	4	6	5$1\frac{1}{2}$	4^{hd}	7$\frac{1}{2}$	7$\frac{1}{2}$	6^2	Howard R	25.30
25Jly72 9Aqu5	Navy Lieutenant	b 4 116	1	1	3$\frac{1}{2}$	5^1	3$\frac{1}{2}$	5$\frac{1}{2}$	7^4	Belmonte E	10.90
25Jly72 7Aqu4	Head Table	3 113	10	5	4^1	3^1	5$\frac{1}{2}$	9^{10}	8^2	Baeza B	7.50
17Jly72 8Del3	Mongo's Image	3 111	5	4	1$1\frac{1}{2}$	1$\frac{1}{2}$	1^1	3^{hd}	9^{10}	Nelson E	28.70
21Jly72 7Aqu5	Chartered Course	b 4 116	6	10	10	10	10	10	10	Arellano J	16.70

Time, :23$\frac{1}{5}$, :46$\frac{2}{5}$, 1:09$\frac{4}{5}$, 1:34$\frac{3}{5}$, 1:40$\frac{4}{5}$ (Against Wind in Backstretch). Course firm.

$2 Mutuel Prices:

2-(B)- SCRIMSHAW	6.80	3.60	3.20
8-(H)- GAY GAMBLER		7.00	4.80
7-(G)- FAST JUDGE			5.60

B. g, by Jaipur—Ivory Tower, by Hill Prince. Trainer Lake R P. Bred by Vanderbilt A G (Md).

IN GATE AT 5.23; OFF AT 5.23 EASTERN DAYLIGHT TIME. Start Good Won Handily

SCRIMSHAW, taken back after breaking alertly, swung out to go after the leaders on the far turn, quickly drew off and was never seriously threatened. GAY GAMBLER, void of early foot, was unable to split horses entering the stretch, altered course to the extreme outside and finished strongly. FAST JUDGE, reserved behind the leaders, split horses leaving the far turn but was not match for the top pair. STRAIGHT TO PARIS prompted the pace much of the way and weakened during the drive. SEARCH THE FARM failed to menace. CHRISAWAY raced within easy striking distance while outside horses much of the way but lacked a late response. NAVY LIEUTENANT, a factor to the stretch while saving ground, gave way. HEAD TABLE was finished leaving the far turn. MONGO'S IMAGE stopped badly after showing to midstretch.

Owners— 1, Vanderbilt A G; 2, Whitney C V; 3, Wygod M J; 4, Rokeby Stable; 5, Nadler Evelyn; 6, Steinman Beverly R; 7, Sommer S; 8, Happy Hill Farm; 9, Reynolds J A; 10, Camijo Stable.

Trainers— 1, Lake R P; 2, Poole G T; 3, Nickerson V J; 4, Burch Elliott; 5, Nadler H; 6, Fout P R; 7, Martin F; 8, Wright F I; 9, Reynolds J A; 10, King W P.

Overweight: Head Table 2 pounds.

On August 12 Scrimshaw won the first division of the Bernard Baruch Handicap. One half-hour later Chrisaway took the second division at 50–1. A few days later Chartered Course won a daily double race paying $25. On the same card Gay Gambler—probably the best bet of the year—took the sixth race. Straight to Paris shipped to Monmouth for his win; Fast Judge, Search the Farm, and Navy Lieutenant raced out of the money in their next starts at Saratoga but won on the rebound at Belmont in September. Mongo's Image won a high-class allowance race at the end of the Saratoga meeting at 8–1.

The only horse that didn't race back during this period was Head Table. For weeks I hunted through the *Racing Form* hoping to find his name among the entries. I was prepared to fly anywhere. But he never showed up.

Believe it or not, Head Table returned to the races on April 21, 1973, nine months after the Key Race. Yes, you guessed it: Head Table won by six. That's weird.

10.
An Edge in Class

At Charles Town racetrack in West Virginia, where the racing is cheap and the betting action takes exotic forms, the horseplayer seldom has a chance to see a top-drawer horse in action. Nevertheless, the player would be making a serious mistake if he failed to incorporate notions about class into his handicapping.

On a typical racing program at a minor-league track like Charles Town, the majority of races are for $1,500–$2,000 claiming horses—the lowest level of horsedom. These are horses that have seen their better days or are just not fast enough to compete in the higher-class claiming events found at the major one-mile racetracks.

Actually, that is not quite true. A respectable number of Charles Town horses can run fast—and a select few can run very fast—but they are too short-winded or too battle-scarred to be able to sustain their speed in three-quarter-mile races at the majors. After all, there are no four-furlong races for three-year-olds and up at Arlington Park, and there are no six-furlong races for $1,500 horses either.

For all the wrong reasons, major-track handicappers tend to have a snobbish attitude toward their compatriots at the minors, thinking perhaps that the cheaper racing is less formful, less predictable. I can assure you, however, that there are more winning players per capita at "bull ring" tracks like Charles Town than there are at Aqueduct or Hollywood Park.

Far from being the indecipherable mess that it seems on the surface, minor-track racing offers some of the most attractive betting opportunities in all of racing. Examining the class factor will show exactly why this is so, and for the astute player the applications extend to a large body of races at the major tracks as well.

The first step toward success at Charles Town is to use the result charts to construct a record of the eligibility conditions of all the cheapest races. About 90 percent of Charles

Town claiming events have restrictive clauses which resemble the eligibility conditions found in allowance (nonclaiming) races at the major one-mile tracks.

For example, the third, sixth, eighth, and tenth races at Charles Town on August 4, 1976, were $1,500 claiming races for three-year-olds and up, but any bettor who assumed that these races were for the same class of horse was on his way to a disastrous evening of betting.

The first $1,500 claiming race was limited to horses "which have not won a race in 1976"; the second, "for nonwinners of three races in 1976"; the third, "for nonwinners of two races lifetime"; and the final $1,500 race, "for nonwinners of a race in 1975 or 1976," the lowest $1,500 race in captivity.

The next evening there were four more $1,500 claiming races with four additional sets of eligibility conditions. Confusing? Perhaps. But it turns out that there is a measurable difference between each of the restricted $1,500-class races. This difference is not only reflected in the average winning times for each separate restricted class but is greater than the difference between the average $1,500 and $2,000 race. In other words, it is more difficult to advance within the same $1,500 claiming class than it is to step up to the $2,000 claiming level!

Whenever a $1,500 horse wins at Charles Town, it loses its chance to compete in the same restricted class. The claiming price remains the same—even the purse tends to be the same—but the horse must now face other horses that have also graduated from the lower restricted level.

Naturally, the next level (within the same $1,500 claiming class) will include other horses with recent victories. This makes for much tougher competition.

Indeed, most Charles Town horses have a very hard time scoring two wins back to back, and some never advance until all the better $1,500 horses win their way into the next level of competition. In a very real sense, the slower horses are hopelessly trapped, and some remain trapped for months.

For the purpose of identification, it is helpful (if not essential) to formulate a classification system for all $1,500 and $2,000 races. (At the major tracks, where allowance races are written with similar restrictive eligibility clauses, the purses attached to each race are scaled in proportion to the quality of the field. A classification code is therefore unnecessary, provided of course that the player refers to the charts to note the purse values. The purse values are in themselves a ready-made classification system.)

CHARLES TOWN CLASSIFICATION CODE FOR $1,500 OR $2,000 CLAIMING RACES

O—open race, unrestricted eligibility (top class)

A—Nonwinners of 2 races in the past two months
or 3 races in the past three months

B—Nonwinners of 2 races in three to five months

C—Nonwinners of 2 races in six to nine months
or 3 races in nine to twelve months

D—Nonwinners of 2 races in nine to twenty-four months

E—Nonwinners of a race in nine to twenty-four months

M—Nonwinners lifetime (maidens)

As you can see, the increments *between* class levels at the same $1,500 claiming price are quite steep. It takes a pretty decent $1,500 horse to make its way up the ladder during a calendar year.

The easiest class jump is maiden to E class (nonwinners of a race in nine to twenty-four months). It is no coincidence that the majority of Charles Town repeaters occur at this rock-bottom level. Most E-class horses have very little ability and are always forced to meet recent maiden graduates. Generally speaking, a recent maiden graduate, especially a lightly raced maiden graduate, is a very dependable Charles Town bet. At the very least, the recent victory is a positive sign of current condition. In the spring of 1976 I charted two months of Charles Town races and found fifteen repeaters of this type in thirty-four E-class races. The average mutuel payoff was $8.60.

With minor revisions, the Charles Town classification code will prove useful at any minor-class racetrack and at any major track where similar eligibility conditions are written into the cheapest races.

Tracks like River Downs, Thistledown, Waterford Park, Lincoln Downs, Green Mountain Park, Penn National, Finger Lakes, Commodore Downs, Longacres, and Fonner Park all fit into this category, and there are at least a dozen others spread across the country.

From practical experience at a few of these minor racetracks, I cannot stress enough the value of the classification code. Of course, you might have to set up slightly different categories depending upon the particular eligibility conditions of races in your area, but you will reward yourself many times over for the effort. Some results will in fact astound you.

At Green Mountain Park, for example, where I enjoyed many an evening during the mid-1960s while working as a counselor at nearby Camp Watitoh, one of the most satisfying bets of my entire career came in the first week that I put the classification code to work.

To my amazement I spotted a 14–1 shot in a $2,000 D-class race that had flashed some high early speed in a $1,500 A-class race. Believe it or not, despite the apparent raise in claiming price, the horse was dropping down sharply in company. He won by nine lengths!

And if you're wondering how this classification code works in today's overexpanded racing marketplace, a good friend of mine, Dick White, has been using this method at Charles Town for the past two years, and he confirms that the identical "dropdown" phenomenon takes place every few weeks.

There are other fundamental applications to consider as well. Very often a $1,500 horse will be entered in an A- or B-class race when it is still eligible for a weaker C- or D-class event. Such a horse can be safely and automatically thrown out. The horse is just out for the exercise, or the trainer is purposely trying to darken its form. (If the horse is really that good, the trainer will invariably raise its selling price.)

Conversely, horses that have been showing signs of life in A- or B-class races make excellent wagers when they are properly placed in less demanding D- or E-class events. This type of hidden class maneuver is the most powerful dropdown angle in all of racing, and you can also expect to see it in a slightly different form at the major tracks.

An allowance race at Aqueduct or Santa Anita or any other major track is probably the toughest kind of race for the novice or intermediate horseplayer. In order to handicap such a race properly, the player must have a fix on the local pecking order. He must know which horses on the grounds are the best sprinters, the best routers, the best turf horses, the best three-year-olds, and so forth. He must also know the approximate breaking point when a claiming race is equal to or better than the allowance race in question.

Allowance race conditions like those $1,500 claiming races at Charles Town are restricted events. A two-time stakes winner or a three-time winner of a $10,000 purse is not allowed into any field that is designed for a band of recent maiden graduates.

Moreover, the major-track trainer of an allowance horse will often do what the Charles Town trainer of a

$1,500 claimer does. He will race the horse against more experienced winners and then drop it back to a level where its best race could make it a top contender. Because the major-track trainer can sometimes hide this maneuver by using top-price claiming events ($40,000+ in New York and California, $25,000+ in Illinois and New Jersey, $15,000+ in Maryland and Michigan, and so on), he can often fool the unsophisticated bettors into thinking the horse is stepping up in company when it goes from a claiming to an allowance race. Many times over the opposite is true.

FIFTH   RACE

AP

June   8, 1976

6 FURLONGS. (1:08⅗). ALLOWANCES Purse $8,500 Fillies. 3- and 4-year-olds which have never won two races other than maiden or claiming. 3-year-olds, 115 lbs.; 4-year-olds, 123 lbs. Non-winners of a race other than maiden or claiming since April 13 allowed 3 lbs.; such a race since March 13. 5 lbs.

Value to winner $5,100; second, $1,700; third, $935; fourth, $510; fifth, $255. Mutuel Pool, $128,595.

At Arlington Park in June and July 1976 there were thirty such allowance races. Fourteen were won by horses that showed good form in claiming races. It shouldn't surprise you to learn that the purse values for all $25,000 claiming races at Arlington are higher than the purse value listed for this category of allowance race. Without result charts, the Arlington player might never have known that. The suspicion is that few people do, because the average price paid by those fourteen winners was $9.

The same sort of oversight happens at Aqueduct and Santa Anita, where a solid $45,000 claiming winner can usually beat three-quarters of the allowance horses on the grounds. A solid $30,000 claimer can similarly handle the weaker allowance horses. Smart trainers know this, and without result charts to expose the true class levels of each race, the player is at the trainer's mercy.

Caspar Milquetoast **113** **Dk. b. or br. c (1973). by Our Michael—Backseat Driver, by Traffic Judge. Breeder. C. Wetherill (Ky.).**

Owner, Leonard Henry. Trainer Philip G. Johnson.

1976	12	5	1	2	$45,020
1975	5	1	1	0	$7.340

10 Aug76 ^{2}Sar	7 f	$:22^{2}$ $:45^{1}1:24^{2}$sy	8-5	▲122	3^{4}	3^{5}	3^{1}	$1^{2\frac{1}{2}}$	MapleE^{1}	60000	83	CsprMilqetst122	Adm'sActn	5
16 Jly 76 ^{6}Aqu	1	$:45^{3}1:10^{1}1:35^{4}$sy	8-5	▲113	$5^{9\frac{1}{2}}$	$4^{5\frac{1}{2}}$	2^{1}	$1^{1\frac{1}{2}}$	MapleE^{1}	55000	87	CasparMilqtst113	MldNedle	6
2 Jly 76 ^{7}Aqu	1	$:46^{4}1:11^{1}1:35^{4}$ft	$3\frac{3}{4}$	112	$4^{8\frac{1}{2}}$	$4^{4\frac{1}{2}}$	$3^{4\frac{1}{2}}$	$3^{2\frac{3}{4}}$	SantiagoA^{4}	Alw	84	Political Coverup 112	Bakor	6
24 Jun76 ^{2}Bel	7 f	$:23^{1}$ $:46^{1}1:23^{1}$ft	$4\frac{1}{2}$e	122	8^{8}	6^{12}	4^{4}	1no	MapleE^{4}	40000	86	CasparMilqutst122	Rbrt'sBy	8
6 Jun76 ^{4}Bel	7 f	$:23^{1}$ $:46^{4}1:23$ ft	$3\frac{3}{4}$e	117	3^{2}	3^{1}	1^{h}	1no	MapleE^{6}	40000	87	CsprMilqtst117	FnncialWhiz	7
19 May76 ^{6}Bel	7 f	$:23^{2}$:47 1:24 sy	4	117	5^{3}	4^{3}	2^{2}	1^{3}	VasqezJ^{3}	30000	82	CasparMilqtst117	ArcticLck	8
6 May76 ^{5}Bel	1	$:46^{2}1:13^{1}1:37^{1}$ft	$3\frac{3}{4}$	117	$4^{3\frac{1}{2}}$	2^{h}	$1^{\frac{1}{2}}$	$2^{\frac{1}{2}}$	VasqezJ^{4}	30000	81	Mr.Interntnl117	CsprMilqtst	9
23 Apr76 ^{4}Aqu	7 f	$:23^{1}$ $:46^{3}1:25$ gd	$8\frac{1}{2}$	117	6^{6}	$6^{7\frac{1}{2}}$	$5^{6\frac{1}{4}}$	$4^{1\frac{3}{4}}$	VsquezJ^{2}	35000	74	ForestStrm117	Drover'sDwn	7
10 Apr76 ^{5}Aqu	6 f	$:22^{3}$ $:46^{1}1:10^{4}$ft	24	115	5^{5}	5^{5}	$5^{5\frac{1}{2}}$	$5^{5\frac{3}{4}}$	HoleM^{3}	Alw	83	Bonge 117	Distinctively	9
18 Mar76 ^{7}Aqu	1	$:45^{3}1:10^{2}1:36^{3}$ft	$6\frac{1}{4}$	115	7^{13}	7^{11}	$7^{9\frac{1}{4}}$	$6^{9\frac{1}{2}}$	HoleM^{7}	Alw	73	HailLiberty115	HenryBrooks	8
6 Mar76 ^{6}Aqu	1	$:47\ 1:11^{3}1:36^{3}$ft	8-5	▲115	$9^{6\frac{1}{2}}$	$7^{6\frac{1}{2}}$	4^{8}	$4^{6\frac{1}{2}}$	CordroAJr^{3}	Alw	77	Resilient 115	Ship Trial	9

Aug 24 Sar trt 4f ft :49h **July 27 Bel 6f ft 1:14⅘h** **July 11 Bel trt 4f ft :49⅖b**

The chart below refers to Caspar Milquetoast's most recent race, a $60,000 claiming event with a purse of $15,000.

SECOND RACE
Sar
August 10, 1976

7 FURLONGS. (1:21). CLAIMING. Purse $15,000. 3-year-olds. Weight, 122 lbs. Non-winners of a race since July 15 allowed 3 lbs.; a race since July 1, 5 lbs. Claiming price, $60,000; for each $2,500 to $55,000, allowed 2 lbs. (Races when entered to be claimed for $50,000 or less not considered.)

Value to winner $9,000; second, $3,300; third, $1,800; fourth, $900. Mutuel Pool, $66,701. Off-track betting, $61,941.

Last Raced	Horse	Eqt	A	Wt	PP	St	¼	½	Str	Fin	Jockeys	Owners	Odds to $1
16 Jly 76 ^{6}Aqu^{1}	Caspar Milquetoast	b	3	122	1	5	3^{2}	3^{2}	3^{5}	$1^{2\frac{1}{2}}$	EMaple	L D Henry	1.60
5 Aug76 ^{7}Sar^{1}	Adam's Action	b	3	118	2	1	2^{4}	1h	$1^{\frac{1}{2}}$	2^{nk}	JVelasquez	Exeter Stable	2.10
2 Aug76 ^{2}Sar^{1}	Austin	b	3	113	5	2	1^{h}	2^{5}	$2^{\frac{1}{2}}$	$3^{7\frac{1}{2}}$	ACorderoJr	Harbor View Farm	2.60
1 Aug76 ^{7}FE^{3}	Salim Alicum		3	122	3	3	4^{h}	$4^{\frac{1}{2}}$	4^{1}	4	RTurcotte	G R Gardiner	6.00
10 Jly 76 ^{7}Aks^{9}	Le Punch	b	3	117	4	4	5	5	5	Eased.	RHernandez	E C Cashman	10.00

OFF AT 2:01 EDT. Start good. Won driving. Time, :22⅖, :45⅕, 1:11, 1:24⅖. Track sloppy.

$2 Mutuel Prices:			
2-CASPAR MILQUETOAST	5.20	2.80	2.20
3-ADAM'S ACTION		2.80	2.20
6-AUSTIN			2.20

Dk. b. or br. c, by Our Michael—Backseat Driver, by Traffic Judge. Trainer, Philip G. Johnson. Bred by Cortright Weterill (Ky.).

CASPAR MILQUETOAST raced wide into the stretch while rallying and drew clear after catching ADAM'S ACTION near the final sixteenth. The latter saved ground while vying for the lead with AUSTIN to midstretch and weakened. AUSTIN weakened from his eary efforts. SALIM ALICUM was always outrun. LE PUNCH, outrun to the stretch, was eased during the late stages.

Corrected weight—Salim Alicum, 122.

Claiming Prices (in order of finish)—$60000, 55000, 55000, 60000, 60000.

Scratched—Buttonbuck, Gabe Benzur.

The next chart is the result chart for the race in which Caspar was entered with the past performances as shown at top this page. Note the lower purse value and the restriction built into the eligibility conditions. This is a classic example of the hidden class dropdown, expertly manipulated by trainer P. G. Johnson.

SEVENTH RACE
Bel
August 31, 1976

6 FURLONGS. (1:08⅖). WISE MARGIN PURSE. ALLOWANCES. (Purse $10,000.) 3-year-olds and upward which have never won a race other than maiden, claiming or starter. 3-year-olds, 118 lbs.; older, 122 lbs. Non-winners of a race other than claiming since Aug. 1 allowed 3 lbs.; such a race since July 15, 5 lbs.
Value to winner $6,000; second, $2,200; third, $1,200; fourth, $600.
Mutuel Pool, $138,757. Off-track betting, $96,245. Exacta Pool, $177,505. Off-track betting Exacta Pool, $191,008.

Last Raced	Horse	EqtAWt PP St	¼	½	Str Fin	Jockeys	Owners	Odds to $1
10 Aug76 2Sar1	Caspar Milquetoast	b3 113 6 5	71½ 4½	2½	11¾	EMaple	L D Henry	1.90
20 Aug76 7Sar3	Bold Needle	b3 113 5 4	4½ 51	55	2¾	PDay	Willwynee Stable	7.20
28 Jly 76 6Aqu2	Balancer	4 117 9 1	21 2½	3h	3¾	MVenezia	Mrs D E Kerr	5.10
23 Aug76 7Sar3	Master Jorge	3 115 8 2	31 31	4½	41	JVelasquez	E Ubarri	5.40
23 Aug76 7Sar7	Private Thoughts	b3 113 2 3	1½ 1h	1h	55½	TWallis	R L Reineman	7.40
7 Aug76 9Sar7	Ferrous	3 113 4 6	82 83	6½	6¾	ACorderoJr	J Allen	6.10
31 Jly 76 4Aqu1	Irish Era	4 119 1 7	5½ 6½	72	74	RHernandez	V J Cuti Jr	9.30
6 Aug76 1Sar1	Uphold	b4 117 7 8	6h 7h	82	81½	HGustines	Darby Dan Farm	44.70
20 Aug76 1Sar1	Iroquois Tribe	3 118 3 9	9 9	9	9	GMartens	T Veale II	18.60

OFF AT 4:38 EDT. Start good. Won ridden out. Time, :23, :46⅗, 1:11⅕. Track fast.

$2 Mutuel Prices:

6-CASPAR MILQUETOAST	5.80	3.60	2.60
5-BOLD NEEDLE		6.80	3.80
9-BALANCER			3.60

$2 EXACTA (6-5) PAID $49.20.

Dk. b. or br. c, by Our Michael—Backseat Driver, by Traffic Judge. Trainer, Philip G. Johnson. Bred by Cortright Wetherill (Ky.).

CASPAR MILQUETOAST raced wide into the stretch while rallying and proved clearly best under intermittent urging. BOLD NEEDLE, between horses to the stretch, finished with good energy to gain the place. BALANCE raced forwardly to midstretch and weakened. MASTER JORGE made a run between horses leaving the turn but hung. PRIVATE THOUGHTS was used up making the pace. FERROUS raced very wide. IRISH SEA saved ground to no avail.

Corrected weight—Master Jorge, 115.
Scratched—Clean 'Em Up, Kool as Ice.

Occasionally, an aggressive trainer will take a recent graduate or a limited winner and step it right up to top allowance-class or stakes competition. In most cases this is not beneficial to the horse, but unlike the cheap races at Charles Town, the player should not automatically assume that the horse is out for the exercise. That is the most likely explanation, but a careful look at one horse's brief career suggests a different story.

6th Belmont Park

SEPTEMBER 6, 1975

WIDENER TURF COURSE
1 1-16 MILES
BELMONT PARK
FINISH

1 1⁄16 MILES (turf). (1:40⅕). TUDOR ERA PURSE. ALLOWANCES. Purse $20,000. 3-year-olds and upward which have not won four races other than maiden, claiming or starter. 3-year-olds. 118 lbs.; older, 122 lbs. Non-winners of $25,000 at a mile or over since July 12 allowed 2 lbs.; $15,000 at a mile or over since July 2, 4 lbs.; $9,000 at a mile or over since July 26, 6 lbs. (Claiming races not considered in allowances.) 3-year-olds which have never won at a mile or over allowed 3 lbs.; older, 5 lbs.

COUPLED: SHREDDER and DROLLERY; JACQUES WHO and CHRISTOFORO; NALEES RIALTO and BRANFORD COURT.

*Appell II.
111 B. c (1971), by El Centauro—Amichevole, by Tatan.
Breeder, Haras Arjo (Argentina). 1975 5 0 2 0 $7,136
Owner, Green Mill Farm. Trainer, T. J. Gullo. 1974 9 4 2 0 $19,978
31 Aug75 4Bel 6 f :231 :46 1:103ft 3¼ 116 62½ 63¼ 43 53 TurcotteR3 Alw 86 Ramahorn 113 Townsand 6
6 Aug75 7Sar 7 f :23 :46 1:33 ft 2½ 114 11 3½ 32 66 TurcotteR6 Alw 89 QueenCityLad120 BigMoses 6
28 Jly 75 4Sar 7 f :221 :4421:223ft 2¼ 116 21 21½ 32 53¼ TurcotteR4 Alw 89 OurTalisman112 Christofro 8
17 Jly 75 8Bel 6 f :223 :4531:101ft 8½ 113 21 44½ 42½ 2½ TurcotteR6 Alw 91 NativeBlend 113 Appell II. 8
6 Jan75 9Maro a 1 1:351ft 119 Uruguay 22¼ SangttiV Stk Brac 119 Appell II. 12
24 Nov74 7Pal a 1 1:354ft 3-4 ▲118 Argentina 1nk SangttiV Stk Appell II. 118 Get Sun 6
9 Nov74 6S.I. Ⓣ a 1 1:332fm 3 119 Argentina 54¼ SangttiV Stk Grand Guignol 119 Ctonal 19
1 Sep74 6Pal a 1⅜ 2:15 ft 3 126 Argentina 925 SangttiV Stk El GranCapitan 126 Envite 10
4 Aug74 6Pal a 1 1:353hy 8-5 ▲123 Argentina 41 SangttiV Stk Telefonico 123 Pinino 21
20 Jly 74 6Pal a 7½ f 1:29 ft 2 121 Argentina 15 SangttiV Stk Appell II. 121 Pinino 8
Aug 28 Bel 4f ft :49⅘b Aug 16 Sar 3f ft :36⅕b Aug 14 Sar 3f ft :36⅘b

Shredder
112 Ch. c (1972), by Stage Door Johnny—Cut It Up, by Tudor Minstrel.
Breeder, Greentree Stud, Inc. (Ky.). 1975 2 1 0 0 $5,400
Owner, Greentree Stable. Trainer, J. M. Gaver. 1974 2 M 0 2 $2,160
23 Aug75 1Sar Ⓣ 1⅛ :47 1:1041:463fm 6¼ 117 11½ 11½ 14 19 BrccleVJr1 Mdn 94 Shredder 117 CopprKingdm 12
16 Aug75 9Sar 6 f :222 :46 1:104ft 9-5 ▲118 75 86 68 513 BracleVJr2 Mdn 73 YuWipi118 SomethingGold 11
Sep 9-743Bel 6 f 1:11⅕ft 1 ▲121 88¾ 64½ 41½ 32¾ Turc'tteR6 Mdn 84 Doug 121 Lucky Limey Shredder 11
Sep 2-743Bel 6 f 1:10⅖sy 7-5 ▲121 1h 1h 2h 34 Turc'tteR7 Mdn 87 Lefty 121 Co Host Shredder 7
Sept 5 Bel 4f ft :47b Sept 1 Bel 5f ft 1:03b Aug 28 Bel 5f ft 1:02b

Candle Stand
116 B. c (1971), by Round Table—Terentia, by Bold Ruler.
Br., W. H. Perry & Claiborne Farm (Ky.). 1975 6 2 1 0 $19,800
Owner, W. H. Perry. Trainer, D. A. Whiteley. 1974 5 2 1 0 $9,576
31 Aug75 8Bel Ⓣ 7 f :223 :45 1:222fm 12 110 910 98¾ 89¾ 610 WdhuseR5 HcpS 82 BeauBugle113 RibotGrande 10
26 Jly 75 7Bel Ⓣ 1 1/16 :48 1:13 1:463sf 4-5 ▲116 37 42 2½ 1nk VasquezJ3 Alw 68 Candle Stand 116 Meon Hill 6
5 Jly 75 9Bel Ⓣ 1 1/16 :4521:0941:412fm 7 116 59½ 35 63¾ 22 MapleE1 Alw 92 PamperdJbnh116 CndleStnd 10
7 Jun75 5Bel 1 1/16 :47 1:12 1:432ft 5¼ 116 77 64 65½ 66¼ VasquezJ7 Alw 79 Christoforo 116 Co Host 8
15 May75 8Aqu 1 :4521:0921:344ft 7-5 ▲116 48½ 45½ 44½ 44½ VasquezJ2 Alw 87 Hunka Papa 114 Phrenology 6
18 Apr75 8Aqu 6 f :222 :45 1:101ft 8¼ 116 54½ 55 52 11¼ VasquezJ5 Alw 92 Candle Stand 116 Erwin Boy 8
Sep18-742Ayr Ⓣ 1⅜ 2:25⅘sf 6-5 ▲119 Ireland 1½ CarsonW Stk CandleSt'nd108 Jimsun Mids'mer Star 7
Aug13-743Cur Ⓣ 1½ 2:43⅗yl 4½ 108 Scotland 48½ BurnsTP Stk Rich'dGrenville122 ConorPass Mistigri 9
Jun 1-741Leo Ⓣ 1¼ 2:10⅘gd 112 ▲126 Ireland 44 PiggottL Stk Conor Pass 133 Silk Buds Klairvimy 7
May15-743Cur Ⓣ 1½ 2:382gd 14 122 Ireland 2no MurphyT Stk Klairvimy 139 Candle Stand Tameric 6
Apr 6-746Cur Ⓣ 1 1:45 gd 6-5 ▲119 Ireland 11 Pigg'tL Mdn C'dleSt'd126 Archd'eFerd'de Retr'ved 26
Aug 30 Bel 3f ft :37b Aug 28 Bel 3f ft :36b Aug 24 Bel 4f ft :48⅕b

Intrepid Hero
118 B. c (1972), by Forli—Bold Princess, by Bold Ruler.
Breeder, O. M. Phipps (Ky.). 1975 8 4 2 1 $143,110
Owner, O. M. Phipps. Trainer, J. W. Russell. 1974 1 M 0 0 (——)
2 Aug75 8Mth 1⅛ :4621:1021:493ft 4¼ 115 32 2½ 2h 2nk ShmkerW7 InvH 92 Wajima 118 Intrepid Hero 8
13 Jly 75 8Hol Ⓣ 1½ :4821:1342:29 fm 7¾ 126 13½ 1½ 11½ 1¾ PierceD5 InvSc 83 Intrepid Hero 126 Terete 7
21 Jun75 8Atl Ⓣ 1 1/16 :47 1:1021:413fm 4 110 3½ 2h 11 12 WoodheR2 AlwS 98 IntrepidHero110 King ofFls 8
16 Jun75 7Bel [T] 1¼ :4911:1412:044gd 3 114 11 1h 1h 2h TurcotteR1 Alw 76 BrianBoru116 IntrepidHero 6
2 Jun75 7Bel 1 1/16 :4611:10 1:421ft 7½ 114 2½ 31 42 35 TejadaV4 Alw 86 Nalee'sKnght118 AllOurHpes 6
30 Apr75 5Aqu Ⓣ 1⅛ :4911:1341:504fm 36 121 31½ 1h 1h 1no TejadaV7 Alw 81 Intrepid Hero 121 Northerly 9
12 Apr75 5Aqu 1⅛ :4821:1221:504ft 6 122 32½ 43 35 47¼ TejadaV2 Alw 74 Old Vic 122 Gunpowder 6
6 Mar75 3Aqu 1 :232 :4531:371ft 23 116 21½ 23 21 1½ TejadaV2 Mdn 80 IntrepidHero116 NobleRctor 7
Dec14-744Aqu 6 f 1:12⅘ft 15 122 77¼ 812 711 711 Mont'yaD8 Mdn 68 Cockbird 122 Alishamar Trounce 8
Sept 1 Bel tc 1f fm 1:39⅗h Aug 22 Sar trt 5f ft 1:07b Aug 17 Sar trt 5f ft 1:03b

Nalees Rialto
112 B. c (1972), by Ribot—Nalee, by Nashua.
Breeder, Mrs. G. M. Humphrey (Ky.). 1975 8 2 2 1 $26,340
Owner, Mrs. G. M. Humphrey. Trainer, E. Burch. 1974 7 1 4 1 $14,620
16 Aug75 8Sar 1⅛ :4721:1121:511ft 2¼ 108 34 33 2½ 13† MontoyaD2 Alw 79 Nalees Rialto 108 First Slice 6
†Disqualified and placed second.
12 Jly 75 8Bel 1⅛ :4531:0931:482sy 7¼ 112 85½ 88½ 710 712 MontyaD8 HcpS 73 Valid Appeal 110 Wajima 8
7 Jun75 7Bel 1½ :48 1:1222:281ft 19 126 55 611 711 817 MntyaD9 ScwS 62 Avatar 126 Foolish Pleasure 9
26 May75 7Aqu 1⅛ :4831:1221:493ft 2 110 13 12 13 12¾ MontoyaD4 Alw 87 Nale'sRlto110 TrmpterSwan 7
17 May75 9Aqu 1⅛ :4721:1121:494ft 2 ▲114 55 42½ 21½ 12½ MontoyaD6 Alw 86 Nalee's Rialto 114 HvnForbd 11
19 Apr75 7Aqu 1⅛ :47 1:1031:483ft 9-5 ▲113 21½ 22 22 22½ MontoyaD1 Alw 89 KaysRoman115 Kp thePmise 8
4 Apr75 9Aqu 1⅛ :49 1:1421:524ft 5½ 114 2h 2½ 2½ 44 MontoyaD8 Alw 67 Media117 Keep thePromise 7
Sept 3 Bel 5f ft :58⅘h Aug 30 Bel 5f ft :59⅘h Aug 27 Bel 3f ft :33⅘h

Drollery
116 Dk. b. or br. g (1970), by Tom Fool—Persian Garden, by Bois Roussel.
Breeder, Greentree Stud, Inc. (Ky.). 1975 11 1 3 4 $61,785
Owner, Greentree Stable. Trainer, J. M. Gaver. 1974 6 1 1 1 $13,800
20 Aug75 8Sar Ⓣ 1⅝ :4831:11 2:42 fm 3 111 21 32 32 32 BccleVJr8 HcpS 77 SnowKnight 118 GoldenDon 8
10 Aug75 8Sar Ⓣ 1⅛ :4831:1231:494fm 7e 112 812 87¼ 54 31¾ BrcceVJr7 HcpS 76 SaltMarsh116 WardMcAlstr 8
5 Jly 75 8Bel Ⓣ 1⅜ :4921:14 2:134fm 9½ 112 24 31½ 69½ 67 BrcleVJr4 HcpS 89 Brigand 112 Prod 9
14 Jun75 8Bel Ⓣ 1½ :51 1:4212:321fm 3¾ 113 52½ 52½ 31½ 21 BrcleVJr5 HcpS 58 Barcas 113 Drollery 6
2 Jun75 8Bel [T] 1¼ :4811:13 2:03 gd 7½ 114 511 69½ 46 21¼ BrcleVJr4 AlwS 84 Telefonico 120 Drollery 9
10 May75 8Pim Ⓣ 1½ :4831:1542:332yl 7¾ 114 1225 912 611 36 BrcleVJr1 HcpS 75 Bemo 114 Outdoors 13
6 Apr75 7SA Ⓣ a 1¾ :4721:1122:521yl 12 115 812 62½ 54 45¾ BracleVJr4 InvH 60 La Zanzara 114 Astray 12
26 Mar75 8SA Ⓣ 1¼ :4741:1232:261fm 3¼ 120 64 42½ 42 2no BrcleVJr2 HcpS 84 El Botija 117 Drollery 6
4 Mar75 9Hia Ⓣ 1½ 2:272fm 9-5e▲111 710 89½ 66¾ 42¾ SmithRC5 HcpS 91 Outdoors 112 Barcas 13
Sept 5 Bel 4f ft :48⅘b Sept 1 Bel 7f ft 1:29b Aug 25 Bel 5f sy 1:02⅖b

The conditions for the above race clearly suggest a top-drawer field. It was in fact more than that. The field was loaded with stakes-class stock, including some of the nation's best grass horses, several of which appear along with the race winner.

Shredder, a recent graduate of a maiden race, was a lead-pipe cinch. And the best bettors in the crowd knew it. Coupled in the betting with the multiple stakes winner Drollery, Shredder's mutuel price was naturally reduced by a few points. But on the evidence of his lone turf race win, there was no way he would have paid more than 4–1 no matter what he was going to run against.

Shredder was a freak. A champion that never got crowned. In the Eclipse Award balloting, I voted him the top turf horse of 1975, simply on the basis of his two grass races. And I don't think I overstated his credentials. They were both incredible performances. Let's examine them.

In his maiden victory romp Shredder ran on his own courage throughout, raced to a nine-length victory under wraps. Jockey Bracciale never moved a muscle. And if you weren't there to see it, the following two result charts tell an interesting tale.

24th Day. WEATHER CLEAR. TEMPERATURE 73 DEGREES.

FIRST RACE **1 ⅛ MILES.(turf). (1.45⅗) MAIDEN SPECIAL WEIGHT. Purse $9,000. 3– and 4-year-olds. Weight: 3-year-olds, 117 lbs., 4-year-olds, 122 lbs.**

Saratoga

AUGUST 23, 1975

Value of race $9,000, value to winner $5,400, second $1,980, third $1,080, fourth $540. Mutuel pool $101,518.

Last Raced	Horse	Eqt.	A.Wt	PP	St	¼	½	¾	Str	Fin	Jockey	Odds $1
16Aug75 9Sar5	Shredder		3 117	1	1	11½	11½	11½	14	19	Bracciale V Jr	6.30
3Aug75 5Sar2	Copper Kingdom	b	3 117	6	12	12	7hd	34	21½	21½	Cruguet J	2.70
3Aug75 5Sar3	Spasoje		3 117	8	11	10hd	9½	6hd	52	3no	Velasquez J	9.50
18Aug75 1Sar2	Braulio		3 117	7	4	4½	5hd	41½	41½	42½	Amy J	13.90
9Aug75 9Sar7	Count Nijinsky	b	3 117	5	7	111½	11½	8½	62	5nk	Turcotte R	a-8.00
13Aug75 1Sar5	Jack Barrett	b	3 117	2	2	31½	2½	2hd	31½	63¾	Hole M	8.30
12Aug75 1Sar7	Off The Record	b	3 110	3	5	8½	6½	101	74	73	Campanelli T7	a-8.00
4Oct74 6Bel7	Vincent	b	3 117	4	3	7hd	8½	9½	8hd	81¾	Ruane J	12.20
13Aug75 1Sar2	Blue Cross	b	3 117	12	8	6½	12	12	101½	91¾	Baeza B	5.10
9Aug75 2Sar4	Sweet Basil	b	3 117	9	10	92	101	112	12	10nk	Maple E	9.80
13Aug75 1Sar10	Bridaled Tern	b	3 110	11	9	51½	41	5½	9hd	116	Long J S7	48.00
16Aug75 9Sar3	The Irish Lord		3 110	10	6	2½	3½	71	111½	12	Martens G7	13.00

a–Coupled: Count Nijinsky and Off The Record.

OFF AT 1:30 EDT. Start good, Won ridden out. Time, :22⅘, :47, 1:10⅘, 1:35, 1:46⅗ Course firm.

Official Program Numbers↘

$2 Mutuel Prices:

2–(B)–SHREDDER	14.60	7.60	5.20
5–(G)–COPPER KINGDOM		4.60	3.20
7–(I)–SPASOJE			4.20

Ch. c, by Stage Door Johnny—Cut It Up, by Tudor Minstrel. Trainer Gaver J M. Bred by Greentree Stud Inc (Ky).

SHREDDER sprinted right to the front, made the pace under good handling and drew away rapidly after entering the stretch. COPPER KINGDOM, outrun away from the gate, moved around horses to reach contention racing into the far turn but was no match for the winner. SPASOJE rallied mildly. Barulion, well placed early, lacked a late response. COUNT NIJINSKY, very wide into the stretch, failed to be a serious factor. JACK BARRETT raced forwardly to the stretch and flattened out. OFF THE RECORD saved ground to no avail. BLUE CROSS was through early. SWEET BASIL was always outrun. BRIDALED TERN gave way after going five furlongs. THE IRISH LORD, a factor to the far turn, stopped badkly.

Owners— 1, Greentree Stable; 2, Live Oak Plantation; 3, Tartan Stable; 4, Blum P E; 5, Hexter Stable; 6, Rokeby Stable; 7, Reineman R L; 8, Hobeau Farm; 9, Sturgis J R; 10, Rosenthal Mrs M; 11, Humphrey Mrs G M; 12, Phipps Ogden.

Trainers— 1, Gaver J M; 2, Kelly T J; 3, Nerud J A; 4, Jerkens S T; 5, Freeman W C; 6, Burch Elliott; 7, Freeman W C; 8, Jerkens H A; 9, Veitch S E; 10, Johnson P G; 11, Miller Mack; 12, Russell J W.

Scratched—Paul's Impulse (13Aug75 ^{1}Sar^{11}); Special Project (3Aug75 ^{5}Sar^4); Triple Optimist (9Aug75 ^{9}Sar^5); Survey (16Aug75 ^{1}Sar^{10}); Rapid Transit II (16Aug75 ^{1}Sar^{11}); Red Grasshopper (18Aug75 ^{1}Sar^4).

An allowance race later that day.

SEVENTH RACE
Saratoga
AUGUST 23, 1975

1 $\frac{1}{16}$ MILES.(turf). (1.39$\frac{3}{5}$) ALLOWANCE. Purse $15,000. 3-year-olds and upward which have not won three races other than maiden, claiming or starter. Weight: 3-year-olds, 117 lbs., Older, 122 lbs. Non-winners of $9,000 at a mile or over since July 26 allowed 2 lbs., $7,200 at a mile or over since July 12, 4 lbs., $6,000 twice at a mile or over since June 25, 6 lbs. (Claiming races not considered in allowances.) 3-year-olds which have never won at a mile or over allowed 3 lbs.; older, 5 lbs.

Value of race $15,000, value to winner $9,000, second $3,300, third $1,800, fourth $900. Mutuel pool $165,739, OTB pool $82,881. TrackExacta Pool $140,551. OTB Exacta Pool $180,996.

Last Raced	Horse	Eqt.A.Wt	PP	St	¼	½	¾	Str	Fin	Jockey	Odds $1
6Aug75 ^{3}Sar^2	Great Above	3 101	5	2	$2^{2\frac{1}{2}}$	$2^{1\frac{1}{2}}$	1^3	$1^{2\frac{1}{2}}$	1^{nk}	Velez R I^7	3.70
28Jly75 ^{6}Sar^1	One On The Aisle	b 3 115	8	7	$7^{\frac{1}{2}}$	4^1	$2^{\frac{1}{2}}$	2^2	2^6	Maple E	2.00
16Aug75 ^{6}Sar^2	American History	3 110	6	4	$5^{1\frac{1}{2}}$	6^{hd}	6^1	$4^{\frac{1}{2}}$	$3^{1\frac{3}{4}}$	Velasquez J	3.00
28Jly75 ^{6}Sar^3	In The Swing	b 4 116	7	5	$4^{1\frac{1}{2}}$	$3^{\frac{1}{2}}$	3^2	3^4	4^{nk}	Bracciale V Jr	13.00
6Aug75 ^{3}Sar^3	Co Host	b 3 113	4	6	6^1	8	7^3	5^2	5^5	Vasquez J	5.60
25Jly75 ^{8}Bel^5	Port Authority	3 111	3	3	1^2	1^{hd}	$5^{\frac{1}{2}}$	6^3	6^3	Turcotte R	12.20
8Jly75 ^{7}Com^1	Montsalvat	3 111	2	8	8	$7^{1\frac{1}{2}}$	4^2	7^4	$7^{3\frac{1}{2}}$	Ruane J	13.50
6Aug75 ^{3}Sar^5	Campaigner	4 116	1	1	3^1	$5^{\frac{1}{2}}$	8	8	8	Cruguet J	17.20

OFF AT 4:53, EDT. Start good, Won driving. Time, :23$\frac{4}{5}$, :48, 1:11$\frac{4}{5}$, 1:35$\frac{2}{5}$, 1:41$\frac{3}{5}$ Course firm (=1:48)

$2 Mutuel Prices:			
5-(E)-GREAT ABOVE	9.40	4.80	2.80
8-(I)-ONE ON THE AISLE		3.60	2.40
6-(F)-AMERICAN HISTORY			2.80

$2 EXACTA 5-8 PAID $28.80.

dk b or br. c, by Minnesota Mac—Ta Wee, by Intentionally. Trainer Nerud J A. Bred by Tartan Farms Corp (Fla).

GREAT ABOVE prompted the pace in hand, took over when ready racing into the far turn, quickly sprinted clear and lasted over ONE ON THE AISLE. The latter, unhurried early, rallied from the outside approaching the stretch and finished strongly. AMERICAN HISTORY, steadied along between horses nearing the end of the backstretch, was going well at the finish.IN THE SWING, never far back, made a run approaching the far turn, remained a factor to the upper stretch and flattened out. CO HOST lacked room between horses midway along the backstretch and failed to be a serious factor. PORT AUTHORITY tired badly from his early efforts. MONTSALVAT, sent around horses racing into the far turn, continued wide and lacked a further response.

Owners— 1, Tartan Stable; 2, Rokeby Stable; 3, Mangurian H T Jr; 4, Brookfield Farm; 5, Schiff J M; 6, Cody M; 7, Steinman Beverly R; 8, Garren M M.

Trainers— 1, Nerud J A; 2, Burch Elliott; 3, Root T F; 4, Kelly E I; 5, Kelly T J; 6, Preger M C; 7, Fout P R; 8, Puentes G.

Overweight: American History 2 pounds; Co Host 2.

Scratched—Grand Salute (13Aug75 ^{6}Sar^6).

On a time-comparison basis, Shredder wins hands down. It was the third fastest 1⅛-mile turf race ever run at Saratoga. Note the final eighth-mile in 11⅗ seconds. That is superhorse time. Most horses are incapable of running the last eighth in 12 seconds flat.

Now let's look at what Shredder did to all those top-drawer stakes horses he met in his next start, his final appearance of the season.

SIXTH RACE
Belmont
SEPTEMBER 6, 1975

1 1/16 MILES.(turf). (1.40⅗) ALLOWANCE. Purse $20,000 3-year-olds and upward which have not won four races other than maiden, claiming or starter. Weights 3-year-olds, 118 lbs.; older, 122 lbs.; non-winners of $25,000 at a mile or over since July 12, allowed 2 lbs.; $15,000 at a mile or over since July 2, 4 lbs.; $9,000 at a mile or over since July 26, 6 lbs. (Claiming races not considered in allowances.) 3-year-olds which have never won at a mile or over allowed 3 lbs.; older, 5 lbs.

Value of race $20,000, value to winner $12,000, second $4,400, third $2,400, fourth $1,200. Mutuel pool $439,287, OTB pool $93,203.

Last Raced	Horse	Eqt.	A.	Wt	PP	St	¼	½	¾	Str	Fin	Jockey	Odds $1
23Aug75 ^{1}Sar^1	Shredder		3	112	2	2	2^3	$2^{1\frac{1}{2}}$	1^{hd}	1^3	1^5	Bracciale V Jr	a-1.40
31Aug75 ^{8}Bel^6	Candle Stand		4	116	4	4	6^{hd}	6^1	4^1	$4^{1\frac{1}{2}}$	$2^{\frac{3}{4}}$	Vasquez J	12.10
2Aug75 ^{8}Mth^2	Intrepid Hero		3	118	5	5	$5^{\frac{1}{2}}$	$4^{1\frac{1}{2}}$	3^1	2^1	$3^{2\frac{1}{4}}$	Cordero A Jr	1.20
31Aug75 ^{4}Bel^5	Appell II		4	111	1	1	$1^{\frac{1}{2}}$	$1^{\frac{1}{2}}$	2^1	$3^{\frac{1}{2}}$	$4^{\frac{1}{2}}$	Turcotte R	12.00
29Aug75 ^{8}Bel^7	Jacques Who	b	5	111	3	9	9	9	7^1	5^3	5^{nk}	Martens G^5	23.60
20Aug75 ^{8}Sar^3	Drollery		5	116	9	6	8^5	8^2	$6^{\frac{1}{2}}$	7^{12}	6^4	Velasquez J	a-1.40
16Aug75 ^{8}Sar^2	Nalees Rialto	b	3	112	6	8	7^2	5^{hd}	5^3	$6^{\frac{1}{2}}$	7^{15}	Maple E	7.40
31Aug75 ^{4}Bel^6	Bold and Fancy	b	4	116	7	3	3^1	$3^{\frac{1}{2}}$	8^4	8^1	8^{nk}	Castaneda M	44.80
13Aug75 ^{6}Sar^6	Grand Salute	b	4	118	8	7	4^1	7^3	9	9	9	Ruane J	56.80

a-Coupled: Shredder and Drollery,

OFF AT 4:18, EDT. Start good, Won handily. Time, :22⅘, :46⅘, 1:11, 1:35⅘, 1:41⅘ Course firm.

$2 Mutuel Prices:				
	1-(B)-SHREDDER (a-entry)	4.80	3.60	2.20
	5-(D)-CANDLE STAND		8.80	2.60
	6-(E)-INTREPID HERO			2.20

Ch. c, by Stage Door Johnny—Cut It Up, by Tudor Minstrel. Trainer Gaver J M. Bred by Greentree Stud Inc (Ky).

SHREDDER, eased back off APPEAL II soon after entering the backstretch, moved through inside that rival to take over on the turn and drew off with authority. CANDLE STAND finished with good courage along the inside to gain the place. INTREPID HERO, unhurried early, loomed a threat from the outside approaching the stretch but weakened during the drive. APPELL II tired badly from his early efforts. DROLLERY was always outrun. NALEES RIALTO rallied nearing the stretch but lacked a further response. BOLD AND FANCY was through soon after going a half. GRAND SALUTE showed some early foot.

Owners— 1, Greentree Stable; 2, Perry W H; 3, Phipps O M; 4, Green Mill Farm; 5, Wimpfheimer J D; 6, Greentree Stable; 7, Humphrey Mrs G M; 8, Vogel Marcus; 9, Steinman Beverly R.

Trainers— 1, Gaver J M; 2, Whiteley D A; 3, Russell J W; 4, Gullo T J; 5, Sedlacek W; 6, Gaver J M; 7, Burch Elliott; 8, Barrera L S; 9, Fout P R.

Scratched—Christoforo (31Aug75 ^{8}Bel^4); T. V. Newscaster (29Aug75 ^{7}Bel^6); Branford Court (31Aug75 ^{8}Bel^7).

I would not like to leave this brief look at allowance races with the notion that all winners come from dropdown maneuvers or have Shredder-type records. The truth is in many allowance races neither factor comes into play. Such allowance races cannot be handicapped without considering track bias, trainer patterns, and other relevant data. Nevertheless, the player who appreciates the subtle power of the hidden class dropdown and is able to incorporate purse values, classification codes, and Key Race studies into his handicapping is almost certain to move many lengths ahead of the crowd. And that's what the game is all about.

11.
$E = MC^2$

In the previous chapter I made a point to introduce the importance of time as it relates to class. At Charles Town the cheapest $1,500 claiming race is usually run in slower time than the next step up in the classification code. At Arlington Park an allowance race for limited winners is usually run somewhat slower than a $20,000 claiming race. And at Saratoga Shredder proved he was no ordinary maiden graduate by running the fastest race of the day.

Although this orderly relationship between class and final times extends through every class level at every racetrack in America, it is nevertheless true that the official time of a race is worthless information by itself.

In order to make sense out of time, in order to make it a meaningful piece of information, the player must be able to answer four intriguing questions:

1. What is a good time or slow time for that distance and that class at that track?
2. How fast or slow was the racetrack the day the race was run? That is, to what extent must the time of the race be adjusted to compensate for the speed of the track itself?
3. To what extent, if any, is final time influenced by track bias, by fractional times, or by unusual pace tactics? And to what extent is it possible to detect a fluky time?
4. When is it most useful to know how fast the horse ran and under what conditions is time a waste of time?

Very few fans ever bother to take these questions seriously. It's an understandable failing. The majority of so-called experts don't do it either. Besides, the past performance profiles seem to provide ready-made answers in the track condition labels, in the speed ratings, and in the track variant figures published in some editions of the *Form*.

Jose Eduardo   **117** Gr. g (1972), by Drone—Fleet Airline, by Count Fleet.
Breeder, R. W. Wilson, Estate (Ky.).   1975 25 5 3 5 $42,900

Owner, Lady Luck Stable. Trainer, W. F. Schmitt. $40,000

21 Nov75	6Aqu	1 :45	1:09	31	:36	2sy	3-5	▲117	1½	1¹	1³	17¾	PcayLJr³	30000 84 JoseEduardo117 Abve theBlt 7
8 Nov75	4Bel	1¹⁄₁₆	:45	31:10	1:42	1sy	4½	117	2¹½	2¹½	4²	2¹½	PncyLJr⁵	30000 89 FramptnDlight110 JseEdrdo 8
1 Nov75	3Bel	6 f	:22	4 :46	41:11	2ft	2¼	▲117	2ʰ	8²½	7¹¹	7¹⁶	VenziaM²	32500 69 JacksonSqre117 CardinlGrge 8
18 Oct/5	5Bel	6 f	:22	2 :46	21:10	2sy	3	117	2¹	2¹	2½	13¾	PincyLJr⁵	27500 90 JoseEduardo117 RealGeorge 6
9 Oct75	7Bel	6 f	:22	3 :46	1:11	3ft	9-5	▲116	2½	2ʰ	2ʰ	1½	PincyLJr⁵	27500 84 JoseEduardo 116 MacCorkle 11
1 Oct75	9Bel	6 f	:22	3 :46	11:11	3ft	4¾	116	1ʰ	2½	3½	3ʰ	PincyLJr¹	30000 84 Balancer 116 Danny Boy 12
22 Sep75	2Bel	6 f	:22	4 :46	21:11	gd	9½	112	1¹½	1¹½	1½	2¹	VenziaM³	27500 86 CenturyGold116 JseEduardo 8
7 Sep75	9Bel	7 f	224	:46	1:25	2ft	7½	116	1ʰ	1½	1¹	1½	VneziaM⁸	22500 75 JoseEduardo116 TingleKing 12

Unfortunately, a "fast" racetrack can have a wide range of speed conduciveness—from lightning fast to not very fast at all. And there are so many flaws built into the *Daily Racing Form*'s speed ratings and track variants that they border on the ridiculous. They can also cost the unsuspecting player a lot of money.

Speed ratings are the *Daily Racing Form*'s attempt to provide the player with a means of comparing the speed of different horses at different distances. The ratings earned by Jose Eduardo, for example, were computed by comparing his time in each race with the appropriate track record for the distance. In the *DRF* speed-rating system, the track record is always worth 100 speed-rating points, and one point is deducted for each fifth of a second slower than the track mark. According to the time-honored notion that a length equals a fifth of a second, Jose Eduardo's worst race (November 1, 1975) was computed this way:

Belmont 6-furlong track record	= 1:08⅖ = 100 speed rating
Time of race winner	= 1:11⅖ = 85 speed rating
Beaten 16 lengths (deduct 16 points)	= 1:14⅗ = 69 speed rating

---

Here is a partial list of Belmont Park track records in effect for the 1976 racing season. Each track record is worth 100 speed-rating points. Each horse racing at Belmont earned its speed ratings by comparisons with these times.

There are several things wrong with this method. Two of the most important appear below the chart.

TRACK RECORDS AT BELMONT PARK

DISTANCE	HORSE	AGE	WGT.	TIME	DATE
5½ Furlongs	Raise a Cup	2	118	1:03	June 8, 1973
6 Furlongs	Sailor's Watch	5	114	1:08⅖	July 3, 1975
6½ Furlongs	Cohasset Tribe	4	114	1:15⅕	May 19, 1973
7 Furlongs	King's Bishop	4	114	1:20⅖	May 19, 1973
1 Mile	Stop the Music	3	122	1:33⅗	May 19, 1973
1¹⁄₁₆ Miles	Everton II	4	112	1:40⅖	Aug. 28, 1973
1⅛ Miles	Secretariat	3	124	1:45⅖	Sept. 15, 1973

First, some track records are set on extremely fast racing days, by horses of varying ability. Although each track record equals 100 speed-rating points, at Belmont Park it is considerably more difficult for a horse to earn an 85 rating at seven furlongs and 1⅛ miles than it is at any other distance. King's Bishop and Secretariat ran much faster races to establish their track records than Cohasset Tribe and Everton II did to establish theirs.

Second, a length does not equal a fifth of a second at all distances and at all rates of speed. Mathematically speaking, a length equals a fifth of a second only when horses travel a furlong in 15 seconds. The only horses that go that slow charge 10 cents a ride.

Not surprisingly, the same sort of inconsistencies among track records can be shown to exist at most race-tracks. And the error is compounded in the editions of the *Form* that feature track variant figures.

These variants—which purport to measure the relative speed of the track—are computed by averaging all winning speed ratings earned at that track that day. The average for the day is then subtracted from 100 to produce the track variant.

If the average winning speed rating for November 1, 1975, was 88, then the *DRF* track variant would be listed as 12. In the Eastern edition of the *Form*, Jose Eduardo's past performance line for that race would include his 69 rating, but it would read 69–12.

The only time these *DRF* variants provide any worthwhile information is when the variant is very large or very small. A variant above 30 would clearly indicate a slow racing strip. A variant under 10 would suggest a concrete highway. Otherwise these figures are useless to serious students of time because it is impossible to tell whether a moderate variant was the result of fast horses racing over a slow track or slow horses racing over a fast track. So much for *Daily Racing Form* speed ratings.

Those of you who are genuinely interested in winning may well achieve that special level of skill without studying the subject of time in great detail. There are other windows to look through, other methods to determine which horse is best suited to the task and most likely to win. But if you are mathematically inclined and wish to explore the racetrack puzzle from a semiscientific base, you will need to become familiar with speed figures—an ingenious process that translates the answers to the first two questions about time (see page 106) to a workable set of numbers, par times, and parallel time charts.

SPEED FIGURES

The very best speed-figure method I have ever seen was created by Sheldon Kovitz, a math wiz who divided his time at Harvard in the early 1960s between his classes, the track, and the nearest IBM computer. I never met Kovitz, but my good friend Andy Beyer learned the method firsthand and refined it for practical use ten years later. In its present form, it involves a two-step research project that may seem tedious but will do a great deal to broaden your understanding of the hows and whys of racing in your area. And if you're as crazy about handicapping as I am, you might even love it.

STEP 1 : Using a complete set of result charts from the previous meeting, compile a list of all final times recorded on "fast" racetracks at every class level and distance. If back copies of the *Form* are unavailable, or too expensive to consider, a trip to the nearest library file of daily local newspapers will suffice. *Daily Racing Form* chart books, costing $22.50 per month, are another alternative.

For the purpose of this research project you are not concerned with anything but age, sex, class of race, distance, and fast-track final times. But for dependable results you should study a minimum of fifteen races at each class and distance. Obviously, the more races you use to work up the data, the more reliable the data will be.

STEP 2 : Obtain the *average* winning time for each class and distance.

Logically, to determine a good time for a six-furlong, $8,000 claiming race, you must determine the *average* time for that class and distance. These averages will then serve as the par, or standard, for each class and distance. The following is a sample of six-furlong average times for New York tracks:

Three years and up stakes - - - - - - - - - - - - - - - 1:10
Three years and up $20,000 allowance - - - - - - 1:10⅖
Three years and up $15,000 claiming - - - - - - - 1:11⅗
Maiden special weight (all ages) - - - - - - - - - 1:12

The average winning times at several distances at another racetrack produced the following results:

$15,000 CLAIMING RACE—KEYSTONE RACETRACK				
6 FURLONGS	6½ FURLONGS	7 FURLONGS	1 MILE, 70 YARDS	1 1/16 MILE
1:11⅗	1:18	1:24⅗	1:44⅗	1:46⅕

These average winning times are the building blocks for establishing an accurate track variant. They are all equal to a single measurement of average speed—the average speed of a $15,000 claiming horse at Keystone racetrack. We may now compare all final times at Keystone with that average or we may go a step further and plot the averages for every class and construct a parallel time chart, a chart that could help us make accurate time comparisons swiftly.

For convenience, Kovitz created a mathematically sound rating system to simplify comparisons between horses running different times and distances. In this rating system the value of a fifth of a second is proportionately greater in faster races and at shorter distances. It also assigns the appropriate number of points for each beaten length.

I will spare you the mathematics behind this idea and refer you to the Appendix for a step-by-step method to compute a satisfactory version of the Kovitz-Beyer speed-figure system. For those of you who are interested in this subject, I strongly recommend Beyer's beautifully written book *Picking Winners,* which is one of the few handicapping books worth serious attention. The time charts, class pars, ratings, and beaten-length charts for New York racetracks included in the Appendix of this book were adapted from *Picking Winners,* reproduced with Andy's special permission. And if you wonder whether the effort to learn how to derive speed figures is worth the trouble, the next chapter should set your head straight.

12.
The Race Is to the Swift

When is time important? How potent is speed-figure handicapping? What about fractional times? Does "pace make the race," as so many handicappers believe?

It is rare that a horseplayer gets a chance to confront a major mystery of the racetrack puzzle. Being naturally bent toward such mysteries helps. I confess. I am always willing to put my most effective handicapping methods aside and experiment with new tools and test out new ideas.

It was in that spirit that I incorporated Andy Beyer's speed figures in my handicapping in 1972, and it was in the same spirit that I stopped using them in the second year of my handicapping broadcasts in 1974.

In the first season the results said 176 winners in 310 picks. Fifty-three percent. A flat bet profit in all categories.

Of course, I relied on numerous handicapping concepts, but so long as speed figures were available on a daily basis, I wasn't sure how much they contributed.

I designed an informal test to find out.

For the first three months of the new season I continued using figures and made note of when they seemed to be the major reason for a selection. For the next three months I operated without using them at all. And for the remainder of the year I used them only when the results of previous use suggested their relevance. Fortunately, I was able to keep my 50 percent win record intact throughout the experiment.

Certainly, a more scientific survey needs to be done here, but in the meantime I think the results I obtained under fire are worth keeping in mind.

These are my present thoughts on the subject.

1. Speed figures, by definition, tell how fast the horse ran at a given racetrack at a given distance on a given day. They do not automatically tell how fast a horse *will* run, especially at a different distance. But the top speed-figure horse in the race does win approximately 35 percent of the

time at a slight loss for every $2 wager. With no handicapping at all, speed figures produce more winners than public favorites and at slightly better prices.

2. By computing the *par times* for each distance and class at a specific racetrack, the player will know which claiming horses have been meeting better stock than the allowance horses. He will know at a glance whether a $10,000 claiming race is better than a low-grade allowance race without having to consult the purse values in the result charts. He will also know at what class a field of fillies is faster than colts.

3. By computing speed figures on a regular basis, the player will have an important handicapping tool in the following cases.

When maiden graduates are entered in races for winners, their speed figures will often indicate their suitability to the class. The horse that graduates with a mediocre speed figure is not likely to repeat the feat in higher company. The graduate that has earned a superior speed figure may not be overmatched in any company. Below is the past performance record of a horse that graduated with an extremely high speed figure. Here he is entered in the 1975 Belmont Futurity against the best two-year-olds in the country. He ran the same speed figure as his maiden win and won by daylight.

Soy Numero Uno

122 B. c (1973), by Damascus—Tasma, by Crafty Admiral.
Breeder, Nuckols Bros. (Ky.).   1975 1 1 0 0 $5,400

Owner, J. R. Straus. Trainer, H. C. Pardue.

25 Aug75 4Bel   6 f :22² :45²1:09⁴ft 4-5 ▲120 3¹ 2ʰ 1² 1⁴ VasquzJ¹⁰ Mdn 93 SoyNumeroUno120 SecretCll 10
  Sept 5 Bel trt 3f ft :36⅖b   Sept 1 Bel 5f ft :58⅗h   Aug 24 Bel trt 3f ft :37⅖b

When a field of maidens is mixed between horses with minimum racing experience and first-time starters, the figures for the horses who have already raced will tell how difficult it will be for the first-timer to win. If the horses with racing experience have been producing above-par figures for the class, the first-timer has to be a tiger to compete. If the figures are subpar, a nicely bred, fast-working first-timer could be an excellent wager.

When a horse has consistently produced superior figures—when its *lowest* figure is better than the *best* figure of the competition—it will win at least 80 percent of the time! (This happens approximately once in every 250 races.)

If the top speed-figure horse in the race is also the horse most likely to get a clear early lead, it deserves a solid edge, providing of course it is not racing far beyond its normal distance capabilities or is not pitted against a stretch-running track bias. On a front-running track bias this kind of horse will usually outrun its apparent distance limitations.

4. Speed figures can be used effectively in the following circumstances.

Prior speed figures can be a valuable clue in spotting the inherent weakness of a betting favorite. If the figures are low for the class or low versus the competition, the player must have well-thought-out reasons to select such a horse at short odds—trainer pattern, visual evidence, vastly improved workouts, and so on.

When a horse is stepped up in claiming price, prior speed figures can be an important clue to its winning potential. If it has run fast enough in the past, the class raise may only be an illusion. Most of the time there will be additional evidence to support the class raise.

See Chapter 18 for an illustration of the value of speed figures in spotting horses in the above two situations.

5. If a horse is likely to get a clear early lead for the first time in its recent racing record, the player should expect a minimum of two lengths' improvement over its customary speed figures. Even more important, whenever such a horse is in a particularly slow-breaking field or has a bias in its favor, no other horse in the race can be played with confidence. An example of this type of straightforward betting situation is also presented in Chapter 18.

6. The traditional handicapping notion that "pace makes the race" is only true in special circumstances.

In the vast majority of sprints the early fractional times do not seem to affect the final time of the race winner. But if the pace is contested by two or more horses, regardless of the early fractions, the chances are good that the leaders will tire in the stretch. Some horses, however, respond to competition by running harder, and the player should have no trouble spotting these game creatures in the past performance records.

Pension Plan ✻ **116** Dk. b. or br. g (1970), by Olden Times—Lo May, by Khaled.
Breeder, R. C. Ellsworth (Ky.).

1975	15	6	4	2	\$60,601
1974	24	6	9	3	\$86,370

Owner, B. Federico. Trainer, K. Grusmark.

13 Oct75	^{8}Bel	6 f :22^3 :45^{3}1:09^{4}ft	17	134	1^h	2^h	2½	4^3	CaplboP^2	HcpS	90	Honorable Miss 133	No Bias	15
5 Oct75	^{9}Suf	6 f :22^1 :45^{2}1:11^{1}ft	3-5	▴124	1^h	1^h	1^h	1^{nk}	CapabloP^1	Alw	85	Pension Plan 124	Bow Ski	7
22 Sep75	^{9}Suf	6 f :22 :45^{1}1:11 ft	6-5	▴126	1^h	3^{nk}	2^h	2no	CapalboP^1	HcpO	86	RobertM.Shrt120	PnsionPln	8
13 Sep75	^{8}Bow	6 f :22^1 :44^{3}1:09^{4}ft	7-5	▴116	2^2	2^{3½}	2^4	2^3	CaplboP^2	HcpS	91	Scam 113	Pension Plan	8
6 Sep75	^{7}Bel	6½ f :23^3 :46^{3}1:17^{3}ft	3¾	123	1^h	1½	1^h	1½	CapalboP^7	Alw	88	PensionPlan123	FrkieAdams	7
23 Aug75	^{8}Rkm	1 1/16 :46^{3}1:10^{4}1:42^{4}ft	3¾	118	1^h	1^h	3^2	4^6	CapalboP^4	HcpS	90	Kiss andRun115	ContinousCt	6
2 Aug75	^{8}Rkm	1^{70} :45^{3}1:10^{1}1:40^{1}ft	4¾	115	2^h	1½	1^h	1^{nk}	CapalboP^6	HcpS	95	PensionPlan115	AlmostGrwn	7
19 Jly 75	^{8}Rkm	1^{70} :46 1:10^{2}1:41 ft	5½	115	3^{nk}	1^h	1^h	2^{1¼}	CapalboP^5	HcpO	90	ContinuousCt123	PensionPln	7
5 Jly 75	^{8}Rkm	6 f :22 :44^{3}1:09^{2}ft	2½	▴118	2^h	2^h	1½	1^{nk}	CapalboP^3	HcpO	97	PensionPln118	PrceDrlingtn	8

Oct 30 Suf 3f ft :35⅗h **Oct 26 Suf 3f m :36⅘h** **Oct 22 Suf 3f ft :35⅘h**

In route races pace can influence the final time as well as the final result. A very slow early pace may or may not prejudice the final time depending upon the action that follows, but it will help a front runner to reach the stretch with more gas in the tank. Naturally, a very fast or highly competitive pace will frequently bring about the opposite result. The very best horses, however, are prone to use that fast pace as a springboard to track records.

EIGHTH RACE
AP 35688
August 24, 1968

1 MILE (chute). (Buckpasser, June 25, 1966, 1:32⅗, 3, 125.) Forty-first running WASHINGTON PARK HANDICAP. $100,000 added. 3-year-olds and upward. By subscription of $100 each, which shall accompany the nomination, $250 to pass the entry box and $750 additional to start, with $100,000 added, of which $20,000 to second, $15,000 to third and $10,000 to fourth. The winning owner to receive a trophy. Closed with 27 nominations.
Value of race $112,700. Value to winner $67,700; second, $20,000; third, $15,000; fourth, $10,000.
Mutuel Pool, $282,271.

Index	Horses	Eq't	A	Wt	PP	St	¼	½	¾	Str	Fin	Jockeys	Cl'g Pr.	Owners	Odds to $1
35524Sar1	—Dr. Fager		4	134	9	1	6^{1}	2^{h}	$1^{\frac{1}{2}}$	1^{3}	1^{10}	B Baeza		Tartan Stable	.30
35415AP1	—Racing Room		4	116	2	7	$4^{\frac{1}{2}}$	3^{2}	2^{3}	$2^{1\frac{1}{2}}$	$2^{1\frac{1}{2}}$	J Sellers		Llangollen Farm	10.40
35553AP4	—Info		4	112	3	6	8^{2}	6^{2}	3^{1}	3^{3}	3^{1}	E Fires		Mrs E J Brisbine	37.00
35580AP1	—Out the Window	b	4	115	5	8	9^{6}	9^{7}	7^{2}	$5^{\frac{1}{2}}$	4^{nk}	H Moreno		J R Chapman	13.90
35625AP3	—R. Thomas	b	7	118	1	9	5^{1}	1^{h}	4^{2}	4^{2}	5^{6}	J Nichols		Wilson-McDermott	24.80
35553AP6	—Cabildo		5	114	8	10	10	10	10	10	6no	M Sol'mone		Mrs J W Brown	a-13.60
35625AP2	—Angelico		5	111	6	5	1^{h}	$4^{\frac{1}{2}}$	$5^{\frac{1}{2}}$	7^{3}	7^{nk}	L Pincay Jr		Foxcatcher Farm	16.00
35606Atl2	—Hedevar		6	112	10	2	$3^{\frac{1}{2}}$	8^{h}	6^{h}	6^{2}	$8^{1\frac{1}{4}}$	T Lee		Mrs Edith W Bancroft	47.60
35625AP1	—High Tribute	b	4	112	7	3	$7^{\frac{1}{2}}$	$7^{1\frac{1}{2}}$	9^{5}	9^{2}	$9^{1\frac{3}{4}}$	D Brumfield		Elmendorf	18.40
35433AP3	—Kentucky Sherry		3	112	4	4	$2^{\frac{1}{2}}$	$5^{\frac{1}{2}}$	8^{1}	8^{h}	10	J Combest		Mrs J W Brown	a-13.60

a-Coupled, Cabildo and Kentucky Sherry.
Time, :22⅘, :44, 1:07⅗, 1:32⅕ (new track and world record). Track fast.

$2 Mutuel Prices:

8-DR. FAGER	2.60	2.20	2.20
3-RACING ROOM		3.80	3.20
4-INFO			5.20

B. c, by Rough'n Tumble—Aspidistra, by Better Self. Trainer, J. A. Nerud. Bred by Tartan Farms (Fla.).
IN GATE—5:36. OFF AT 5:36½ CENTRAL DAYLIGHT TIME. Start good. Won easily.
DR. FAGER, away alertly but hard held to be reserved just off the lead, moved with a rush while still under restraint to take command leaving the backstretch, continued slightly wide to shake off RACING ROOM on the final turn, commenced lugging in while drawing off through the stretch run and won with something left.

The reliability of speed figures as a handicapping tool is significantly lower in route races whenever established running styles figure to create a superfast or slow, snail-like pace.

EIGHTH RACE
Bel
June 4, 1976

1⅛ MILES (chute). (1:45⅖). Twentieth running MOTHER GOOSE. SCALE WEIGHTS. $75,000 added. Fillies. 3-year-olds. Weight, 121 lbs. By subscription of $150 each, which shall accompany the nomination; $375 to pass the entry box; $375 to start, with $75,000 added. The added money and all fees to be divided: 60% to the winner, 22% to second, 12% to third and 6% to fourth. Trophies will be presented to the winning owner, trainer and jockey. Closed with 14 nominations.
Value of race $80,850. Value to winner $48,510; second, $17,787; third, $9,702; fourth, $4,851. Mutuel Pool, $328,981. Off-track betting, $129,405.

Last Raced	Horse	EqtAWt	PP	St	¼	½	¾	Str	Fin	Jockeys	Owners	Odds to $1
22 May76 ^{8}Bel^4	Girl in Love	3 121	4	5	5	5	5	2^7	$1^{1\frac{1}{4}}$	JCruguet	Elmendorf	4.00
22 May76 ^{8}Bel^2	Optimistic Gal	3 121	2	2	2^5	2^5	1^2	1^2	2^{11}	BBaeza	Mrs R B Firestone	1.00
29 May76 ^{8}GS^1	Ancient Fables	b3 121	5	1	4^{10}	4^8	4^2	$3^{\frac{1}{2}}$	$3^{6\frac{3}{4}}$	ACorderoJr	Brazil Stable	18.50
22 May76 ^{8}Bel^5	Artfully	b3 121	3	4	3^2	3^4	3^3	4^2	$4^{3\frac{1}{4}}$	GPIntels'noJr	R N Webster	30.40
22 May76 ^{8}Bel^1	Dearly Precious	3 121	1	3	$1^{\frac{1}{2}}$	$1^{\frac{1}{2}}$	2^3	5	5	JVelasquez	R E Bailey	1.20

OFF AT 5:02½ EDT. Start good. Won driving. Time, :22⅕, :44⅖, 1:08⅘, 1:35⅕, 1:48⅘. Track fast.

$2 Mutuel Prices:			
4-GIRL IN LOVE	10.00	4.00	4.40
2-OPTIMISTIC GAL		2.60	2.20
5-ANCIENT FABLES			3.80

Ch. f, by Lucky Debonair—Lover's Quarrel, by Battle Joined. Trainer, John P. Campo. Bred by Elmendorf Farm (Ky.).

GIRL IN LOVE, badly outrun on the backstretch, commenced to rally after going five furlongs, raced wide into the stretch, continued to advance under left-handed pressure and proved clearly best after catching OPTIMISTIC GAL. GIRL IN LOVE pulled up lame. OPTIMISTIC GAL, bothered by DEARLY PRECIOUS while racing outside that rival on the backstretch, took over while racing well out in the track on the turn, quickly opened a clear lead but wasn't able to withstand the winner. ANCIENT FABLES failed to be a serious factor. ARTFULLY raced within striking distance to the stretch and flattened out. DEARLY PRECIOUS ducked out into OPTIMISTIC GAL after the start, made the pace while bearing out into that rival throughout the run down the backstretch and was finished soon after going six furlongs.

7. Except for the top speed figure with front-running tendencies mentioned earlier (see point 3 above), the presence of a powerful, one-dimensional track bias of any kind makes speed figures as irrelevant as the times they are based on.

On a stretch runners' track the final quarter-mile time is somewhat helpful, but the dominant handicapping considerations are stamina, class, condition, and post position.

On a front runners' track the early fractions and early position calls in the running line are the best clues to the cashier's window.

If the bias is also to the inside part of the track, post position is the player's best means of separating contenders.

Virtually every racetrack in America provides aberrant conditions like the ones described here sometime during the racing season. The player who can recognize these prevailing situations and then adjust his handicapping will have the best shot at the equivalent of a perfect game. It's possible to sweep the card on days like that.

NOTE: *The early speed in the Schuylerville Stakes, the sample race exhibited in Chapter 4 (pages 41–42), was Our Dancing Girl. This determination was made by noting the first call position of Our Dancing Girl in her race with the great Ruffian. Post number two didn't hurt either. The next best speed in the race seemed to be Secret's Out and the top closer But Exclusive. This was the result.*

SEVENTH RACE
Saratoga
JULY 29, 1974

6 FURLONGS. (1.08) 57TH RUNNING THE SCHUYLERVILLE. $25,000 Added. 1st Division. Fillies, 2–year–olds. By subscription of $50 each, which shall accompany the nomination; $125 to pass the entry box; $125 to start, with $25,000 added. The added money and all fees to be divided 60% to the winner, 22% to second, 12% to third and 6% to fourth. Weights, 119 lbs. Non–winners of a sweepstakes allowed 3 lbs.; maidens, 7 lbs. Starters to be named at the closing time of entries. A trophy will be presented to the owner of the winner. Closed Monday, July 15 with 30 Nominations. Value of race $27,625, value to winner $16,575, second $6,077, third $3,315, fourth $1,658. Mutuel pool $108,621, OTB pool $46.764. Exacta Pool $79.247. OTB Exacta Pool $98.708.

Last Raced	Horse	Eqt.	A.	Wt	PP	St	¼	½	Str	Fin	Jockey	Odds $1
10Jly74 ^{8}Aqu^{3}	Our Dancing Girl	b	2	116	2	1	1^{2}	$1^{2\frac{1}{2}}$	1^{2}	1no	Bracciale V Jr	10.20
19Jun74 ^{8}Mth^{5}	Secret's Out		2	119	5	3	2^{1}	2^{2}	2^{3}	$2^{2\frac{1}{2}}$	Vasquez J	4.70
12Jly74 ^{4}Aqu^{2}	But Exclusive		2	116	7	7	$6^{\frac{1}{2}}$	5^{4}	5^{5}	3^{1}	Cordero A Jr	3.60
8Jly74 ^{6}Crc^{1}	Some Swinger	b	2	116	4	4	5^{2}	$4^{1\frac{1}{2}}$	$3^{\frac{1}{2}}$	$4^{1\frac{1}{4}}$	Velasquez J	6.00
20Jly74 ^{3}Mth^{1}	My Compliments		2	116	1	5	3^{2}	$3^{\frac{1}{2}}$	4^{hd}	5^{6}	Venezia M	1.60
14Jly74 ^{6}WO^{2}	La Bourrasque	b	2	116	3	6	7	6^{5}	6^{5}	$6^{7\frac{1}{2}}$	Turcotte R	5.90
15Jly74 ^{3}Aqu^{2}	Precious Elaine	b	2	112	6	2	4^{hd}	7	7	7	Santiago A	15.60

OFF AT 4:42 1/2 EDT. Start Good, Won driving. Time, :22⅕, :45⅕, 1:11⅕ Track fast.

$2 Mutuel Prices:				
	2–(B)–OUR DANCING GIRL	22.40	7.00	4.60
	5–(E)–SECRET'S OUT		5.00	4.00
	7–(H)–BUT EXCLUSIVE			3.20

$2 EXACTA 2–5 PAID $80.40.

B. f, by Solo Landing—Amber Dancer, by Native Dancer. Trainer Rigione J. Bred by Elcee H Stable (Fla).

OUR DANCING GIRL quickly sprinted clear, saved ground while making the pace and, after settling into the stretch with a clear lead, lasted over SECRET'S OUT. The latter prompted the pace throughought, lugged in slightly nearing midstretch and finished strongly, just missing. BUT EXCLUSIVE, off slowly, finished well while racing wide. SOME SWINGER rallied along the inside leaving the turn, eased out for the drive but lacked the needed late response. MY COMPLIMENTS had no excuse. LA BOURRASQUE was always outrun after breaking slowly. PRECIOUS ELAINE broke through before the start and was finished early.

Owners— 1, Elcee-H Stable; 2, Schott Marcia W; 3, Levin W A; 4, Mangurian H T Jr; 5, Reineman R L; 6, Levesque J L; 7, Brodsky A J.

Trainers— 1, Rigione J; 2, Picou J E; 3, Imperio D A; 4, Root T Jr; 5, Freeman W C; 6, Starr J; 7, Conway J P.

Scratched—Elsie Marley (30Apr74^{4}Aqu^{1}).

13.
Theory vs. Experience

For each and every piece of information in the past performance profile, there is a popular theory purporting to measure its exact significance. The interesting thing about that is I know of no winning player who subscribes to any such rigid approach to any aspect of the game.

WEIGHT

The old saying that "weight will stop a freight train" is true enough. But except for a few special cases, it is pure conjecture that a fit racehorse can be stopped or slowed by the addition of a few pounds. Weight is simply the most overrated factor in handicapping.

Perhaps 105 pounds will help a horse run a fifth of a second faster than 110 pounds and two-fifths of a second faster than 115. But there is no proof to demonstrate the validity of such a rigid relationship. Indeed between 105 and 115 pounds the amount of weight carried by the horse is demonstrably unimportant.

Beyond 115 pounds, the effect of added weight on performance is an individual thing.

Some horses can't handle 120 pounds; others are able to run just as fast and as far with considerably more. Past performance profiles usually provide sufficient clues to make such determinations; but because the betting public tends to automatically downgrade the chances of a top-weighted horse, the reward for a more flexible attitude is generally generous mutuel prices.

Gallant Bob **126** **Dk. b. or br. g (1972), by Gallant Romeo—Wisp O'Will, by New Policy.**
Breeder, J. L. Homan (Ky.). **1975 16 12 1 2 $229,213**
Owner, R. Horton. Trainer, J. D. Morquette. **1974 10 3 4 0 $58,118**

22 Nov75	^{8}Key	6 f	$:22^1$	$:45^1$	$1:09^4$gd	3-5	▲119	$2\frac{1}{2}$	$1\frac{1}{2}$	$1\frac{1}{2}$	$1^{1\frac{1}{2}}$	GalltnoG^3	AlwS	93	GallantBob119	BearerBond	8
4 Oct75	^{8}Key	$6\frac{1}{2}$ f	:22	$:44^4$	$1:16^3$ft	2-5	▲119	$3\frac{1}{2}$	2^1	$1^{1\frac{1}{2}}$	1^2	GalltnoG^3	AlwS	94	Gallant Bob 119	Talc	6
6 Sep75	^{8}Key	7 f	$:21^4$	$:44^1$	1:24 ft	6-5	▲129	3^1	3^2	2^h	1^3	GalltnoG^7	HcpO	89	Gallant Bob 129	Talc	9
13 Aug75	^{8}Mth	6 f	$:20^4$	$:43^4$	$1:09^2$ft	2	▲129	2^7	$2^{3\frac{1}{2}}$	$2\frac{1}{2}$	$1^{1\frac{1}{4}}$	GalltnoG^5	HcpO	93	Gallant Bob 129	Talc	7
5 Jly 75	^{8}Bow	6 f	$:22^3$	$:45^4$	$1:10^2$ft	2-5	▲127	2^h	$1^{1\frac{1}{2}}$	1^3	$1^{3\frac{1}{2}}$	GalltnoG^5	HcpO	91	GallantBob127	FrchWhistler	6
21 Jun75	^{8}AP	7 f	:22	$:44^3$	$1:23^2$ft	$4\frac{1}{2}$	124	1^h	$1\frac{1}{2}$	1^2	1^1	GallitnoG^5	AlwS	85	Gallant Bob 124	Doug	11
1 Jun75	^{8}Del	$1\frac{1}{16}$	$:46^2$	1:12	$1:46^1$ft	3-2	▲117	1^h	1^h	5^6	5^{12}	GallitnoG^5	AlwS	66	GreyBeret111	Dr'sEnjyDollrs	10
24 May75	^{8}Del	6 f	$:21^4$	:45	$1:11^1$ft	4-5	▲124	2^h	2^h	2^h	$1\frac{1}{2}$	GallitnoG^4	AlwS	89	Gallant Bob 124	Bold Gun	7
22 Mar75	^{8}Pim	6 f	$:22^4$	$:46^1$	$1:11^1$ft	1	▲122	$3\frac{1}{2}$	2^h	1^1	2^h	GallitnoG^8	AlwS	90	BombayDuck122	GallantBob	9
15 Mar75	^{8}Aqu	7 f	$:22^3$	$:45^3$	$1:23^4$sy	$2\frac{3}{4}$	▲119	2^h	2^h	$1\frac{1}{2}$	$3\frac{3}{4}$	GallitnoG^8	AlwS	81	Lefty 113	Tass	8
1 Mar75	^{8}Aqu	6 f	$:21^4$	$:45^2$	$1:09^4$ft	3	117	1^h	1^1	$2\frac{1}{2}$	$3^{3\frac{1}{2}}$	GallitnoG^9	AlwS	90	Singh 114	Laramie Trail	10
22Feb75	^{8}Key	7 f	$:22^1$	:45	$1:25^3$ft	2-5	▲119	1^3	1^6	1^8	1^{10}	GallitnoG^1	AlwS	81	GallantBob119	WickedPark	11
15 Feb75	^{8}GS	6 f	$:22^1$	$:45^4$	1:11 gd	2-5	▲122	1^h	1^3	1^5	1^9	GallitnoG^6	AlwS	88	GallantBob122	LuckeyLeaf	7
1 Feb75	^{8}Bow	6 f	$:22^4$	$:46^3$	1:12 gd	4-5	▲124	1^3	1^5	1^5	$1^{4\frac{1}{2}}$	GallitnoG^6	AlwS	83	GallantBob124	PendulmSam	6
25 Jan75	^{8}Key	6 f	$:22^2$	$:46^1$	$1:13^2$sy	4-5	▲119	$1\frac{1}{2}$	1^h	$1\frac{1}{2}$	1^2	GallitnoG^6	AlwS	75	Gallant Bob 119	Sgt. Hunt	7

Nov 29 Key 4f ft :48$\frac{4}{5}$b

Give me an obviously sharp horse with a proven superiority over the contenders and I'll gladly support him carrying 120, 125, or 128 pounds, providing of course that he has successfully carried that kind of weight before. Give me a horse that is not in shape and I don't care what weight he carries.

A few years ago I remember getting 6–1 on a horse that had beaten the same field of starter handicap horses five straight times. The betting crowd was so afraid of the horse's 134-pound weight assignment that it failed to accept him at face value.

If the fans had bothered to look up his record, they might not have been so apprehensive. The season before the horse won a similar-class event under 136 pounds. To a certain extent the same kind of situation occurs several times a season at every racetrack in America.

Of course, common sense dictates paying some attention to large weight shifts or to heavy weight assignments, especially when two or more closely matched contenders are involved.

1¼ MILES—SUBURBAN HANDICAP, AQUEDUCT, JULY 20, 1974

True Knight * **127** Dk. b. or br. h (1969), by Chateaugay—Stealaway, by Olympia.
Breeder, J. W. Galbreath (Ky.). 1974 .. 8 3 3 0 $283,638
Owner, Darby Dan Farm. Trainer, T. L. Rondinello. 1973 .. 12 3 2 2 $200,858

Jly 13-74^{8}Mth	1 1-4	2:02	ft	8-5	▲124	9^{13}	4^{3}	$1^{1\frac{1}{2}}$	$1^{3\frac{3}{4}}$	Riv'aMA^{5}	HcpS	92	TrueKnight124 EcoleEtage HeyRube	9
Jun16-74^{9}Suf	1 1-8	1:48⅗	ft	3-5	▲121	7^{18}	7^{19}	$5^{8\frac{1}{2}}$	4^{3}	C'd'oAJr^{6}	HcpS	95	BillyComeLately109 Forage NorthSea	7
May27-74^{8}Bel	1	1:34⅖	ft	7	125	8^{22}	8^{13}	$7^{9\frac{3}{4}}$	$6^{8\frac{1}{4}}$	Riv'aMA^{5}	HcpS	88	ArbeesBoy112 Forego Timel'ssMom'nt	8
Apr 6-74^{8}GS	1 1-4	2:06	sl	6-5	125	$6^{8\frac{3}{4}}$	4^{3}	$2^{1\frac{1}{2}}$	$1^{\frac{3}{4}}$	C'd'oAJr^{4}	HcpS	70	TrueKnight125 ProveO't PlayTheF'ld	6
Mar23-74^{9}Hia	1 1-4	2:01⅕	ft	9-5	124	7^{19}	$7^{7\frac{1}{2}}$	$3^{2\frac{1}{2}}$	2^{1}	C'd'oAJr^{3}	HcpS	91	Forego 129 True Knight Play the Field	7
Mar 9-74^{8}Bow	1 1-4	2:05⅖	ft	3-5	▲123	14^{15}	10^{10}	$5^{4\frac{3}{4}}$	$1^{\frac{1}{2}}$	C'd'oAJr^{4}	HcpS	96	True Knight 123 Delay Ecole Etage	14
Feb23-74^{9}GP	1 1-4	1:59⅘	ft	1	▲123	6^{16}	$4^{5\frac{1}{2}}$	2^{h}	$2^{\frac{1}{2}}$	C'd'oAJr^{4}	HcpS	97	Forego127 TrueKnight GoldenDon	6
Feb 9-74^{9}GP	1 1-8	1:48⅗	ft	2¼	123	5^{16}	5^{16}	4^{6}	2no	C'd'oAJr^{3}	HcpS	91	Forego125 TrueKnight Proud andBold	5
Nov22-73^{8}Aqu	1 3/16	1:55	ft	4½	126	$11^{9\frac{1}{4}}$	$9^{7\frac{1}{2}}$	$3^{\frac{1}{2}}$	1^{2}	C'd'oAJr^{9}	HcpS	87	TrueKnight126 Triangular NorthSea	12
Oct27-73^{7}Aqu	2	3:20	ft	4½	124	5^{12}	3^{8}	3^{17}	4^{18}	C'd'oAJr^{2}	WfaS	78	Prove Out 124 Loud Twice A Prince	6
Oct15-73^{8}Aqu	1 1-8	1:47	ft	4	122	8^{11}	$5^{5\frac{1}{2}}$	3^{6}	$3^{4\frac{3}{4}}$	Cast'daM^{7}	HcpS	96	Riva Ridge 130 Forage True Knight	9
Sep22-73^{8}Bow	1 1-8	1:49⅘	ft	5½	120	9^{14}	8^{10}	1^{1}	1^{4}	C't'daM^{5}	HcpS	102	TrueKnight 120 Delay BurningOn	12

July 19 Bel 3f ft :39b July 12 Bel 4f ft :50b July 8 Bel 6f ft 1:16b

Forego **131** B. g (1970), by Forli—Lady Golconda, by Hasty Road.
Breeder, Lazy F Ranch (Ky.). 1974 7 5 2 0 $322,378
Owner, Mrs. Edward F. Gerry. Trainer, S. W. Ward. 1973 18 8 3 3 $188,909

Jly 4-74^{8}Aqu	1 3/16	1:54⅘	ft	2-5	▲129	6^{15}	4^{8}	2^{h}	$1^{\frac{3}{4}}$	Gust'sH^{6}	HcpS	88	Forego129 BillyComeLately ArbeesBoy	7
Jun26-74^{8}Aqu	7 f	1:21⅕	ft	2-3	▲132	6^{12}	6^{12}	$5^{6\frac{1}{2}}$	$2^{\frac{1}{2}}$	G'tinesH^{2}	HcpS	94	Timel'ssM'm'nt112 Forego N'rthSea	6
May27-74^{8}Bel	1	1:34⅖	ft	6-5	▲134	6^{11}	2^{h}	$1^{1\frac{1}{2}}$	2^{2}	G'tinesH^{2}	HcpS	94	ArbeesBoy112 Forego Timel'ssMom'nt	8
May18-74^{8}Bel	7 f	1:22⅕	ft	7-5	▲129	8^{9}	$6^{3\frac{1}{2}}$	$1^{1\frac{1}{2}}$	$1^{2\frac{1}{4}}$	Gust'sH^{7}	HcpS	91	F'r'go129 Mr.Pr'sp'ct'r Tim'l'sM'm'nt	8
Mar23-74^{9}Hia	1 1-4	2:01⅕	ft	4-5	▲120	5^{10}	$1^{\frac{1}{2}}$	$1^{1\frac{1}{2}}$	1^{1}	G'tinesH^{5}	HcpS	92	Forego 129 True Knight Play the Field	7
Feb23-74^{9}GP	1 1-4	1:59⅘	ft	7-5	127	4^{8}	2^{2}	1^{h}	$1^{\frac{1}{2}}$	G'stinesH^{2}	HcpS	98	Forego127 TrueKnight GoldenDon	6
Feb 9-74^{9}GP	1 1-8	1:48⅗	ft	2-3	▲125	4^{6}	$3^{2\frac{1}{2}}$	2^{1}	1no	G'tinesH^{2}	HcpS	91	Forego125 TrueKnight Proud andBold	5
Dec 8-73^{8}Aqu	1 1-8	1:47⅕	ft	3-5	▲127	5^{6}	3^{4}	$1^{1\frac{1}{2}}$	$1^{\frac{3}{4}}$	G'tinesH^{6}	HcpS	99	For'go127 MyG'll'nt Key to theK'gd'm	7
Nov24-73^{8}Aqu	1 3/16	1:54⅗	ft	2	▲123	4^{5}	$3^{2\frac{1}{2}}$	1^{3}	1^{5}	Gust'esH^{9}	HcpS	89	Forego123 MyGallant Twice aPrince	10
Nov10-73^{6}Aqu	7 f	1:22⅗	ft	4-5	▲122	$3^{5\frac{1}{2}}$	3^{6}	3^{4}	3^{4}	GustinesH^{2}	Alw	84	North Sea 115 Tap The Tree Forego	5

July 19 Bel 3f ft :35⅕b July 15 Bel 7f ft 1:24h July 13 Bel 3f ft :36⅘b

Two honest, hard-hitting stakes horses.

The difference between Forego and True Knight was never more than a length or two. In Florida during the winter of 1974 Forego won three straight races over True Knight, each by a narrow margin. In the spring Forego was twice unsuccessful in attempts to carry 130 or more pounds. And he was, in fact, meeting weaker horses than True Knight. Either he had lost some of his edge in condition or as a four-year-old was inhibited by such heavy weight loads. True Knight, on the other hand, was razor sharp; and on July 13, 1974, one week before the Suburban, True Knight put in his best lifetime race.

Given True Knight's obvious edge in condition, the spread in the Suburban weights and Forego's 131-pound impost were plus factors that deserved to be taken into account. Somehow, and I don't believe it yet, True Knight paid $10.60.

There is one special circumstance in which a rigid approach to the weight factor is supported by fact. Few people know about it.

Before the turn of the century the Jockey Club Scale of Weights was created as a concession to the natural maturation rate of horses. It is a common fact that a horse is not as well developed at age three as it is likely to be at age four.

Racing secretaries use the scale of age-linked weight concessions as a guide when carding races for horses of mixed age groups.

7th Arlington Park

1 1/16 MILES (inner turf). (1:41⅘). CLAIMING. Purse $5,500. 3-year-olds and upward. 3-year-olds. 113 lbs.: older. 122 lbs. Non-winners of two races since May 20 allowed 2 lbs.; a race, 4 lbs. Claiming price, $13,000; 2 lbs. allowed for each $1,000 to $11,000. (Races where entered for $10,000 or less not considered.)

4th Detroit Race Course

6 FURLONGS (chute). (1:08). CLAIMING. Purse $2,500. 3- and 4-year-olds, non-winners of two races. 3-year-olds. 115 lbs.: 4-year-olds. 120 lbs. Non-winners of a race in 1974 allowed 3 lbs.; a race since Nov. 10, 5 lbs. Claiming price, $2,500.

THE JOCKEY CLUB SCALE OF WEIGHTS

DISTANCE	AGE	JAN. & FEB.	MAR. & APR.	MAY	JUNE	JULY	AUG.	SEP.	OCT.	NOV. & DEC.
½ Mile	2	...	...	...	...	...	105	108	111	114
	3	117	119	121	123	125	126	127	128	129
	4	130	130	130	130	130	130	130	130	130
	5 & up	130	130	130	130	130	130	130	130	130
6 Furlongs	2	...	...	...	...	...	102	105	108	111
	3	114	117	119	121	123	125	126	127	128
	4	129	130	130	130	130	130	130	130	130
	5 & up	130	130	130	130	130	130	130	130	130
1 Mile	2	...	...	...	...	...	...	96	99	102
	3	107	111	113	115	117	119	121	122	123
	4	127	128	127	126	126	126	126	126	126
	5 & up	128	128	127	126	126	126	126	126	126
1¼ Miles	2	...	...	...	...	...	...	...	...	...
	3	101	107	111	113	116	118	120	121	122
	4	125	127	127	126	126	126	126	126	126
	5 & up	127	127	127	126	126	126	126	126	126
1½ Miles	2	...	...	...	...	...	...	...	...	...
	3	98	104	108	111	114	117	119	121	122
	4	124	126	126	126	126	126	126	126	126
	5 & up	126	126	126	126	126	126	126	126	126
2 Miles	3	96	102	106	109	112	114	117	119	120
	4	124	126	126	126	126	125	125	124	124
	5 & up	126	126	126	126	126	125	125	124	124

NOTE: *Fillies are entitled to a five-pound sex allowance in races against colts.*

For reasons I cannot fathom, there is a great deal of controversy in racing circles about the legitimacy of age-linked weight concessions. Every season there is talk of abolishing or amending the scale of weights. Most say that three-year-olds should not get automatic weight concessions in the late summer or fall. Nonsense. It seems to me the old-timers had a pretty good idea. The effectiveness of the scale and the need for the concessions are made abundantly clear in the following remarkable statement, checked out in a research project that included several thousand races.

When a three-year-old is assigned actual top weight in a race for horses three years and up, the three-year-old has little or no chance of winning. I suggest you read that again.

In all stakes and allowance races run at seven of the nation's most popular tracks during 1973 there were only two exceptions to this maxim. In all of 1974 there were only three exceptions. In 1975 and the first half of 1976 there were but five more exceptions to the rule.

All ten horses that defied the scale of age-linked weight concessions were curiously unable to repeat the feat at any other time, and only one was able to win a follow-up race of any kind during the next two months of competition. Ten exceptions and over 400 top-weighted three-year-olds that were unable to give away weight to their elders. That's information worth keeping in mind.

SEX

In Europe fillies race against colts and win with absolute impunity. In America most trainers are reluctant to match the so-called weaker sex against males. Ruffian's tragic demise in the match race against Foolish Pleasure didn't help reverse the trend. But to his credit, it didn't change Frank Whiteley Jr.'s commitment to the experiment. Only two of Honorable Miss's races shown in the p.p.s below were against members of her own sex.

Honorable Miss **120** B. m (1970), by Damascus—Court Circuit, by Royal Vale.
Breeder, Mrs. T. Bancroft (Ky.).
Owner, Pen-Y-Bryn Farm. Trainer, F. J. Whiteley, Jr.

								1976	8	3	2	1	$100,148
								1975	13	7	2	0	$183,857

30 Aug76 8Bel	6 f :223 :4541:10 ft	7-5 ^130	97½ 53½ 1h	14½ ShmrW10	HcpS 92 HonorableMiss130	Lachesis 10
25 Jly 76 8Aqu	7 f :232 :47 1:242ft	1 ^118	61² 69 42	31½ VsquezJ2	HcpS 78 El Fitirre 114 Nalee'sKnight 6
12 Jly 76 4Atl	6 f :221 :4441:09 ft	1 ^119	1010¹012 910 56	VasqzJ10	HcpS 91 North Call 115 Our Hero 10
4 Jly 76 8Aqu	6 f :22 :4441:092ft	1 ^125	51⁴ 411 47	51½ VsquezJ5	HcpS 95 Red Cross 118 Shy Dawn 5
27 May76 8Bel	6 f :223 :4541:102ft	2-5e^123	61¹ 65 2¹	13¾ VasquezJ1	Alw 90 Honorable Miss 123 Lachesis 6
15 May76 8Bel	7 f :222 :4421:21 ft	9-5 ^121	91² 99½ 57½	26¼ VsquezJ1	HcpS 91 LordRebeau115 HonorbleMiss 9
1 May76 8Aqu	7 f :221 :4421:222sy	4¾ 122	81¹ 81³ 57	2¾ VasquezJ5	HcpS 88 DueDiligence111 HnrbleMiss 8
23 Apr76 8Aqu	6 f :222 :4541:103gd	1 ^123	61⁴ 610 33	1¾ VasquezJ3	Alw 90 ℗HonrbleMiss123 FltVictrss 6
1 Nov75 8Bel	7 f :22 :4431:224ft	7-5e^125	11171012 58½	45½ VasquezJ9	HcpS 82 No Bias 116 Step Nicely 11
13 Oct75 8Bel	6 f :223 :4531:094ft	9-5e^133	14111161 5⁰½	1² VasqzJ15	HcpS 93 Honorable Miss 133 No Bias 15
25 Sep75 8Bel	7 f :224 :4531:231sy	1-2 ^119	48¼ 46 3½	22¾ VasquezJ1	Alw 83 ℗FltVictress112 HnrbleMiss 4

Sept 14 Bel 4f ft :46⅗h   Sept 10 Bel 4f ft :46⅘h   Sept 5 Bel 4f ft :48b

Because of a variety of economic factors, it is true that a filly of $15,000 claiming class will usually run one- or two-fifths of a second slower than a colt of the corresponding claiming class. But if the filly is in a race with colts and is intrinsically the fastest horse in the field, my research shows that there is nothing linked to sex differences that will prevent her from proving her superiority on the track. Simply put, a fast filly will beat a slow colt and a fast colt will beat a slow filly.

One caution: During the late spring and early summer, female horses tend to go into heat. Occasionally that will bring out excessive kidney sweating and other nervous habits. A filly acting in that manner during the post parade is telling you she has other things beside racing on her mind. (This can happen in a race carded exclusively for fillies too.)

WORKOUTS

The racetrack is open for training in the early morning hours, and the *Daily Racing Form* clockers have a tough job. As many as thirty horses can be out on the racetrack at the same time, and there are no names or numbers on the saddlecloths to help identify the horses.

DELAWARE PARK - Track Fast

Three Furlongs			**Four Furlongs**			Amystar	1:01⅖	h	Spanish Dew	1:00⅖	h
A Long Way	:40	b	Bog Road	:49⅘	b	Army Hitch	1:04	b	WilmingtonFlask	1:01⅗	hg
Arctic Ability	:36⅖	h	Boldinthepark	:50⅗	bg	Black Power	1:01⅘	b	Woulda Coulda	1:03	b
Decladation	:38	bg	Chinese Trumpet	:49⅕	b	Blackjack Davis	1:03	b	You'reSensationl	1:03⅖	b
Deep	:38	b	Count Knave	:49	bg	Cold Voyage	1:05	bg	Zasperilla	1:03⅖	b
Don Miguel	:40	b	**Custers LastStand**	:48	h	Double Chop	1:03⅗	b	**Six Furlongs—1:09**		
Fair Toe	:38⅖	bg	Demonic	:52	b	Gun Cotton	1:07	b			
GlitterandGlmor	:38⅗	b	Dim Royalty	:51⅗	b	Hillybob	1:00	h	Cellini	1:16	b
Grundgy Twerp	:36	h	Double Nymph	:51	b	I'm A Lady Pilot	1:03	b	**Mickey Solo**	1:15	h
Long Tall Texan	:37	b	Ercildoun	:51⅗	b	Kintla's Folly	1:01	h	Plant Native	1:18	bg
Loom's Boy	:37	b	FurtherMoreLdy	:51	b	Las Profesoras	1:02	b	Sinister Knight	1:16⅗	b
No No Niki	:38	b	Grassisgreener	:51	b	Lassie Dear	1:00⅘	h	Tim Lee Lad	1:16	bg
Royal Exstasy	:38	b	Haf Pro	:50	b	Late Spring	1:05	b	**Seven Furlongs**		
Satan's Speed	:38	bg	Landing Field	:49	b	Mercado II	1:00	h			
Some Duce	:37	b	LuckyThirtyThre	:49	bg	Over the Stile	1:03⅖	bg	Bee Abe	1:29	b
Summer Secret	:38⅗	b	Lynne Baby	:52	b	Pilgrim's Plight	1:04⅘	b	**Better Arbitor**	1:27	h
Sweet Chutney	:38⅖	bg	Norton Priory	:48⅘	b	Pinch Pie	1:03⅘	b	**1 Mile—1:35⅕**		
Tiger Castle	:36⅖	h	Princess Hairan	:50⅗	b	Prince Berry	1:03	bg			
Two Coats	:38	b	Real Terror	:52	b	Prophetic	1:03⅖	b	**T. V. Vixen**	1:39⅖	h
White Skies	:36	h	**Five Furlongs—**	:57⅕		Ready Axe	1:03⅖	b	The Eclipser	1:45⅖	b

HILLYBOB & LASSIE DEAR (5) were in company. PINCH PIE (5) was given an easy trial. LAS PROFESORAS (5) was given an easy trial. MERCADO II (5) was impressive. BETTER ARBITOR (7) is being brought to hand in good fashion. T. V. VIXEN (1M) went very smartly. Her fractions were 23, 35, 48.3, 1:01, 1:13, 1:27 & 1:39.2. And was allowed to gallop out one mile. one eighth in 1:53.1.

ITEM: Because of typographical mistakes and omissions, workouts that appear in the daily tabulator listings are frequently more accurate than works appearing below the past performance profile. In addition, these tabular listings often contain the clocker's comments about some of the more noteworthy training drills of the day.

ITEM: When a horse ships from a section of the country serviced by one edition of the *Form* to another serviced by a different edition, the out-of-town workouts will frequently be omitted from the past performances. I have complained about this to the publisher of the *Daily Racing Form,* but aside from a smattering of California workouts that now make their way into the Eastern edition and vice versa, the response has not been satisfactory. Maybe if we all scream about this together we will get better results.

ITEM: The absence of workouts from any past performance profile does not mean the absence of training. Some works are missed, missing, or misidentified. A few trainers have access to private training tracks. Until all states adopt a rule requiring local workouts, the player is simply going to have to keep a record of the trainers who like to sneak their hot horses past the public.

For obvious reasons, this practice is most often attempted with first-time starters in cheap maiden claiming races and is particularly rampant in Maryland, a breeding state where the racing commission is not known for its compassion for the fan, and where there are almost fifty private training tracks within a 100-mile radius of Bowie, Laurel, and Pimlico.

ITEM: The times of workouts are as accurate as the clockers are skillful and honest. Because the vast majority of clockers are honest and skillful but not well paid, the player should expect a few of the best workouts to be misrepresented.

The most accurate clocking crews operate in New York (under the direction of Frenchie Schwartz), in California (where a workout identification system is used), and in Florida during the high-class winter meets. At all but a few racetracks, however, 95 to 99 percent of the workouts accorded to established stakes horses, and 70 to 80 percent of the rest are as accurate as a hand-held stopwatch can report them. In Maryland and Kentucky I would not be willing to stand by that statement.

ITEM: Some tracks offer an auxiliary training track to handle the overflow of horses on the grounds. These training tracks tend to be considerably deeper and slower than the main track, and the following table of times should be adjusted accordingly.

MAJOR-TRACK TABLE OF NOTEWORTHY WORKOUT TIMES

DISTANCE	BREEZING (WITHOUT SERIOUS WHIPPING)	HANDILY	FROM GATE	MUD
3 Furlongs	.35⅘b	.35⅖h	Add ⅖ sec.	Add ⅘ sec.
4 Furlongs	.48b	.47⅗h	Add ⅖	Add 1
5 Furlongs	1:00⅗b	1:00⅕h	Add ⅖	Add 1⅕
6 Furlongs	1:13⅗b	1:13h	Add ⅖	Add 1⅖
7 Furlongs	1:27b	1:26⅖h	Add ⅖	Add 1⅗
1 Mile	1:41b	1:40⅖h	Add ⅖	Add 1⅘
1⅛ Miles	1:56b	1:55⅖h	Add ⅖ sec.	Add 2 sec.

Admittedly, the value of the above chart is limited. It is only a guide. On lightning-fast racetracks the standards should be adjusted by at least one full second, and at minor tracks few horses will ever work fast enough to spark the player's attention.

The value of workouts is not restricted to speed. Indeed, a fast workout is not often conclusive evidence of improved physical condition; nor is a series of short, speedy drills of any special import to a horse that consistently shows high early speed in its races. Instead the player should consider the value of workouts in the light of the following principles; they are the concepts many of the best trainers use, and the ones many of the best players use as well.

1. Pay special note to the frequency of workouts and give a horse extra credit for positive physical condition if it has several good workouts to its credit or has raced well recently and has worked four furlongs or longer at least once in the interim. This is especially true at minor racetracks and for horses that have been out of action sometime during the recent past.

Royal Rhett **115** Ch. g (1973), by Royal Union—Sweet Straw, by Jackstraw.
Breeder, Al Rossi (Ill.). 1976 4 3 0 0 $6,787

Owner, Lepere Stable. Trainer, Ron O. Goodridge.

10 Sep76^{10}Cka	5 f :22^2	:46^2	:59^{2}ft	13	118	1^h	1^1	1$^{1\frac{1}{2}}$	1$^{1\frac{1}{2}}$	WolfC^5	Alw 90	RoyalRhett118	DarkAvenger	8
28 Jly 76 ^{8}FP	5½ f :23^2	:48^2	1:07^{4}ft	7-5	▲118	2$^{\frac{1}{2}}$	3^2	4^2	5$^{2\frac{1}{2}}$	WolfC^4	Alw 80	MeanMr.Green114	SadiesMn	7
19 Jly 76 ^{5}FP	6 f :23	:47	1:13^{2}ft	8-5	120	1$^{3\frac{1}{2}}$	1$^{3\frac{1}{2}}$	1$^{4\frac{1}{2}}$	1^5	WolfC^7	Alw 80	RoyalRhett 120	GreatPeach	8
29 May76 ^{3}FP	5½ f :23	:47^2	1:07 gd	8-5	▲120	1$^{1\frac{1}{2}}$	1$^{2\frac{1}{2}}$	1^4	1^3	WolfC^1	Mdn 87	RoylRhett120	AbleScrtaryJr.	10

Sept 9 Cka 4f ft :51⅖b Sept 2 Cka 5f ft 1:00⅕hg Aug 27 Cka 5f ft 1:02⅗bg

2. A recent fast workout at three or four furlongs is a positive sign if the horse has shown little early speed in its recent races (or has been racing in a route and is now attempting a sprint). Conversely, if the horse has been showing high early speed in its races or is attempting a significantly longer distance, a longer, slower workout would suggest the trainer's attempt to build staying power. In the

first example below, Princely Song showed high speed in his training drill of July 11 and won a sprint off that work four days later. In the case of Bold Forbes, trainer Laz Barrera had employed several long slow workouts in his strategy to prepare the colt for a maximum effort in the Kentucky Derby. His workout prior to the Preakness, a blazing-fast half-mile, did nothing to advance the horse and may have put him too much on edge. For the Belmont, the workout line shows that trainer Barrera was very conscious of the stamina factor. A masterpiece of horsemanship on display.

Princely Song * **114** Dk. b. or br. c (1972), by Cornish Prince—Songster, by Jester.
Br., Warnerton Farm of Ky., Ltd. (Ky.). 1976 4 1 1 0 $12,150
Owner, A. & Christine Willcox. Trainer, L. Rettele 1975 3 2 0 0 $8,809

3Jly 76	^{5}Hol	Ⓣ 1	:47^{4}1:11^{3}1:36^{2}fm	$3\frac{1}{2}$	114	5^2	$4^{3\frac{1}{2}}$	$6^{2\frac{1}{2}}$	7^3	OlivaresF^7	Alw	85	Chindo115	EarlyCotton	7
26Jun76	^{7}Hol	1	:45^{4}1:10 1:35^{2}ft	40	114	3^2	2^h	$2\frac{1}{2}$	$2\frac{1}{2}$	OlivaresF^7	Alw	88	HomeJerome114	PrincelySong	7
4Jun76	^{7}Hol	6 f	:22 :44^{2}1:08^{2}ft	$2\frac{3}{4}$	115	6^4	$6^{6\frac{1}{2}}$	7^{11}	6^{11}	HawleyS^7	Alw	86	Maheras116	RestlessRestless	7
20May76	^{7}Hol	6 f	:22 :44^{2}1:09^{3}ft	1	▲115	$1\frac{1}{2}$	$1\frac{1}{2}$	$1\frac{1}{2}$	1^{nk}	HawleyS^1	Alw	91	PrincelySng115	Chief'sHolday	7
22Nov75	^{8}Key	6 f	:22^1 :45^{1}1:09^{4}gc	7	114	$3^{3\frac{1}{2}}$	$3^{1\frac{1}{2}}$	4^2	4^3	TrctteRL^8	AlwS	90	GallantBob119	BearerBond	8
10Nov75	^{6}Key	7 f	:22^1 :45^{4}1:23^{3}sy	2-3	▲114	$1\frac{1}{2}$	$1^{1\frac{1}{2}}$	1^6	1^5	TurctteRL^1	Alw	91	PrincelySong114	Bee aTipper	7
27Oct75	^{9}Key	$6\frac{1}{2}$ f	:23 :46^{2}1:17^{3}ft	3	119	1^h	$1^{1\frac{1}{2}}$	1^3	1^8	TrctteRL^8	Mdn	89	PrincelySong119	CourtRportr	10

*July 10 Hol 4f ft :46$\frac{2}{5}$h June 20 Hol 6f ft 1:16h June 17 Hol 5f ft 1:01h

Bold Forbes **126** Dk. b. or br. c (1973), by Irish Castle—Comely Nell, by Commodore M.
Br., Eaton Farms & Red Bull Stable (Ky.). 1976.. 7 4 1 2 $318,890
Owner, E. R. Tizol. Trainer, L. S. Barrera. 1975.. 8 7 0 1 $62,749

15 May76	^{8}Pim	$1\frac{3}{16}$	:45 1:09 1:55 ft	1e	126	1^2	1^2	2^h	3^4	CoroAJr^4	ScwS	91	Elocutionist126	Play theRed	6
1 May76	^{8}CD	$1\frac{1}{4}$	:45^{4}1:10^{2}2:01^{3}ft	3	126	1^5	$1\frac{1}{2}$	$1\frac{1}{2}$	1^1	CrdroAJr^2	ScwS	89	BoldForbes126	HonestPlesre	9
17 Apr76	^{8}Aqu	$1\frac{1}{8}$	:46 1:09^{4}1:47^{2}ft	2-5	▲126	1^3	$1^{1\frac{1}{2}}$	1^4	$1^{4\frac{3}{4}}$	CdroAJr^5	ScwS	98	Bold Forbes 126	On The Sly	7
20 Mar76	^{8}Aqu	7 f	:22^1 :44 1:20^{4}ft	8-5	119	2^h	1^2	1^7	$1^{7\frac{3}{4}}$	CdroAJr^7	AlwS	97	Bold Forbes 119	Eustace	8
28 Feb76	^{8}SA	1	:45^{3}1:09^{3}1:35 ft	2	117	1^2	2^1	1^4	1^3	PincyLJr^5	AlwS	94	BoldForbes117	Grandaries	7
14 Feb76	^{8}SA	7 f	:22 :44^{3}1:21^{4}ft	8-5	▲119	1^h	$2\frac{1}{2}$	$1^{2\frac{1}{2}}$	$3\frac{3}{4}$	PincyLJr^7	AlwS	93	ThrmlEnrgy117	StaindGlass	7
24 Jan76	^{8}SA	6 f	:22^1 :45 1:09^{3}ft	6-5	▲120	$2\frac{1}{2}$	2^2	$2\frac{1}{2}$	2no	PincyLJr^2	AlwS	91	Sure Fire 114	Bold Forbes	6
31 Dec75	^{4}SA	$5\frac{1}{2}$ f	:21^4 :44^{2}1:03 ft	1-3	▲122	$1\frac{1}{2}$	$2\frac{1}{2}$	2^h	3^5	PincayLJr^1	Alw	94	Sure Fire 114	Beau Talent	5
3 Aug75	^{8}Sar	6 f	:21^4 :44^{1}1:09^{4}ft	1-10	▲120	1^2	1^8	1^{10}	1^8	V'squezJ^5	AlwS	91	BoldForbes120	FamilyDoct'r	5
23 Jly 75	^{8}Bel	6 f	:22^2 :45^{2}1:09^{2}ft	8-5	120	$1^{1\frac{1}{2}}$	1^2	1^4	1^5	PincyLJr^2	AlwS	96	Bold Forbes 120	Iron Bit	5
15 Jun75	^{7}PR	6 f	:22^2 :44^{3}1:10^{3}ft	1-6	▲118	1^2	1^4	1^5	1^{13}	HiraldoJ^2	Stk	101	Bold Forbes 118	Lovely Jay	4
4 Jun75	^{4}PR	6 f	:23 :45^{3}1:11^{2}ft	1-4e	▲114	1^2	$1^{3\frac{1}{2}}$	1^5	1^8	HiraldoJ^3	Alw	97	Bold Forbes 114	Lovely Jay	10
25 Apr75	^{1}PR	5 f	:22 :45^3 :59^{1}ft	1-6	▲116	1^4	1^5	1^6	$1^{8\frac{1}{2}}$	HiraldoJ^3	Alw	95	Bold Forbes 116	Lovely Jay	5
11 Apr75	^{1}PR	5 f	:22 :45^3 :58^{4}ft	1-3	▲115	1^5	1^5	1^5	1^5	HiraldoJ^4	Alw	97	Bold Forbes 115	Lovely Jay	5
12 Mar75	^{1}PR	5 f	:22 :45^4 :59^{2}ft	35	116	1^5	1^6	1^8	1^{17}	HiraldoJ^2	Mdn	94	BoldForbes116	MyDad'sBrdy	8

June 1 Bel 1m ft 1:50$\frac{3}{5}$bq May 27 Bel $1\frac{1}{2}$m ft 2:43$\frac{2}{5}$b May 13 Pim 4f ft :45$\frac{2}{5}$h

3. A workout of any distance at any reasonable speed one or two days before a race is a useful "blowout" and can often be interpreted as a positive sign of trainer intention. To obtain Sunday workouts, which are not included in the

Monday *Daily Racing Form* (published Saturday evening), check the racing secretary's office on entering the track. Some tracks announce these workouts over the public address system or post them in a designated location in the grandstand.

Speed Burgoo **116** B. f (1972), by Scotland—Queen Corona, by Bernburgoo.
Breeder, K. Blitsch (Ill.). 1976 . . 10 1 0 1 $2,010
Owner, S. Wheeler. Trainer, Rex Loney. $2.500 1975 . . 12 1 4 1 $3,3C0

9 Sep76 9Lat	1 1/16 :491 1:181 1:534sy	16	117	103	1022	1017	817	MurchisnJ8	2500		ClassyCanuck109	KennyLeVn	12
2 Sep76 9ElP	6 f :24 :49 1:17 sl	26	120	78½	88½	57½	33	MurchsnJ3	2500	62	J.Artest114	Day ofComfree	8
23 Aug76 9ElP	1 :48 1:134 1:403ft	8e	117	55¼	88¾	919	828	MurchsnJ7	2000	51	Quarnos 120	O Song	8
12 Aug76 9ElP	1¼ :492 1:152 2:092ft	53	120	31½	67¼	69½	615	MurchisnJ1	2000	59	Phil's Regret 115	Controblss	7
3 Aug76 6ElP	1 :474 1:133 1:403ft	8¼	115	35	45½	69	622	McDowlM7	2000	57	JacCourt120	LilThermo	7
26 Jly 76 2ElP	1 :483 1:142 1:43 ft	5¾	116	41½	31	3½	11½	MurchisnJ1	2000	67	SpeedBurgoo116	HeACrook	10
19 Jly 76 6ElP	6 f :231 :464 1:122ft	26	115	54¼	54¼	56	57½	CrtwrhtN1	3500	78	FairDiamond115	BoxcrBetty	6
13 Jly 76 2ElP	6 f :23 :47 1:143ft	27	112	57	66¾	75¾	95¼	CwrightN1	2500	72	Go Go Liza 112	Karen Lou	10
7 Jly 76 9ElP	6 f :23 :47 1:13 ft	26	118	53¼	41½	52½	55	MurchisnJ4	2000	80	Ⓕ Oh Katy 113	Roy's Choice	9
2 Jly 76 2ElP	6 f :23 :461 1:12 ft	35	112	1113	1214	119¼	1117	CrtwrghtN6	2500	73	Dr. Mills 114	Bixby Imp	12
8 Nov75 2CD	6 f :231 :473 1:152sl	58	115	97¾	910	89	811	BeechJJr7	3000	58	Wa Tonka 117	Vent Du Sud	12

July 25 ElP 3f ft :38⅕b

4. Most stakes-class horses work fast, and with a well-trained horse every training drill has a purpose. The following past performance profile shows the great Kelso preparing for the Washington, D.C., International, a 1½-mile classic run each fall on Laurel's grass course. In this particular case, Kelso, who was never 100 percent comfortable on the grass, lost by a narrow margin to Mongo, one of the top grass horses of the past twenty-five years. The defeat was surely no disgrace and certainly not the fault of trainer Carl Hanford, who made all the right moves.

Kelso X **126** Dk. b. or br. g (1957), by Your Host—Maid of Flight, by Count Fleet.
Breeder, Mrs. R. C. duPont. 1963 . . 11 9 1 0 $544,762
Owner, Bohemia Stable. Trainer, C. H. Hanford. 1962 . . 12 6 4 0 $289,685

Oct 19-637Aqu	2 3:22 ft	1-6	▲124	41¾	12	16	14	Val'z'lal1	WfaS 87	Kelso 124	Guadalcanal 124	Garwol	7
Sep28-637Aqu	1 1-4 2:00⅘ft	1-4	▲126	34	2½	1½	13½	Val'z'lal2	WfaS 96	Kelso126	NeverBend120	CrimsonSatan	5
Sep 2-637Aqu	1 1-8 1:49⅘ft	2-3	▲134	32	31	12	15½	Val'z'lal7	AlwS 92	Kelso134	CrimsonSatan129	Garwol	8
Aug 3-636Sar	1 1-8 1:50⅖ft	1-3	▲130	43	42½	11	12½	Val'elal2	SpwS 93	Kelso130	Saidam111	SunriseCounty	7
Jly 4-637Aqu	1 1-4 2:01⅘ft	2-5	▲133	32	31½	11½	11¼	Val'z'lal7	HcpS 91	Kelso 133	Saidam 111	Garwol	7
Jun19-637Aqu	1 1-8 1:48⅘ft	1-3	▲132	33½	31	12	11½	Val'uelal3	AlwS 97	Kelso 132	Lanvin 114	Polylad	5
Mar23-638Bow	1 1/16 1:43 ft	4-5	▲131	55	33	21½	1¾	Val"z'lal5	HcpS 98	Kelso131	CrimsonSat'n124	G'sh'gWind	6
Mar16-638G.P	1 1-4 2:03⅕ft	1-5	▲130	2h	12	12	13¼	Val'uelal2	HcpS 83	Kelso 130	Sensitivo 112	Jay Fox	6
Feb23-637Hia	1 1-4 2:01⅘ft	2-5	▲131	31	42½	23	22¼	Val'z'lal5	HcpS 87	BeauPurple125	Kelso131	Heroshogala	9
Feb 9-637Hia	1 1-8 1:48⅘ft	2¼	128	45	42	12	12¾	Val'z'lal1	HcpS 91	Kelso 128	Ridan 129	Sensitivo	6
Jan30-638Hia	7 f 1:22⅘ft	2½	128	2h	32	43½	45½	Val'z'lal4	HcpS 89	Ridan 127	Jaipur 127	Merry Ruler	5
Dec 1-628G.S	1 1-2 2:30⅕ft	2-5	▲129	1h	13	13	15	Val'z'lal2	AlwS 105	Kelso 129	Bass Clef 117	Polylad	5

Nov 5 Lrl tc 1 1-8m fm 1:50⅘h Nov 4 Lrl tc 3f fm :37⅖b Nov 1 Lrl 7f m 1:27⅖b

5. A horse that races regularly, particularly one in good form, does not necessarily need any workouts to stay in shape. A prior victory without workouts is sufficient proof of this.

Mrs. Herman **119** B. m (1971), by Map Maker—Lana Belle, by To Market.
Breeder, Mrs. R. C. duPont Jr. (Md.).
Owner. Janet Greenberg.Trainer, H. Jacobson.

1976	10	3	1	1	$16,810
1975	9	3	0	1	$15,360

15Jly 76	5Aqu	1 :45⁴1:10²1:36⁴ft	2¾	117	1½	1³	1⁶	11½	VeneziaM⁶ 18000 82 Ⓕ Mrs.Herman117 IceStar II. 8
8Jly 76	2Aqu	7 f :22² :45²1:25 gd	3¾	113	3²	1½	1⁴	13¾	VenezaM² 13000 76 Ⓕ Mrs.Herman113 MagcalLdy 8
1Jly 76	9Aqu	1 :45⁴1:09⁴1:35³ft	3	⁴117	1½	1⁵	1⁸	1⁹	VeneziaM⁷ 7500 88 Ⓕ Mrs.Hrmn117 T.G.ForEthyl 10
24Jun76	1Bel	6 f :23¹ :46³1:11²ft	4½	115	1ʰ	1²	1¹	2ⁿᵏ	VeneziaM⁴ 7000 85 Ⓕ QckPassage113 Mrs.Hermn 10
31May76	9Bel	6 f :22³ :46¹1:12³ft	13	112⁵	3¹	3¹	2²½	5²½	MrtinJF¹¹ 9500 77 Ⓕ Form inColor112 Gynarchy 11
19May76	1Bel	7 f :23² :47³1:25³sy	2½	⁴110⁵	2¹	1ʰ	35½	5¹⁰	MartinJE⁸ 9500 64 Ⓕ Sarmaletta118 LoudCry 8
16May76	3Bel	6 f :23 :46³1:12⁴ft 8-5	⁴118	1½	1ʰ	2ʰ	3¾	MontyaD⁴ c7500 77 Ⓕ DoubleSkip114 QuietSuzne 9
10May76	3Bel	6 f :22⁴ :46²1:12¹ft	7½	113	2³	2½	1ʰ	4½	MontoyaD⁷ 8500 80 Ⓕ Sarmaletta115 AuntBud 11

NO WORKOUTS SINCE→June 12 Aqu 3f ft :38b

---

6. To better determine the readiness of a first-time starter or an absentee, the player should review the daily tabular workout listings for additional clues. In maiden special-weight (nonclaiming) races at the top-class race-tracks, very few first-timers win without showing snappy speed in one or more training trials or drawing at least one rave review from the clockers. Even fewer win without showing at least one very good workout at five furlongs or longer among other trials that stretch back over four, six, or eight weeks of preparation. A good workout from the starting gate is also reassuring.

In cheap maiden races superfast workouts are rarely to be trusted. In fact, the most promising workout line for claiming maidens is the one that contains a few closely spaced workouts of modest speed. A workout line that contains no training drills, however, is a signal to watch the tote board. In sharp hands such a horse can be expected to run a top race.

In either case—in the high-grade maiden race or the low-grade maiden claimer—first-time starters are bad risks if the field contains a lightly raced horse with proven ability. Conversely, the more proven losers in a field, the greater credit one should give to a well-bred, well-trained first-time starter.

Little Riva   **118** B. c (1973), by First Landing—Iberia, by Heliopolis.
Breeder, Meadow Stud, Inc. (Va.).   1975 . 0 M 0 0   (—)

Owner, Meadow Stable.   Trainer, L. Laurin.

June 3 Bel 3f ft :35h   May 29 Bel 3f ft :59⅗h   May 24 Bel 5f ft 1:00h

---

On the Belmont Stakes day card of 1975 Riva Ridge's half-brother—the horse you see above—was fit and ready to run a top race at first asking. The following workouts predate those included in his past performance profile.

May 20—Bel 4f ft 47⅕b . . .
May 16—Bel 3f ft 35b . . .
May 10—Bel 6f ft 1:13⅕h . . . COMMENT: "Little Riva showed good speed."
May 7—Bel 5 f ft 1:02⅖b . . .
May 1—Bel 4f 48b . . . COMMENT: "Little Riva is coming to hand."

In California the *Form* not only provides accurate workouts but also includes the latest six workouts in the past performance profile of a first-time starter. This is an excellent idea, and I wish the *Form* would supply such information as a matter of course for all its editions.

The two past performance examples below show the kind of training program necessary to get a claiming-class maiden ready for a winning try. Note the subtle but real difference in workout times between the maiden trying to win a $20,000 claiming event and the more expensive colt.

Hollywood Park is a lightning-fast racetrack. For a top-class maiden event, a first-timer would need to show much faster training trials.

Elroy Braun **118** Dk. b. or br. c (1974), by Old Bag—Marcy Lynx, by Mount Marcy.
Breeder, R. E. Schleicher (Ky.). 1976 0 M 0 0 ——
Owner, R. E. Schleicher. Trainer, S. Martin. $20,000
July 11 Hol (TR) 5f ft 1:01⅕hg July 7 Hol 4f ft :50h July 2 Hol 4f ft :49⅖h
June 27 Hol (TR) 5f ft 1:02hg June 22 Hol 4f ft :48⅗h June 17 Hol 4f ft :48⅗hg

---

Devil's Bluff **114** Dk. b. or br. c (1974), by Big Bluffer—Witchy Norma, by Crimson Satan.
Breeder, Braugh Ranches (Texas). 1976 0 M 0 0 ——
Owner, Braugh Ranches. Trainer, L. Regula. $30,000
July 22 Hol 4f ft :48⅘h July 18 Hol 1(TR) 5f ft :59⅗hg July 14 Hol 4f ft :47⅘h
July 10 Hol 6f ft 1:15⅖h July 4 Hol 1(TR) 5f ft 1:00⅗h June 27 Hol (TR) 5f ft 1:02⅕hg

---

It may seem hard to believe, but when Seattle Slew, the unanimous two-year-old champion of 1976, made his debut at Belmont Park on September 20, 1976, he had no published workouts in the Western edition of the *Form*. A few mediocre works were listed in the Eastern *Form* but they were no indication of his true ability. The heavy play he received on the tote board suggested that his subsequent dynamite performance was not a surprise to his trainer. W. H. Turner is nobody's fool.

Seattle Slew **122** Dk. b. or br. c (19794), by Bold Reasoning—My Charmer, by Poker.
Breeder, B. S. Castleman (Ky.). 1976 0 M 0 0 (——)
Owner, Karen L. Taylor. Trainer, William H. Turner, Jr.

---

7. A workout on the turf course is an extremely valuable clue to trainer intention. A good drill on the turf is excellent evidence of the horse's ability to handle such footing. Sometimes the trainer will enter such a horse in a grass race immediately following a good turf work; sometimes he will wait until the workout is no longer listed in the past

performances. As a rule, it makes good sense to keep a special record of all good turf works.

BELMONT PARK –
(Turf) Course Firm (Dogs Up)

Four Furlongs		**Thirty Years**	**:47⅖ h**	Hosanna II	1:04⅗ h	Our Doctor	1:15 b
Captain Max	:49⅕ b	Yvetot	:50⅖ b	Ode to Romeo	1:04⅖ b	PoliticalCoverup	1:18 b
Duveen	:48 h	**Five Furlongs**		**Spanish Dagger**	**1:00⅖ h**		
Inward Bound	:49⅘ b	Alibhai's Luck	1:02⅕ b	**Six Furlongs**		**Seven Furlongs—1:20⅘**	
Manifest	:48⅘ b	Carlogie	1:02⅗ h	**Go Double**	**1:14⅗ h**		
Ruling All	:48⅘ h	Close to Noon	1:01⅗ h	Herculean	1:15 h	**Barcas**	**1:32⅖ b**
Run Tara Run	:49⅖ h	Evening Dance	1:02⅕ h	I'm All	1:17 b	I Encircle	1:33 b

SPANISH DAGGER (5) looks good.

The following horse gave ample evidence of her ability to handle turf racing in two workouts prior to her winning turf race on July 13, 1976.

Miss Gallivant **113** B. f (1973), by Gallant Man—Year Around, by Hill Prince.
Breeder, L. R. Miller (Md.).
Owner, Dr. S. or L. Miller. Trainer, L. Rettele.

1976	7	2	1	1	$16,180
1975	0	M	0	0	——

18Jun76	^{6}Hol	$1\frac{1}{16}$	:47 1:11^{1}1:42^{2}ft	3½	116	1^h	1½	1^4	1^6	HawleyS^2	Alw 83	Ⓕ MissGallivnt116	Save aLtle	7
11Jun76	^{6}Hol	6 f	:22^1 :45^{1}1:09^{2}ft	5	114	3½	1½	1½	1^3	HawleyS^5	Mdn 92	Ⓕ MsGallivant114	Shanagoldn	7
5Jun76	^{4}Hol	6 f	:22^1 :45^{2}1:09^{4}ft	7¼	114	5$^{1\frac{3}{4}}$	2½	3$^{3\frac{1}{2}}$	3^8	HawleyS^5	Mdn 82	Ⓕ MadamGaylady114	Deploy	9
26Mar76	^{4}SA	1	:46^{2}1:12^{1}1:38^{4}ft	3¼	116	1½	1^1	6^7	9^{22}	ValdezS^3	Mdn 53	Ⓕ BidBoldly116	Shamara	9
13Mar76	^{3}SA	$1\frac{1}{16}$	:46^{3}1:12^{2}1:46^{3}ft	8-5	▴116	1$^{1\frac{1}{2}}$	5^3	9^{15}	9^{37}	ToroF^3	Mdn 32	Ⓕ Chavalarious116	BidBoldly	9
22Feb76	^{3}SA	6 f	:21^3 :44^{3}1:10^{4}ft	6-5	▴117	4$^{3\frac{1}{2}}$	4$^{4\frac{1}{2}}$	4$^{5\frac{1}{2}}$	5$^{5\frac{3}{4}}$	HawleyS^2	Mdn 79	Ⓕ ContingentFee117	Jaunting	10
25Jan76	^{3}SA	6 f	:22 :45 1:10^{3}ft	2	▴117	8$^{7\frac{1}{2}}$	6^5	5$^{4\frac{1}{2}}$	2$^{2\frac{1}{2}}$	PincayLJr^6	Mdn 83	Ⓕ Wandle117	MissGallivant	11

July 9 Hol (tc) fm 1:28⅕h ✻July 2 Hol 6f ft 1:13h ✻June 26 Hol (tc) 5f fm 1:00⅖h

---

8. Improving workouts generally denote improving physical condition. With the workout line below, all that Patriot's Dream needs is a slight drop in class.

Patriot's Dream **113** Ch. c (1973), by Gunflint—Ambitious Lady, by Petare.
Breeder, Ocala Stud, Inc. (Fla.).
Owner, H. Allen. Trainer, E. Jacobs.

1976	7	1	1	2	$10,590
1975	5	1	0	1	$6,769

18Jly 76	^{8}Aqu	6 f	:22^1 :45^{1}1:10^{3}ft	16	112	3^3	3^3	5$^{3\frac{1}{2}}$	6$^{4\frac{1}{4}}$	VelasqzJ^2	HcpS 86	ArabianLaw112	FullOut	7
8Jly 76	^{8}Aqu	6 f	:22^2 :45^{1}1:09^{2}ft	11	113	4$^{1\frac{1}{2}}$	5$^{2\frac{1}{4}}$	4$^{2\frac{1}{2}}$	3$^{6\frac{1}{4}}$	MontoyaD^2	Alw 90	SoyNumeroUno111	ArabanLw	6
30Jun76	^{8}Aqu	1	:45^{1}1:08^{4}1:34^{1}ft	40	114	2½	2^1	5^6	6$^{9\frac{1}{2}}$	MontyaD^4	AlwS 85	DanceSpell 114	Zen	6
22Jun76	^{5}Mth	6 f	:22^1 :45^{2}1:11^{4}ft	3-5	113	3^4	3$^{1\frac{1}{2}}$	4^3	3$^{6\frac{3}{4}}$	EdwrdsJW^4	Alw 74	KindIndeed118	SecondTerm	5
15Jun76	^{7}Mth	6 f	:22^1 :44^{3}1:10 ft	2¾	115	2½	2^1	2^3	2$^{3\frac{1}{2}}$	EdwrdsJW^6	Alw 86	SunnyClime120	Patriot'sDrm	6
30May76	^{6}Bel	Ⓣ 1	:45^{4}1:10 1:34^{3}fm	10	115	3^1	9^{12}	10^{20}	10^{26}	HrnandzR^2	Alw 72	FifthMarine115	Burundi	10
21May76	^{7}Bel	6 f	:22^1 :45^{2}1:10 ft	2	114	1^1	1$^{1\frac{1}{2}}$	1^2	1$^{\frac{3}{4}}$	VeneziaM^1	Alw 92	Patriot'sDrm114	FinanclWhiz	7

July 23 Bel (trt) 5f ft :59⅖h July 14 Bel (trt) 5f ft 1:00⅕h July 5 Bel (trt) 4f ft :49b

9. A series of closely spaced workouts or workouts mixed with racing ordinarily points out a horse in sound physical health. Very often the average horseplayer eliminates an active horse with mediocre finishes in his past performance profile without realizing how fit the horse really is. On the other hand, a horse in apparent good form cannot be expected to hold that form if the trainer insists on working the horse hard and fast every few days between starts. Studying the strengths and weaknesses of trainers is the only reliable way to make accurate judgments about this type of training regimen.

This horse is racing fit. She has shown improved speed in her recent starts. Pretty soon she's going to get a field she can lead from wire to wire.

Cameo Girl	116	Ch. f (1972), by Dandy K.—Octopus Girl, by Octopus			
Owner, J. E. Sowards. Trainer, J. E. Sowards.		Breeder, J. E. Sowards (Ky.). $3,500	1975 9 1 1 0		$2,440
			1974 .11 1 3 1		$3,774

7 Nov75	1CD	6 f :23	:4731:153sy	10	115	11	11	741	910	McCllrJW6	3500 58	ⒻMark theSpt115 GameFce 12
3 Nov75	2CD	6 f :222	:4611:123ft	90	116	31	633	833	912	McCllrJW9	5000 71	ⒻImprsiveMry114 Hln'sMsic 9
25 Oct75	2Kee	6 f :223	:4611:121ft	20f	109	31	351	561	612	McCllrJW1	5000 69	Proud Spirit 112 Fuel 10
18 Oct75	2Kee	6 f :23	:4811:142sy	93	114	111	11	671	919	BrmfldD11	5000 51	ⒻMay'sJwll 115 TooMchCrn 12
11 Oct75	7Beu	6 f :23	:4611:113ft	57	119	751	11131	11181	122	UrrutiaJ6	Alw 66	Darby Dale 114 Scott Man 11
17 Feb75	8Lat	6 f :241	:5021:103m	5	108	211	2h	1h	1no	McCulrJW2	Alw 65	Cameo Girl 108 Just Miss 8
8 Feb75	5Lat	6 f :23	:4621:111ft	51	114	32	46	411	421	McCurJW3	Alw 71	Dr.Abs116 Holloway'sMistke 6
18 Jan75	4Cwl	41 :222	:472 :544m	21	114	5	421	22	26	McCurJW4	7500 82	Clemstone 122 Cameo Girl 6
Jan 2-75	8Cwl	61 f 1:253⅖m	64	117	21	21	2h	781	McCu'rJW9		Alw 62	Donda'sMir'e122 CoolItB'e Jan't'sDe't 10

| Nov 1 CD 5f ft 1:05b | Oct 24 Kee 3f ft :37b | Oct 22 Kee 5f ft 1:04b |

This horse is crying for a rest. Instead, he was entered in a stakes race against For the Moment and other top-class juvenile colts.

Heidee's Pal	122	B. c (1974), by Tinajero—Debbys Charm, by Debbysman.			
Owner, M. M. Garren. Trainer, Gilbert Puentes.		Breeder, M. M. Garren (N. Y.).	1976..11 1 2 1		$16,404

3 Sep76	6Bel	6 f :224	:4621:104ft	13	115	631	521	451	473	MapleE6	Alw 80	HeyHyJ.P.115 Albi'sTrckStp 6
19 Aug76	8Sar	6 f :222	:46 1:122ft	10	119	12101	1083	643	22	MapleE6	AlwS 76	FratelloEd115 Heidee'sPal 17
9 Aug76	3Sar	6 f :223	:4631:12 m	63	120	21	3nk	21	53	MapleE5	27500 77	JollyQuill 119 Strtp'sGlitters 8
28 Jly 76	5Aqu	6 f :223	:4641:131ft	20	122	77	99	911	97	SantgoA5	35000 70	Plantaris 119 PrinceNoName 9
17 Jly 76	7Aqu	51 f :22	:4521:044ft	13	115	77	791	612	612	SantiagoA6	Alw 77	Bucksaw 115 Hey Hey J. P. 7
10 Jly 76	3Aqu	51 f :223	:47 1:054sy	51	122	311	211	11	1nk	StgoA8	M25000 84	Heidee'sPal 122 PrinceNoNe 8
2 Jly 76	4Aqu	51 f :23	:47 1:06 ft	21	122	411	43	33	321	StgoA3	M25000 80	Bucksaw 122 Dobrynin 7
24 Jun76	4Bel	51 f :232	:4731:062ft	20	118	31	3nk	21	22	SngoA9	M20000 81	PeppyPeppis122 Heidee'sPal
16 Jun76	3Bel	51 f :23	:44 1:07 ft	14	118	55	983	881	793	SngoA8	M20000 70	Hawaiian'Ways120 Dky'sBlrc
28 May76	4Bel	51 f :224	:4631:053ft	49	1175	871	981	913	917	MartinJE4	Mdn 70	MedievalMn122 FirstPretse !0
21 May76	4Bel	51 f :23	:4641:054ft	53	122	42	551	713	716	TrtteR5	M35000 70	FlagOfficer122 WincomaLss 10

| Sept 9 Bel trt 4f ft :47⅜h | Sept 1 Bel 4f ft :50⅖h | Aug 26 Sar trt 5f ft 1:02h |

10. Consult the clocker's comments, where available, for special mention of noteworthy training drills, fractional times, workouts in company, and other important clues. Pay particular attention to the tone of the clocker's remarks. If the comment is a positive one, you might well expect improvement from the horse in the next race or two. A good "horses to watch" list can be compiled this way, depending of course on the reliability of the clocker in question.

SAMPLE CLOCKER COMMENTS, BELMONT PARK, SEPTEMBER 1976

SEATTLE SLEW is sharp. WARM FRONT had all his speed. DANCE SPELL acts good. HONORABLE MISS was full of run. ASHMORE AND MAITLAND II were in company. BOLD FORBES is doing well. FIGHTING BILL had jockey Day up.

Most of the horses who drew the comments above were well-known stakes horses. However, there were two strangers who worked in company on even terms, and the player might not have paid attention to the modest comment they received. But the moment Ashmore was exposed as a contender for the $350,000 Jockey Club Gold Cup, the value of Maitland II's stock increased.

Workouts in company are particularly useful to the trainer and the horseplayer. Very often a trainer will not know which of two lightly raced horses is the faster. A workout in company may provide a definitive answer. As you might imagine, one of the most reliable workout clues is a victory by the slower of two horses that worked in company. From that moment onward, the faster worker becomes a four-star entry in my "horses to watch" list. A young maiden working on even terms with a known stakes horse is another key clue provided by workouts in company.

SAMPLE CLOCKER COMMENTS, BOWIE, SEPTEMBER 1976

(4) BACAYE still retains her speed. **(4) SILVER FLORIN** had a high turn of speed in his trial. **(5) INCÁ ROCÀ** with jockey Snell in the irons went in fractions of :22.1, :34, :46.1, :59.1 galloping out in 1:12.4. **(5) ROYAL DRAFTSMAN** is ready for another winning effort. **(6) MUM BOLD** had a useful trial. Additional Workout on Oct 6, 75, ALTO REBOT (4F) :50 B.

Most of the above comments are quite helpful and to the point, but I would tend to downgrade the clocker's note on Royal Draftsman unless prior results demonstrated the particular clocker's reliability as a tout.

RUNNING STYLE AND THE DISTANCE FACTOR

While most racehorses tend to have a preferred racing distance and some horses are incapable of winning a race when out of their element, there is great power in the training regimen to alter the distance capability of the horse. In addition, there is a most intriguing and predictable relationship between each different distance and running style.

A good trainer can increase or decrease the distance potential of a horse through workouts, special equipment, and actual races at longer and shorter distances. Allen Jerkens does it all the time; so do hundreds of other trainers of lesser talent. The following two principles illustrate the manner in which the vast majority of horses react to distance manipulations:

1. A horse that has been sprinting will most often race closer to the lead or will even set the pace in a longer, slower-paced route event.
2. A horse that has been on the pace in a longer, slower route may be unable to cope with the faster pace of a sprint but is nevertheless likely to show improved stretch punch.

The past performance profiles below demonstrate both principles at work.

Operating * **112** Ch. m (1971), by Dr. Fager—Cutting, by Bold Ruler.
Breeder, O. Phipps (Ky.). 1976 . 6 1 0 0 $6,440
Owner, Shinrone Farm, Inc. Trainer, Frank Kirby. 1975 . . 1 0 0 0 (——)

3 Aug76	^{7}Aks	6 f :22^1 :45^{4}1:11^{1}ft	4	112	$3^{6\frac12}$	$3^{5\frac12}$	2^2	$1^{1\frac12}$	LivelyJL^5	Alw 81	Operating112	CordialPrince	8
28 Jly 76	^{7}Aks	1^{70} :45^{4}1:12^{2}1:45 gd	5½e	114	1^4	1^4	$2^{\frac12}$	6^8	HarmonB^2	Alw 65	BrotherSasa112	GunChoke	8
16 Jly 76	^{7}Aks	1^{70} :46^{4}1:11 1:41^{3}ft	41	114	$1^{1\frac12}$	1^h	$5^{5\frac12}$	$6^{8\frac14}$	WhtdDW^3	HcpS 82	ⒻRoger'sChce115	RockyTrip	8
23 Jun76	^{7}Aks	1^{70} :48^{1}1:11^{4}1:42^{2}ft	21	114	$7^{4\frac14}$	5^5	9^{12}	9^{11}	McBdeB^{10}	Alw 75	ⒻBaygo 120	Quivira	11
9 Jun76	^{7}Aks	5½ f :21^4 :45^{3}1:05^{1}ft	14e	114	$9^{6\frac34}$	$10^{8\frac34}$	$9^{8\frac12}$	$7^{5\frac14}$	McBdeB^{12}	Alw 79	ⒻFashionNews114	TruxTop	12
20 May76	^{7}Aks	6 f :22^2 :45^{4}1:11^{1}ft	33	114	$5^{5\frac12}$	5^4	7^9	$7^{9\frac14}$	McBrideB^2	Alw 72	ⒻMk andWne120	FashnNws	10
26 Jly 75	^{7}AP	6 f :22^2 :45^{4}1:10^{3}ft	11	114	$9^{8\frac34}$	8^{10}	8^{11}	9^{15}	RubbiccoP^4	Alw 75	ⒻMary Dugan 114	Salus	9

Midnight Tattoo **122** Dk. b. or br. g (1970), by Blue Tattoo—Dainty Joy, by Johns Joy.
Breeder, D. E. Breshears, S. F. 1976 19 2 1 3 $9,296
Cheesman & J. H. Cole (Ark.). 1975 22 5 3 3 $17,980
Owner, W. A. Morris. Trainer, Roy Landis. $7,500

8 Sep76	^{7}Det	1^{70} :48^{2}1:14 1:45^{4}ft	2¾	119	$6^{4\frac34}$	3^1	2^h	1^{nk}	GarciaJR^6	6250 68	MidnightTattoo119	FltMkna	8
30 Aug76	^{6}Det	1 :48 1:13^{4}1:41 ft	2	▲114	5^2	2^h	$2^{\frac12}$	1^{nk}	GarciaJR^6	6500 74	MidnightTattoo114	Rabish	7
7 Aug76	^{3}Det	1$\frac{1}{16}$:47^{2}1:12^{4}1:46^{3}ft	6	109	$3^{1\frac12}$	$4^{3\frac12}$	$4^{3\frac12}$	5^{11}	HrreraA^7	H2500 59	DepndbleMel 110	QckDiscvry	7
16 Jly 76	^{6}Aks	6 f :22^1 :45^{3}1:11^{2}ft	16	116	$9^{9\frac14}$	8^{12}	$5^{4\frac12}$	3^{nk}	StageJL^2	c6500 80	Nu I Shud 119	Nobby Dod	11
3 Jly 76	^{6}Aks	6 f :23 :46^{2}1:11^{2}ft	87	116	10^8	$10^{8\frac14}$	9^{10}	$8^{7\frac12}$	SntgeJL^{10}	7500 72	Terms 122	Sturdy Money	10
23 Jun76	^{6}Aks	6 f :22 :44^{4}1:10^{4}ft	54	116	12^{13}	12^{14}	11^{11}	$11^{9\frac34}$	SangeJL^7	8500 73	Amerix 119	Proud State	12
28 May76	^{6}Aks	6 f :22^3 :46^{2}1:12^{4}sy	20	117	10^{15}	8^{12}	8^9	$6^{9\frac14}$	HreraA^{12}	c6500 64	Twiddley De 112	Tin Horn	12
25 May76	^{6}Aks	6 f :22^1 :45^{4}1:12^{2}ft	26	117	11^{12}	11^{14}	8^7	$4^{2\frac14}$	HerreraA^4	7000 73	Shoeshiner 117	Kenya A.	12
21 May76	^{4}Aks	6 f :22 :44^{4}1:11 ft	21	112	11^{15}	10^{21}	8^{13}	5^{11}	HereraA^{11}	7000 71	Solid Mix 112	City Visitor	11

Kind Tom **113** Ch. g (1970), by Pinnacle—Kindness, by Stymie.
Breeder, Mrs. T. Thompson (Tex.). 1976 20 2 2 5 $5,901
Owner, J. C. Farley. Trainer, Lonnie Abshire. $2,500 1975 26 3 3 3 $11,703

27 Aug76	^{2}RD	1^{70} :49 1:14^{4}1:46^{2}gd	2½	▲122	2^h	1^h	3^2	$4^{6\frac12}$	BrynMW^{10}	2500 61	BigBdGrgry116	SouthnGuest	10
23 Aug76	^{7}RD	1$\frac{1}{16}$:48^{4}1:13 1:46 ft	13	114	$6^{4\frac14}$	4^4	$4^{5\frac12}$	4^{12}	BryanMW^5	3250 67	SecondFrost116	TiffanyFair	8
26 Jly 76	^{2}RD	1$\frac{1}{16}$:48 1:13^{2}1:48 ft	2¾	▲122	1^3	$1^{1\frac12}$	1^h	$3^{1\frac12}$	MelndzJH^7	2500 67	Busy King 116	Perry's Boy	10
18 Jly 76	^{10}RD	Ⓣ1 1:39^{3}fm	22	112	$4^{3\frac12}$	4^6	5^{10}	8^{12}	CostaAJ^6	4500 71	Akaroa 116	I'm Baffled	10
4 Jly 76	^{10}RD	1^{70} :47^{4}1:12^{4}1:44^{3}ft	31	114	1^2	1^2	$1^{2\frac12}$	$3^{1\frac34}$	CostaAJ^{10}	3250 75	Regal Fox 122	Fleet Court	10
18 Jun76	^{2}RD	1$\frac{1}{16}$:48^{3}1:13^{2}1:47^{3}ft	6¾	116	1^h	1^2	$3^{1\frac34}$	$3^{6\frac12}$	SolomonG^4	2500 64	Lancer'sImge122	Paddy'sKn	7
11 Jun76	^{9}RD	1^{70} :48^{1}1:13^{4}1:45^{3}ft	7½	117	1^2	1^2	2^1	$4^{8\frac12}$	WelchH^4	2500 63	Mr. Cad 122	Lancer's Image	7
7 Jun76	^{1}RD	6 f :22^1 :45^{4}1:12^{3}ft	4¾	119	$8^{5\frac34}$	$7^{7\frac34}$	8^{12}	8^8	SolmonG^{11}	2500 72	TexasToy111	ShamrockTim	12
22 May76	^{3}RD	6 f :22^1 :46^{2}1:12^{3}ft	8	116	5^4	$3^{1\frac12}$	6^4	$7^{1\frac14}$	ClinchW^{12}	2500 79	Liberal Man 116	Hesourpet	12
15 May76	^{3}RD	6 f :22^2 :46^{1}1:12^{2}ft	15	116	$3^{2\frac12}$	$2^{2\frac12}$	$2^{2\frac12}$	$2^{6\frac12}$	ClinchW^4	2500 74	PennantRaiser122	KindTom	8

Aug 17 RD 5f ft 1:04b

Kirby Lane **115** Gr. c (1973), by Native Charger—Dancing Puppet, by Northern Dancer.
Breeder, Albert & Stantely (Fla.). 1976 3 2 0 1 $14,520
Owner, Gedney Farm. Trainer, L. S. Barrera. 1975 . . 5 1 2 0 $10,420

21 May76	^{5}Bel	6 f :22 :44^{4}1:08^{4}ft	3¾	113	$3^{3\frac12}$	3^2	1^h	1^2	CordroAJr^2	Alw 98	Kirby Lane 113	Sunny Clime	7
12 May76	^{6}Bel	6 f :23^3 :46^{3}1:10^{3}ft	9-5e	113	5^3	$6^{2\frac34}$	$5^{1\frac34}$	$3^{1\frac14}$	VasquezJ^6	Alw 88	PrlessMcGth106	DeltaLegcy	7
1 Jan76	^{9}SA	1$\frac{1}{16}$:46^{3}1:11^{2}1:44 ft	6-5	▲120	6^6	$3^{\frac12}$	$1^{1\frac12}$	$1^{3\frac12}$	PincyLJr^{10}	Alw 82	Kirby Lane 120	Tregillick	11
24 Nov75	^{4}Aqu	1 :48 1:13 1:37^{4}ft	8-5	▲122	1^2	$1^{\frac12}$	$1^{2\frac12}$	$1^{3\frac14}$	BaezaB^8	Mdn 77	KirbyLane122	FingerPaints	14
13 Nov75	^{5}Aqu	1 :47^{4}1:13^{4}1:38^{2}sy	3	122	$5^{2\frac34}$	$5^{2\frac14}$	3^1	$2^{\frac34}$	BaezaB^3	Mdn 73	L'Heureux 122	Kirby Lane	9
5 Nov75	^{4}Bel	1 :47^{3}1:12^{2}1:37^{3}ft	5¼	122	$1^{\frac12}$	1^h	1^h	$2^{1\frac14}$	BaezaB^2	Mdn 79	Play the Red 122	Kirby Lane	8
25 Oct75	^{1}Bel	6 f :22^3 :46 1:11^{3}sy	10	122	8^7	$8^{7\frac12}$	7^7	$7^{5\frac34}$	VelasqzJ^3	Mdn 78	Just a Dandy 122	QuickCard	9
18 Oct75	^{3}Bel	6 f :23^1 :46^{2}1:11^{2}sy	15	122	7^{11}	8^{12}	7^{11}	$4^{7\frac12}$	BaezaB^4	Mdn 78	PrivateThghts122	LrdHnrbee	8

June 3 Bel trt 3f ft :35⅖h **May 26 Bel trt 1m ft 1:40⅕h** **May 19 Bel trt 4f sy :49b**

Charleston **114** Ch. c (1973), by Graustark—Jitterbug, by Northern Dancer.
Breeder, Greentree Stud, Inc. (Ky.). 1976 . . 10 2 3 0 $20,050
Owner, Greentree Stable. Trainer, John M. Gaver. 1975 . . 1 M 0 0 $540

2 Aug76	^{6}Sar	7 f	:22^4 :45^{3}1:23^{4}ft	5¼	114	1½	4¾	2½	2½	GustinesH^1	Alw 85	Rich asCroesus114	Charlestn	6
26 Jly 76	^{6}Aqu	6 f	:22^2 :45^{2}1:09^{4}ft	12	113	5^{9}	5^{10}	5^{12}	5^{13}	VelezRI^4	Alw 81	SoyNumeroUno113	WatrFwr	5
26 May76	^{6}Bel	1⅛	:46 1:10^{3}1:49^{1}ft	1-3e	▲107^5	1^{4}	$1^{1\frac{1}{2}}$	2^{h}	2^{nk}	VelezRI^3	Alw 81	QuietLittleTable112	Chrlstn	5
29 Apr76	^{7}Aqu	1	:46^{4}1:11^{1}1:36 ft	2½	112	1^{2}	1½	2^{h}	$4^{2\frac{1}{4}}$	GustinesH^5	Alw 84	House of Lords 120	Malign	6
21 Apr76	^{6}Aqu	7 f	:22^4 :45^{4}1:22 ft	7½e	111	$4^{5\frac{1}{2}}$	$3^{5\frac{1}{2}}$	$5^{8\frac{1}{2}}$	$5^{6\frac{3}{4}}$	GustinesH^3	Alw 84	DanceSpll 110	GabeBnzur	7
10 Mar76	^{9}GP	7 f	:22 :44^1 1:21 ft	9	114	$6^{8\frac{1}{2}}$	$5^{6\frac{1}{4}}$	7^{8}	6^{10}	GustinsH^2	AlwS 89	Sonkisser116	GayJitterbug	7
26 Feb76	^{8}Hia	1⅛	:46^{4}1:12^{1}1:49^{3}sy	3-2	▲115	1^{h}	1^{h}	1½	1^{4}	GustinesH^6	Alw 84	Charleston115	ChateauRyale	8
20 Feb76	^{7}Hia	7 f	:22^4 :46^{1}1:24 ft	2¼	▲122	$9^{8\frac{3}{4}}$	$8^{7\frac{1}{2}}$	5^{6}	$5^{6\frac{1}{2}}$	GustinesH^2	Alw 79	Sonkisser 122	Legendaire	11
4 Feb76	^{5}Hia	7 f	:23^1 :46^{1}1:23^{4}ft	2-3	▲115	$5^{4\frac{1}{4}}$	3^{3}	2^{h}	1½	GustinesH^8	Alw 86	Charleston 115	GaitorRatten	9
23 Jan76	^{8}Hia	6 f	:22^2 :45^{2}1:10 ft	2½	115	$5^{4\frac{1}{2}}$	3^{4}	$3^{2\frac{1}{2}}$	2^{2}	GustinesH^2	Alw 91	LoadedOrBsted 122	Charlstn	11
20 Sep75	^{4}Bel	6½ f	:22^4 :45^{3}1:17^{2}sy	6-5e	▲120	$5^{2\frac{1}{2}}$	4^{11}	4^{9}	4^{10}	GustinesH^4	Mdn 79	Meritable 120	Azirae	9

July 25 Bel 3f ft :34⅗h July 21 Bel 6 ft 1:11⅘h July 17 Bel 5f ft 1:03⅖b

Sensitize **119** B. h (1971), by Sensitivo—Ye-Cats, by Mr. Busher.
Breeder, W. J. Fowler & 1976 . . 16 2 2 4 $7,377
Mr. & Mrs. A. N. Winick (Fla.). 1975 . . 7 0 1 1 $1,693
Owner, J. Chaffee. Trainer, Roy Houghton. $2,500

2 Sep76	^{1}Det	6 f	:22^4 :46^{4}1:13^{3}ft	10	119	$3^{1\frac{1}{2}}$	$1^{1\frac{1}{2}}$	1^{1}	2½	MapleS^4	2500 71	Rod N Reel 119	Sensitize	11
26 Aug76	^{1}Det	6 f	:22^2 :45^{4}1:11^{4}ft	5¾	119	3^{4}	3^{4}	5^{6}	6^{12}	JonesK^3	2500 69	Anaconda122	TheCommissar	10
19 Aug76	^{4}Det	1	:48^{1}1:13^{4}1:40^{1}ft	3¾	119	1^{3}	3^{nk}	$3^{5\frac{1}{2}}$	7^{16}	JonesK^3	2500 62	LarbHills119	RomanTudor	9
4 Aug76	^{9}Aks	1$\frac{1}{16}$	:47^{2}1:13^{2}1:46^{4}ft	6¼	122	1^{8}	1^{5}	1^{h}	2^{6}	JonesK^{11}	2500 68	Quatre Blanc 122	Sensitize	12
29 Jly 76	^{1}Aks	6 f	:21^4 :46 1:12^{1}ft	3½	122	$4^{1\frac{1}{2}}$	1^{1}	1^{4}	1^{4}	JonesK^1	2500 76	Sensitize 122	Lori's Jet	12
23 Jly 76	^{1}Aks	6 f	:23^1 :47 1:13^{3}ft	2¾	▲122	$7^{6\frac{1}{4}}$	6^{5}	4^{5}	$7^{7\frac{3}{4}}$	JonesK^7	2500 61	ThunderMug117	Mac'sPrize	11
15 Jly 76	^{1}Aks	6 f	:22^3 :46 1:12^{2}ft	3½	119	$6^{5\frac{1}{2}}$	$5^{6\frac{1}{2}}$	$5^{5\frac{1}{2}}$	3^{2}	JonesK^4	2500 73	Hasty'sPlsre116	Mac'sPrize	12
2 Jly 76	^{2}Aks	6 f	:22^4 :46^{2}1:12^{2}ft	3¾	120	6^{7}	$5^{3\frac{3}{4}}$	$4^{3\frac{1}{2}}$	3^{4}	JonesK^7	2500 71	Hooki Lau 116	C. B's Beau	11
23 Jun76	^{2}Aks	6 f	:22^3 :45^{3}1:12^{3}ft	4½	120	$4^{5\frac{1}{2}}$	$3^{4\frac{1}{2}}$	2^{3}	3^{2}	JonesK^{12}	2500 72	CharmingK. 113	JamSession	12
9 Jun76	^{1}Aks	1$\frac{1}{16}$	:47^{2}1:13^{1}1:48^{4}ft	11	117	2^{1}	2^{1}	4^{6}	11^{17}	JonesK^6	2500 45	Dandy Tiz 115	Sab's History	12

BREEDING

I am not what you might call a student of breeding. Over the years I have found that it makes better sense to study the horse's racing record and pay attention to the trainer's techniques. Nevertheless, I learned rather early in my handicapping adventures to pay more than a little attention to the bloodlines of horses in certain clear-cut situations. So I forced myself and learned to recognize the top two-year-old sires, the top mud sires, and of course the top turf sires. I did that because it was impossible to handicap certain races without knowing which newcomer to the turf or which first-time starter would be more likely to cope with a five-furlong race in April, a muddy track, or a grass race. I now find that there are fewer and fewer cases where breeding knowledge is the significant factor. Consider turf racing.

For the first sixty years of this century turf racing was

not very popular in the United States. Few racetracks had turf courses and those that did scheduled perhaps one grass race every two or three days. Those were the good old days for a student of turf breeding, days when a few European-born sires produced virtually every turf race winner this side of the Atlantic.

During the 1960s American racetrack owners built dozens of turf courses. Belmont Park has two turf courses, as do Arlington Park and a few other tracks. Indeed three out of every five racetracks now card an average of six turf races a week, weather permitting. That's change number one. Change number two is the influence of breeding itself. Fifteen years ago there were only a handful of established turf sires; at present the number is well past 200 and counting.

As more and more horses are imported from Europe and as more and more horses are trained over turf courses, the signal importance of breeding will continue to be diluted and diminished. In the meantime, I have lifted forty of the world's most potent turf course sires. Secretariat is included in anticipation of what I think he will sire; he was the greatest turf racer I ever saw. Asterisks denote extraordinary turf potency. Get them while they last. (*See page 143*)

Mud

Although previous form in the mud (including strong workouts) is the best indication of ability to handle an off-track, a few sires and sire families tend to transmit the trait to nearly all their offspring. The most prominent of these are Bagdad, Better Bee, and the entire Bold Ruler line (especially What a Pleasure and the Bold Commander–Dust Commander wing of that line).

Cinteelo, a son of Jacinto, who in turn was a son of

THE NEARCO FAMILY
*Amerigo
Bold Bidder
Hail to Reason
Indian Hemp
Nasrullah
Neartic
Northern Dancer
Royal Charger
Secretariat
Sir Gaylord
*Sir Ivor
Turn To
T.V. Lark
What a Pleasure

OTHER DOMINANT
TURF SIRES FROM
ASSORTED FAMILIES
Bagdad
Bolero
Dr. Fager
Gallant Man
Herbeger
Intentionally
Mongo
Sea Bird
The Axe II

THE RIBOT FAMILY
Arts and Letters
Graustark
Ribocco
Sir Ribot
*Tom Rolfe

THE HYPERION FAMILY
Alibhai
Assagai
Khaled
Swaps
Vaguely Noble

THE PRINCEQUILLO FAMILY
*Advocator
*Jean Pierre
*Prince John
*Round Table
*Speak John
*Stagedoor Johnny
*Tambourine

NOTE: *The very best turf sire in the country is Stagedoor Johnny. That's particularly interesting because Stagedoor Johnny never raced on a grass course in his life.*

Bold Ruler, is a case in point. In 1976 he was the number-one mud runner in America.

Cinteelo **119** B. c (1973), by Jacinto—Teela, by Cockrullah.
Breeder, J. M. Schiff (Ky.).
Owner, J. M. Schiff. Trainer, T. J. Kelly.

1976	6	2	0	2	$24,600
1975	7	2	0	1	$13,260

19 May76	^{8}Bel	1$\frac{1}{16}$	:46^2	1:11^3	1:43^1	sy	2-3	▲106^5	1^2	1$^{1\frac{1}{2}}$	1^5	1$^{7\frac{1}{2}}$	VelezRI^3	Alw	86	Cinteelo106	BabyFaceBeau	8
1 May76	^{6}Aqu	1	:45	1:09	1:34^3	sy	6-5e	▲104^5	2^h	1^1	1^5	1$^{8\frac{1}{2}}$	VelezRI^4	Alw	93	Cinteelo 104	El Portugues	7
17 Apr76	^{6}Aqu	1	:45^2	1:09^4	1:35^1	ft	2	▲104^5	2^h	2^h	1$\frac{1}{2}$	3$^{2\frac{3}{4}}$	VelezRI^1	Alw	87	RoughPunch112	BrownCat	7
27 Mar76	^{6}Aqu	1	:46	1:09^4	1:35^2	ft	14	112^5	1^h	1^h	2^h	3^4	VelezRI^4	Alw	85	MountSterlng119	NwCollctn	9
3 Mar76	^{6}Aqu	7 f	:23^1	:46^3	1:23^4	ft	3	115	3$^{2\frac{1}{2}}$	3^3	7^{11}	8^{14}	VelasquzJ^5	Alw	68	GabeBenzur117	PlayTheRed	8
24 Jan76	^{5}Hia	Ⓣ 1$\frac{1}{16}$			1:43^2	fm	4$\frac{1}{2}$	119	4^2	3^4	3$^{5\frac{1}{2}}$	5$^{7\frac{1}{4}}$	CruguetJ^1	Alw	74	ControllerIke122	GrstarkLad	8
21 Nov75	^{7}Aqu	1	:44^4	1:08^4	1:34^4	sy	1$\frac{1}{2}$	117	1^3	1^5	1^4	1^6	CruguetJ^4	Alw	92	Cinteelo 117	Play the Red	9
15 Nov75	^{5}Aqu	7 f	:23	:46	1:23^2	ft	37	115	4$^{1\frac{1}{2}}$	5$^{1\frac{1}{4}}$	3^{nk}	4$^{2\frac{3}{4}}$	CruguetJ^2	Alw	81	JumpOvr theMn122	Wn'tYld	8
28 Aug75	^{4}Bel	7 f	:23^1	:47	1:25^1	ft	3-2	▲120	5$^{3\frac{1}{4}}$	2$\frac{1}{2}$	1$^{1\frac{1}{2}}$	1^1	CrugtJ^6	M35000	76	Cinteelo 120	Ahoy John	9

June 3 Bel 3f ft :35b May 30 Bel trt 5f ft 1:01$\frac{3}{5}$h May 26 Bel trt 4f ft :52b

Speed Sires

In early season two-year-old races at three, four, and five furlongs the emphasis is on speed and precocious physical development. If the get of Loom, Mito, Mr. Washington, and other one-dimensional sprint specialists are going to win any top-grade races, they will usually do so in these abbreviated dashes. Many win at first asking. Few hold their form beyond six furlongs.

Stamina Sires

Generally speaking, the staying power of a horse is linked more to its training regimen than to its breeding, but there are a few sires and a few female families that tend to produce long-distance runners. The get of many European sires—Sea Bird, Ribot, and Nijinsky II among others—and the male and female descendents of Princequillo are rarely interested in racing until the distances stretch out to a mile and beyond. However, most top-class American-bred sires, particularly the many sons and grandsons of Bold Ruler, are capable of getting fast, precocious horses that carry their speed as far as their trainers let them. If breeding is your bag, consult the Appendix for a recommended reading list.

OPTIONAL EQUIPMENT

BLINKERS: There is nothing like a pair of blinkers (eye cups) to help keep a horse's mind on its business, particularly a young horse that has had a difficult time running a straight course. Blinkers also tend to improve a horse's gate-breaking ability or early speed; and as a tool of last resort blinkers sometimes help the quitter type—the kind that stops in its tracks the moment another horse challenges it for the lead. If the quitter can't see the competition, it just might hold on long enough to get a piece of the purse.

Although more than half of the 70,000 horses racing in America go to the post with blinkers, "blinkers on" for the first time is generally a very positive sign of trainer intention. "Blinkers off" is not so easy to interpret.

In the case of a speedball, or perhaps a quitter type, the removal of blinkers may help the horse relax a bit and conserve some of its energy for the stretch. A few horses also run better when they can see the competition. For obvious reasons, some trainers remove blinkers when they send a sprinter into a longer race or, conversely, put them on when a router is seriously meant in a sprint.

In the East the oversized edition of the *Daily Racing Form* carries blinker information in the past performance profile, but elsewhere players must rely on result charts to learn about this important piece of equipment.

MUD CAULKS: If the track is muddy, heavy, or slow or the turf course is anything but firm or hard, the addition of mud caulks is a sign of trainer intent; it is also often helpful to the horse itself.

Mud caulks are horseshoes with small prongs for better traction. On fast or hard racing surfaces these shoes can do damage to the horse's ankle or hoof, but on a soggy surface, especially a soggy turf course, mud caulks are a distinct advantage.

The trainer is a cheapskate or a fool if he consistently avoids spending the extra few dollars for mud-caulked horseshoes when conditions are bad enough to warrant them. And the player is taking a big risk if he pays no attention to this information when it is available.

STEEL SHOES AND BAR SHOES: The player takes a bigger risk investing money on horses equipped with steel shoes or bar shoes, unless the horse in question has won with that kind of equipment before. Both types are danger signals. The horse usually has foot problems, and the shoe is an attempt to give more secure footing at the cost of extra, unfamiliar weight.

I am sorry to report that at present there are a number of racetracks that do not care about the fan sufficiently to provide a working shoe board on the grounds. Please yell at the general manager of any such racetrack for me too.

BANDAGES: Many trainers apply bandages on the rear legs as a matter of course to keep a horse from hitting itself in close quarters. But the presence of front leg bandages may have distinctly negative implications: a minor injury or a weak ankle or a sore muscle. Front leg bandages are chiefly used for extra support, and unless the player knows that the horse has raced well with them before (Forego, for example) or is expert at evaluating the horse in motion during the post parade, it is wise to be suspicious.

On muddy racetracks I will not bet a horse with front leg bandages because of the extra weight that is bound to adhere to these wrappings. Try running 100 yards yourself with an ounce of bandages taped to each ankle if you doubt my point. This act of temperance has cost me only four otherwise qualified winners in seventeen years.

PHYSICAL APPEARANCE

It takes a trained eye and many years of experience to reach valid conclusions about physical fitness on sight. A few basics should help; but I caution you to pay close attention to the clues in the *Racing Form* until you have mastered the art.

NEGATIVE SIGNS: Excessive kidney sweat between the flanks. And on cool days, heavy sweating of any kind in the paddock or post parade. Fractious, uncontrollable behavior during the post parade and warm-up period. Unusual swelling at the knee joints. Stiff-leggedness. A gimpy stride, favoring one leg. Cantankerous or listless behavior. A dull coat.

POSITIVE SIGNS: Aggressive but controllable behavior in the post parade and warm-up. A fluid transition from a walking gait to the gallop to the run. Attentive, alert behavior nearing the gate (watch the ears and head). A well-groomed, shiny coat.

JOCKEYS

Most trainers have alliances with one or more jockeys. Some jockeys ride every race for the trainer; others ride only when the trainer is serious. The player should learn who the top jockeys are, who rides for what stable, and who can't ride worth a damn.

Some trainers like to use apprentice jockeys because of the three, five, seven, or ten pounds of weight concession permitted during their apprenticeship.

My standards for jockeys may not meet your standards, but I will play a well-qualified contender ridden by a hot three- or five-pound apprentice, by an established veteran or star, by a rider who has won with the horse before, or by a stable favorite. But under no circumstances will I play a horse ridden by a ten-pound apprentice or a proven incompetent. I do not discriminate against women jockeys, but there are few I am presently impressed with. And there is one more point to be made about jockeys. At one time or another, all of them hit slumps. Terrible slumps. Like zero for thirty-five or two for sixty. Not only should the player avoid these jockeys when they are losing, but he should expect improvement from the horses they rode when a switch is made.

A few years ago Johnny Rotz, a solid twenty-year veteran, was riding so atrociously that the "Rotz off" angle produced six longshot winners in two weeks and a dozen more during the next two months. Mr. Rotz apparently got the message and retired the following winter.

14.
The Drug Factor

SEVENTH RACE
CD 34634
May 4. 1968

1 1-4 MILES. (Northern Dancer, May 2, 1964, 2:00, 3, 126.)
Ninety-fourth running KENTUCKY DERBY. Scale weights. $125,000 added. 3-year-olds. By subscription of $100 each in cash which covers nomination for both the Kentucky Derby and Derby Trial. All nomination fees to Derby winner, $500 to pass the entry box, $1,000 additional to start, $125,000 added, of which $25,000 to second, $12,500 to third, $5,000 to fourth. $100,000 guaranteed to winner (to be divided equally in event of a dead heat). Weight, 126 lbs. The owner of the winner to receive a gold trophy. A nomination may be withdrawn before time of closing nominations. Closed Thursday, Feb. 15, 1968, with 191 nominations.
Value of race $165,100. Value to winner $122,600; second, $25,000; third, $12,500; fourth, $5,000.
Mutuel Pool, $2,350,470.

Index	Horses	Eq't	A	Wt	PP	1/4	1/2	3/4	1	Str	Fin	Jockeys	Owners	Odds to $1
34451Aqu[1]	Dancer's Image		3	126	12	14	14	10$\frac{1}{2}$	8h	1^1	11$\frac{1}{2}$	R Ussery	Peter Fuller	3.60
34402Kee[1]	Forward Pass	b	3	126	13	3^2	4^4	3^4	2^2	2$\frac{1}{2}$	2nk	I Valenz'ela	Calumet Farm	2.20
34402Kee[3]	Francie's Hat		3	126	10	113^{1}12	7^2	7^2	4^2	32$\frac{1}{2}$	E Fires	Saddle Rock Farm	23.50
34402Kee[2]	T. V. C'mercial	b	3	126	2	9$\frac{1}{2}$	8^1	9^1	6$\frac{1}{2}$	5h	4^1	H Grant	Bwamazon Farm	24.00
34307CD[4]	Kentucky Sherry		3	126	4	1$\frac{1}{2}$	1^2	1^2	1h	3^2	5^1	J Combest	Mrs Joe W Brown	f-14.70
34325CD[2]	Jig Time	b	3	126	3	7^{1}16$\frac{1}{2}$	6$\frac{1}{2}$	4h	6h	6$\frac{1}{2}$	R Brouss'rd	Cragwood Stable	36.30
34425GG[2]	Don B.		3	126	7	5^2	5^2	5^1	51$\frac{1}{2}$	74	75	D Pierce	D B Wood	35.50
34307CD[2]	Trouble Brewing		3	126	5	12$\frac{1}{2}$	9^1	11^2	134^1	124	8nk	B Thornb'rg	Coventry Rock Farm	f-14.70
34325CD[1]	Proper Proof		3	126	11	13^{3}121	12^2	112	81$\frac{1}{2}$	94	J Sellers	Mrs Montgomery Fisher	9.90
34325CD[4]	Te Vega	b	3	126	6	8h13h	131	12^2	9^2	10$\frac{3}{4}$	M Mang'llo	F C Sullivan	f-14.70
34307CD[1]	Captain's Gig		3	126	9	2h	2h	.21	3^2	10^2	111$\frac{1}{2}$	M Ycaza	Cain Hoy Stable	6.10
34451Aqu[2]	Iron Ruler		3	126	1	10$\frac{1}{2}$	7$\frac{1}{2}$	8$\frac{1}{2}$	9h	11^1	12^3	B Baeza	October House Farm	5.70
34325CD[3]	Verbatim	b	3	126	8	6h10h	14	14	14	13no	A Cord'o Jr	Elmendorf	37.40
34402Kee[5]	Gl'ming Sword	b	3	126	14	4$\frac{1}{2}$	3$\frac{1}{2}$	4h	10^2	13^1	14	E Belmonte	C V Whitney	31.20

f-Mutuel field.

Time, :22$\frac{1}{5}$, :45$\frac{4}{5}$, 1:09$\frac{4}{5}$, 1:36$\frac{1}{5}$, 2:02$\frac{1}{5}$. Track fast.

$2 Mutuel Prices:

9-DANCER'S IMAGE	9.20	4.40	4.00
10-FORWARD PASS		4.20	3.20
7-FRANCIE'S HAT			6.40

Gr. c, by Native Dancer—Noors Image, by Noor. Trainer, L. C. Cavalaris, Jr. Bred by P. Fuller (Md.).

IN GATE—4:40. OFF AT 4:40$\frac{1}{2}$ EASTERN DAYLIGHT TIME. Start good. Won driving.

DANCER'S IMAGE, void of speed through the early stages after being bumped at the start, commenced a rally after three-quarters to advance between horses on the second turn, cut back to the inside when clear entering the stretch at which point his rider dropped his whip. Responding to a vigorous hand ride the colt continued to save ground to take command nearing the furlong marker and was hard pressed to edge FORWARD PASS. The latter broke alertly only to be bumped and knocked into the winner, continued gamely while maintaining a forward position along the outside, moved boldly to take command between calls in the upper stretch and held on stubbornly in a prolonged drive. FRANCIE'S HAT, allowed to settle in stride, commenced a rally after three-quarters and finished full of run. T. V. COMMERCIAL closed some ground in his late rally but could not seriously menace. KENTUCKY SHERRY broke in stride to make the pace under good rating, saved ground to the stretch where he drifted out while tiring. JIG TIME faltered after making a menacing bid on the second turn. PROPER PROOF was always outrun. CAPTAIN'S GIG tired badly after prompting the issue for three-quarters. IRON RULER failed to enter contention. GLEAMING SWORD broke alertly but sharply to the inside to bump with FORWARD PASS, continued in a forward position for five furlongs and commenced dropping back steadily.

NOTE: DANCER'S IMAGE DISQUALIFIED FROM PURSE MONEY BY ORDER OF CHURCHILL DOWNS STEWARDS, MAY 15, 1968 AND RULING SUSTAINED BY THE KENTUCKY STATE RACING COMMISSION

On the first Sunday in May 1968 the ninety-fourth running of the Kentucky Derby was decided in the laboratory of the state chemist. A small trace of the prohibited painkilling drug phenylbutazone was found in the urine sample of Dancer's Image, the winner of the world's most famous horserace. Thoroughbred racing in America hasn't been the same since.

Today phenylbutazone ("Bute") and the contoversial diuretic furosemide (Lasix) are legal in a dozen racing states (including Kentucky) and are used promiscuously nearly everywhere else. What this means to the future of racing I can only guess, but in the late 1970s there are serious questions about the sport's willingness to adopt an open, well-defined policy on this explosive issue.

Bute tends to reduce swelling in the joints and dulls the horse's sensory apparatus. Lasix, an effective treatment to curb bleeding in the nasal passages, flushes out watery substances with amazing efficiency. The sudden widespread use of these and other drugs, detectable and undetectable, is more than a little bit suspicious.

I have personally conducted studies on horse performance where drug information was made available to the player, and in 1974 and 1975 I published reports in *Turf and Sport Digest* and in *The New York Times*. A special research commission working at the request of the New York State Racing and Wagering Board agreed with my conclusions and offered a few of its own in a 1976 midsummer report. The key facts about drugs as they affect the horseplayer are as follows.

1. Because drugs interfere with the horse's warning system (pain), more horses are breaking down with drugs than without them.

2. Administering Lasix for the first time can and often does create a wake-up effect.

3. Although the regular use of Bute is widespread, it is impossible to measure its value as a handicapping factor.

4. In some cases either or both drugs can act as a screen to the detection of other drugs.

5. The public disclosure of drug information is inadequate in most states and nonexistent in some others. It is

hard to believe, but Kentucky, the blue-blooded breeding state, the home of the Kentucky Derby, is one of the many states that refuse to provide the racegoing public with race-day drug information. I think that is scandalous.

6. The testing procedures used to protect against drug abuse are not sufficient to cope with the variety of sophisticated drugs currently on the market. A multimillion dollar, nationwide, industry-run testing laboratory is the only realistic answer to this problem, but there is presently little interest in that proposal.

7. It is not possible to tell whether trainers who persistently put over dramatic form reversals are in fact training their horses from the bottle. But the player should keep a record of all such horsemen for future reference.

8. If the player is suspicious of the drug factor to the extent that he begins to blame defeats on it, he is probably overstating the case. Nevertheless, he owes it to the sport to take the time to save the past performance profiles of all such defeats. Draft a resume of the circumstances and forward this information to the stewards or the racing commission. Contrary to typical racetrack cynicism, most racing officials are becoming more sensitive to the drug problem. A little fan pressure is the best way to keep these folks on the ball. If all else fails, write to me care of the publisher. I'm no crusader, but this is one issue that's worth fighting about.

15.
To Bet or Not To Bet, and How Much?

When a gambler goes to Las Vegas for a weekend of rou-lette, craps, or blackjack, he should know in advance that the percentages constantly favor the house. Before the payoff odds are calculated, approximately 3 to 6 cents is raked off the top of every dollar wagered and the payoff odds are always lower than the actual mathematical odds.

This of course is the house take, and except for the one-in-a-million blackjack memory expert, no amount of skill will change the odds to the player's favor. I'm sorry folks, but the only way to beat the house is through unabashed luck—the longer one plays craps or roulette, the greater the probability for a wipeout.

A good casino gambler, then, is simply one who knows to quit if he's lucky enough to be ahead.

In betting on pro football and other team sports, the point spread theoretically balances out the action between supporters of two competing teams, and the player usually pays a 10 percent charge, or "vigorish," for the privilege of betting with a bookie. I won't go into the theories of proper football betting strategy in this book other than to say that racetrack bettors should only have it so easy. Consider the following:

By flipping a coin to determine which team should be played, anyone can expect approximately 50 percent win-ners. With any degree of skill at all 60 to 70 percent of spot-play winners is not only possible, but anyone calling himself a professional should be ashamed if he can't do that well. (Are you there Jimmy the Greek?)

At the racetrack the average field has nine horses, most of which have never faced each other before and never will again. The best horse in the race may get into trouble, step on a pebble, lose its jockey, jump a puddle, or decide to go for a swim in the infield lake. The jockey may have a tooth-ache or commit a terrible mistake, or the stewards may have or do the same.

Meanwhile, for all his trouble in researching the complexities of racing, the horseplayer is told that the state and the track will take away some 20 cents per dollar on straight win bets and that much and more on most combination bets like the exacta or big triple. That's a tough nut to overcome. Good handicapping and thorough research help, but sound money management is just as important.

Whether you are a four-time-a-year novice or a once-a-week regular, the way you play your money at the track will determine whether you win or lose and how much you win or lose. Through skill, the odds can be turned to the player's favor, but it takes intelligent handling of betting capital to be in a position to take advantage. At 20 cents on the dollar, you can get wiped out pretty fast if you do not have a healthy respect for your money.

If you know something about two-year-old sprint racing but lack an understanding of stakes, claimers, or routes, it would be smart to concentrate your strongest bets on your specialty. If you use speed figures and know how to recognize a speed-figure standout, it would be foolish to bet the same amounts on races when you have no reason to be so confident. And if you do not know *what* you know, you should spend some time finding out.

Keep a record of your bets. Be honest with yourself.

Do you know how to spot a track bias when you see one? Do you have a feel for turf racing or stakes? Are claiming-class sprints easier than allowance-class routes? Do you have special insights about the winning and losing tendencies of the top trainers in your area? Perhaps you find it easy to narrow the field to live contenders but very difficult to separate the winner from the second- or third-best horse. Can you pass up a race or an entire card, or must you have a bet every half-hour?

Asking questions like those above will do wonders for your profit-and-loss statement. They will also bring to light the strengths and weaknesses in your game.

When I go unprepared to a strange racetrack, I do not

bring very much money. Without the necessary insights about the track, the trainers, and all the other fundamentals that influence results, I am no more likely to win than thousands of other players in the crowd. I have my winning days at such racetracks—I do pay attention—but I have to be lucky and extremely cautious with my money.

When I do prepare for a serious assault on a track, I do the research necessary to uncover any prevailing track bias and learn as much as I can about the trainers, jockeys, and horses I will be asked to compare. At most racetracks that kind of preparation takes about thirty to fifty hours of advance work, requires two hours of daily follow-up, and yields approximately one to three good bets a day; but that is not enough action for me and I know it.

Most racing fans, myself included, like something to root for in almost every race. It's tough to sit through a whole card waiting around for the ninth-race goodie. So most of the time I don't.

Instead, and as a concession to my personality, I separate my money into serious *prime* bets and *action* bets. Nothing would upset my concentration more than a $40 winner that I liked well enough to think about but didn't bet a dime on. Perhaps you feel the same way.

I have two very stiff requirements for a serious prime bet. Bitter experience has taught me that holding to these requirements is the safest way to guard my capital and maximize my skill.

When I think the horse deserves a 50 percent or better chance to win the race, I expect to be right at least 50 percent of the time. That's my first requirement. The second is a payoff price of 8–5 ($1.60–$1.00) or higher.

Fifty percent may seem to be an outrageously high win percentage to achieve, but with the tools and insights I have been detailing in this book it really isn't all that difficult.

King Leatherbury dropdowns coming back after a

month's rest win 60 percent of the time. Front runners on the rail in $1\frac{1}{16}$-mile races at Pimlico win almost as often. Other high-percentage strategies and tools include Van Berg repeaters going up in class, fast Calder front runners shipping into Gulfstream, Tony Basile–trained first-time starters at Keeneland, fit Jerkens–trained horses right back or stretching out in distance, minor track classification codes, hidden class dropdowns in allowance races, speed horses ready to get the lead for the first time, post position studies, Key Races, trainer patterns, clocker's comments, result charts, class pars, speed figures, track bias, and so on. Anyone willing to put in the necessary research time can pick 50 percent spot-play winners with these tools and insights. And the prices will astound you.

I have personally taught much of this material to nine of my friends, including two absolute novices. Within one year all were able to approach or exceed 50 percent results. Nothing is stopping you from achieving as much. If, however, you find your winning average is lower—35 percent, for example—you must adjust your minimum-odds requirement to compensate.

Logically, 35 percent winners would require payoff odds of 5–2 or better, but frankly I am not at all sure it is possible to win at the races without being able to pick a higher percentage of winners. A lower win percentage is an invitation to long losing streaks. I further believe my criteria help create enough selectivity to provide safe but profitable betting opportunities. By these standards an odds-on favorite can never be a prime bet, unless I am playing it to place and getting a bargain minimum of 80 cents on the dollar.

An exacta or daily double can never be a prime bet unless the total investment needed to cover the selected combinations yields a 50 percent chance of cashing a winning ticket at an expected 8–5 or better. To fulfill the two requirements in the case of a key horse wheel, it is sometimes necessary to buy extra combinations on the lowest anticipated payoffs. And in those cases where I am confident to play one horse as a key with two, three, or four others, I reduce my total investment in the exotic bet and place at least some money in the win pool to protect myself. I may also be inclined to use my key horse underneath the three contenders for additional protection. For solid crisscross plays using three or four live contenders, I will rarely invest more than half of my typical prime betting unit. Exactas often present inflated payoff possibilities, but the risk is usually increased as well.

I repeat, a prime bet is an estimated 50 percent chance to cash a winning ticket at 8–5 or better. All other bets are action bets and I separate the two categories in the following manner:

PRIME BETS: A maximum of 5 to 8 percent of total betting capital for the meet per play; 8 percent reserved for superconfident plays. Maximum of three prime bets allowed in one day, unless first two out of three win.

ACTION BETS: A maximum of 2 to 3 percent of total betting capital for the meet per day. On a day with three prime bets, no action bets are permitted beyond a token $2 to $5 per race.

EXPENSES: Deduct 1 percent per day.

For example, if my total available betting capital for the meet is $2,000, a prime bet would be $100 to $160, depending on how well I have been doing at the meet and how much more than a 50 percent edge the horse really has. On that scale I would feel free to play the rest of the card with $40 to $60 on contenders lacking prime betting qualifications, on wild stabs, daily doubles, or exactas.

As capital increases (or decreases) the amount of the bet changes, but not the percentages.

I expect to lose money with my action bets and I do. But I have a lot of fun with them; I watch races more carefully because of them, and they help keep my equilibrium. A small price to pay for peace of mind.

I realize of course that not many racing fans can afford to put aside $2,000 to bet on horseraces. Not many should either. But the truth is many horseplayers lose that much and more in a season, and if you go to the racetrack regularly and want to improve your chances of success, you must take care to plan your betting activity along similar guidelines.

Whether your typical daily capital is $100 or you bring considerably more to the track, the point is to consolidate the power of your money on the races in which you have some insight.

Betting odds-on favorites is taking the worst of it. Betting a large percentage of your capital in the daily double or big triple is a sure-fire way to put yourself in the hole to stay. Betting a disproportionate amount of your money on any one race places too much emphasis on the luck factor. Doubling up your bet to "get even" on the last race is a way to triple your losses in track record time.

Every horseplayer has losing streaks. But there is no reason why a player should lose serious money during such streaks.

Losing three or four prime bets in a row is a warning sign, a sign to cut down all serious play until the problem is solved. Maybe you have lost touch with the track or have failed to note the presence of a hot trainer. Maybe you are bothered by personal problems, or a tough defeat has upset you more than you thought.

Take a day or two off. Go to a ballgame. Rediscover your family and friends. Watch TV, and if that doesn't work, try a few exercises in fundamentals.

Rather than trying to pick the race winner, try instead

to pick the worst horse in the race or the horse most likely to be in front ten strides out of the gate. Check the past three days of racing. Has there been a subtle change in the bias? Has the bias disappeared? It happens.

These exercises can be fun, and like a baseball player who needs to take extra batting practice, you will find they help straighten out many a weakness. Try some of them, or invent others to suit your fancy. Lighten up. It's only a game.

16.
La Prevoyante to Win, My Wife to Place

With the advent of the big triple and other popular, exotic forms of wagering, very few racing fans have been schooled in the finer points of place and show betting. While no argument will be presented here to suggest an emphasis on the minor payoff spots, there are times at the track when it pays handsomely to think second best.

In the early 1960s I remember being at a New York racetrack when so much money was bet on the mighty Kelso to win and so little was bet on him to place that he paid $2.40–$3.60–$2.40 across the board. By thinking win, and win only, the crowd in attendance that day offered one of the safest bets of modern times, an overlay of gigantic proportions. If Kelso was worth 20 cents on the dollar to win the race, which I will not debate, he was surely worth 80 cents on the dollar to finish second or better. It's doubtful Lloyds of London could have offered a better deal.

Of course, most racetrack crowds do not let such absurd situations occur every day, but I've seen enough $3.60 win, $4.00 place payoffs in my lifetime to give the tote board a close look before parting with my money. And if in truth I wasn't always careful to do that, my wife, Laurie, gave me ample cause to do so a few years ago.

At Saratoga during the 1972 racing season Laurie thought it would be a good idea if she came out to the track to see Robyn Smith, a pretty tough cookie and one of the best female jockeys in America. My friend Andy Beyer and I traded in our two reserved seats plus a dollar for three seats together. Andy and I were enjoying a spectacular meeting but didn't know we were about to miss out on the easiest bet of the year.

During the first six races on the card Robyn won one and lost one; so did Laurie. Andy and I had won the one Robyn and Laurie lost and had lost the one they both had won. Not that we were prejudiced against female jockeys or anything; we just figured one race *right* and one race *wrong*.

So the day went. Andy and I had shoved almost half a thousand through the windows to be plus $40 apiece. Laurie had bet maybe $8 and was ahead $50.

I wasn't depressed, far from it, but was glad to see her winning; maybe she would get hooked or something. After all, it would be nice to talk about horses with someone besides Andy. In any case, the point of this setting was the race on deck: the $50,000-added Spinaway Stakes.

La Prevoyante, undefeated and on her way to a two-year-old championship, was the odds-on favorite. Yet in spite of her unblemished record, neither of us thought she was very much horse. She had never run a truly fast race, and she had been beating up on the worst bunch of stakes-class juvenile fillies we had ever seen. She had beaten them pretty badly, though, and she figured to do so again; but there was a new challenger in the field—Princess Doubleday—a shipper from Chicago.

Although Princess Doubleday had finished last in her most recent race in the slop, she had raced strongly in Chicago throughout the summer, winning two races and finishing a close third in a stakes. After checking some out-of-town result charts to determine the quality of the Midwestern juvenile fillies and after one last review of the *Form*, Andy and I concluded independently that Princess Doubleday had a great chance to win the Spinaway at 40–1.

Now it isn't too often that a sound piece of handicapping turns up a 40–1 shot that should really be a solid second choice in the betting, and naturally we were excited. We didn't want to go overboard; we still knew that we had to beat an undefeated 1–5 shot. We each decided to make a maximum-limit action bet—$60—and with just five minutes to post Laurie returned from the saddling area to share in the good news. I was surprised by her response. "It all sounds great," she said, "but shouldn't you bet your money to place?" Almost instinctively my stomach grumbled its reply to this heresy. I agreed that it would certainly be safer to bet to place but patiently explained to her that since the money bet to place on a heavy favorite like La Prevoyante would be returned to her supporters in the place pool, she would deflate the place prices on every other horse in the race. I argued that the value of this longshot was only in the win pool.

"As it is," I said, "we have to beat a filly that has slaughtered her opposition half a dozen times just to win our bet. For us to get a big place price on Princess Doubleday, La Prevoyante would have to run third or worse. Besides," I added, "40–1 on this filly is a tremendous overlay." Convinced by my own logic, my stomach relaxed. Laurie said she understood my position but insisted we would be better off if we followed her advice.

By that time I began to feel that Laurie should have stayed out by the trees or gone to talk to Robyn. Shaking our heads in unison, Andy and I gave up on the talking and headed for the win windows. He went upstairs and I went downstairs.

At the windows, after I had traded serious money for pasteboard, a sudden impulse crossed my brain. I ran as fast as I could to the place line and just did get in a small bet before the bell rang. "And they're off," the PA system said. But I knew exactly what was going to happen.

La Prevoyante breezed to victory as Princess Doubleday rallied to get second money.

Back at the seats, we watched the prices go up on the board. La Prevoyante paid $2.80 to win, $3.00 to place, $2.60 to show. Princess Doubleday paid $15.20 in the middle—at least $6 more than an early reading of the tote board had indicated. Laurie didn't say a word, but just counted her money and smiled. Andy, I found out, had made the same play I had, and our impulsive saver wagers to place gave us each a slight profit on the race. But some fifteen minutes later, while scooping some of Saratoga's great homemade ice cream, I nearly choked on the reality of what had happened.

"We're both idiots," I screamed abruptly, causing Andy to spill his sundae on the floor. "Supposing we had been told La Prevoyante was a late scratch and wouldn't be in the Spinaway. What price would we then have made Princess Doubleday to beat the rest of that weak field? Even money? Seven to five? Well, by ignoring the place pool, by being so longshot conscious, we just passed up the sweetest 6–1 prime bet of the year." We could have made an action bet on her to win and quadrupled the place bet with absolute confidence.

Strangely, my stomach never bothers me anymore when I talk horses with Laurie, and ever since that eye-opening experience I have had no trouble remembering to check the place and show pools very carefully. You just never know when the track is going to give it away.

17.
More on Betting

There are many lessons to be learned about betting, many traps that await the reckless, overconfident player. What follows in this chapter are some additional facts of life that every handicapper should find profitable to recognize.

Above all other repetitious mistakes, the average racetrack crowd will seriously overbet the chances of horses whose records resemble the past performances below. I can't stress enough the folly of playing horses to win when everything in their records says they don't want to do that. Experienced horseplayers have a pet name for horses like these. They call them "sucker" horses. The term applies just as well to the players who bet on them.

Advising Jean * **116** Ch. f (1971), by Noble Jay—Fleet Rhymer, by Flaming Fleet.
Breeder, E. Mull (Md.). 1975 22 0 (12 2) $35,405
Owner, Mrs. W. A. Kelley. Trainer, W. A. Kelley. $12.500 1974 23 3 5 2 $30.531

25 Nov75	3Aqu	1⅛	:47 2 1:12 1:51 1 ft	3½	114	2 5	2 4	2 3	2¾	CruguetJ5	13000	78	ⒻCzarevna111	AdvisingJean	7
10 Nov75	7Key	7 f	:23 3 :45 1 1:24 3 sy	9-5	114	8 4	4 6½	2 5	2 4	LukasM4	13000	82	ⒻSlwBeat116	AdvisingJean	8
9 Oct75	2Bel	1 1/16	:48 1 1:12 4 1:46 ft	6-5	▲116	3 1½	2 1	1½	2¾	CruguetJ1	13000	71	ⒻWittyWays113	AdvisingJn	8
18 Sep75	5Bel	1⅛	:47 2 1:11 1 1:51 1 ft	2	116	2 2	2 3	2½	2 no	CruguetJ8	14000	71	ⒻMssTaub118	AdvisingJean	8
31 Aug75	9Bel	1 1/16	:46 3 1:11 1 1:45 2 ft	4	114	2 h	1 2	1 h	2 h	CruguetJ4	15000	75	ⒻLaVikina116	AdvisingJean	11
15 Aug75	6Sar	7 f	:22 3 :46 1:25 ft	3	116	3 7	3 5½	4 2¼	4 2¾	CruguetJ4	15000	77	ⒻAlla Va 116	La Vikina	8
8 Aug75	1Sar	6 f	:22 1 :46 2 1:12 4 sy	2¾	116	7 14	4 9½	3 6	2¾	CrugutJ1	15000	75	ⒻWiseHeart114	AdvisingJn	7
25 Jly 75	7Bel	6½ f	:22 3 :46 3 1:17 4 sy	17	116	2 4	6 4½	5 5½	4 6½	VenziaM6	22500	80	ⒻBrta'sDandy112	PrcsM.L.	9

Geoffery Vernon **113** Dk. b. or br. g (1973), by Gameus—Dusty Nancy, by Penaction.
Breeder, J. E. Harman (Fla.). 1976 17 1 (5 4) $8,833
Owner, Sharon Maker & B. Hessling. Trainer, George Maker. $6.250 1975 3 M 0 0 $170

15 Sep76	7Det	6 f	:22 2 :46 1 1:12 1 ft	10	118	4 5¼	4 7	4 5	4 4½	GabrielR10	6250	74	Bhagalphur113	SteamingHot	11
8 Sep76	5Det	6 f	:22 2 :46 1 1:12 2 ft	5½	118	5 5½	3 1	2 1	2 1½	MorgnMR2	6250	76	Mr.Brtolini116	GeoffryVrnn	9
2 Sep76	3Det	6 f	:22 4 :47 1 1:13 3 ft	4½	117	3 3	3 2	2 2	2½	GabrielR5	c5000	71	MyFthr'sPde115	GffryVrnon	9
26 Aug76	4Det	6 f	:22 4 :46 2 1:13 3 ft	3¾	117	2 1	1 2	1 3	3 3†	CamiloJF7	5000	69	Boogie Band 115	Son Jay	9
†Disqualified.															
16 Aug76	6Det	6 f	:22 4 :46 2 1:12 2 ft	4	117	2½	2 2	2 1½	3 2½	GabrielR8	6250	75	Chester V. 117	Right Audit	8
11 Aug76	7Det	6 f	:22 3 :46 1 1:12 4 ft	16	117	4 2½	4 2½	5 4¼	5 6¼	CamiloJF2	6500	70	Tin 120	Esha Brown	9
17 Jly 76	7HP	6 f	:23 1 :47 1 1:14 ft	12	114	5 7½	6 5½	7 7½	6 5¾	CamiloJF4	8000	76	SpeedyKlu121	RojaBandera	8
9 Jly 76	8HP	6½ f	:23 2 :47 2 1:20 ft	23	120	2 h	1 1	3 4	7 11	CamiloJF7	Alw	70	SpindleTop115	Baker'sSyrup	7
30 Jun76	5HP	6 f	:23 4 :48 2 1:16 2 m	9¾	120	4 2½	1½	1 3	2 1	CamiloJF6	8000	69	Bhagalphur110	GeofferyVrnn	7
17 Jun76	2HP	6½ f	:22 2 :47 1:21 1 ft	3-2	▲114	2 3	1 3	1 5	1 8	CmiloJF5	M6250	75	GeofferyVernon114	MistySnt	10

July 30 Det 4f sl :50b

Our Kid Dreams **114** B. g (1971), by Crasher—Five Hundred, by Swiv.
Breeder. Trine Stables, Inc. (Mich.). 1976 22 1 (6 5) $9,771
Owner, Jack C. Van Berg. Trainer, Jack C. Van Berg. $2.500 1975 14 0 4 6 $3.556

15 Sep76	5Det	6 f	:22 2 :46 4 1:13 ft	3¼	119	7 14	6 6½	4 3½	2 nk	CatalnoW8	2500	75	AlAckerman117	OurKidDrms	11
6 Sep76	10Det	1 1/16	:49 1 1:15 2 1:50 ft	9-5	▲114	5 11	5 7¼	6 8½	7 14	PerezR5	2500	39	Bucket O'Suds 111	Ludship	8
25 Aug76	5Det	6 f	:22 :47 1:12 4 ft	2¼	▲119	8 6½	9 5¾	6 5½	4 3½	PerezR3	2500	72	NativeDory122	AlAckerman	9
17 Aug76	1Det	6 f	:23 1 :47 1 1:13 1 ft	4¾	122	10 8½	9 9	7 8	3½	PerezR8	2500	73	O'RileyHimself122	TwtyFrKt	12
11 Aug76	4Det	1	:49 1 1:14 2 1:42 1 ft	9-5	▲117	2 2	3 1½	3½	2 no	CatalnoW4	2500	68	Adml'sCmnd122	OurKdDrms	8
2 Aug76	2Det	6 f	:23 :47 1 1:13 4 ft	2¾	▲117	5 6½	4 6	3 5	2½	MapleS5	2500	70	Abreast 119	Our Kid Dreams	10
24 Jly 76	2Det	1	:49 2 1:54 1 1:43 2 ft	8-5	▲117	5 3½	3 2	3 5	3 7	CatalnoW9	2500	55	Timetolight114	SirraGrande	10
7 Jly 76	6HP	6 f	:23 2 :47 3 1:14 3 ft	3¾	116	6 9	6 6	4 3	2 1	CatalnoW4	2500	78	ChoctawRidge121	OrKdDrms	10
2 Jly 76	3HP	6½ f	:23 1 :48 1 1:22 3 sl	7-5	▲116	6 6	5 5	3 4½	5 3½	PerezR7	2500	64	ChoctawRidge116	L.O.Davis	9
25 Jun76	4HP	6½ f	:24 1 :49 2 1:23 4 sl	2	▲116	6 4½	4 2½	1 1	1 2½	PerezR8	2500	62	OurKidDreams116	LordSutn	9
17 Jun76	3HP	6½ f	:23 2 :48 1:21 ft	3¼	116	5 6½	4 5½	2 3	2 nk	PerezR5	2500	76	BroncoBilly121	OurKidDrms	10
2 Jun76	3HP	1	:50 1 1:16 4 1:44 4 ft	5½	115	3 3½	2 h	2 h	2½	BaconJ1	2500	58	ManOfSummr115	OrKdDrms	10

Sometimes the act of wagering on a horse is more than a simple process of translating one's own opinion into cash. At times it becomes a test of will power. Tipsters, touts, and the blinking lights of the tote board can exert an amazing influence on the rational decision-making process, and any player who doesn't have a basic knowledge of the reliability of these enticing sources of information will be busted out of the game every time.

There is such a thing as "smart money," but it is not likely to be aligned with the tipsters and touts who advertise their "expertise" and sell it for a buck. Nor is it likely to be represented by the wildest spenders in the crowd.

Although most players get caught up in the tidal wave of enthusiasm generated by strong late play on the tote, very few moves of that kind are worth any consideration. Let's take the exceptions:

1. A shipper.
2. A first-time starter or absentee with no positive workouts.
3. A stable that has a history of such doings.

Generally speaking, the winning potential of a horse that gets excessive play is logically limited to the winning capacity of the people behind it. Most often there will be ample clues in the past performance profile to suggest an all-out performance. However, certain trainers—people like Kaye Belle in Kentucky and M. C. Preger in New York—rarely win a race unless the tote board says tilt.

On the other hand, the lack of convincing betting action on a seemingly superior, apparently sharp horse, except in stakes races, is a powerful tote board clue to a probable subpar performance. If the horse has won a few recent races or has been in excellent form and is now dropping to a seemingly easy spot, he should attract heavy play. If he does not, if he flirts with 2–1 or 5–2 odds when he should be 4–5, the player would do well to examine the rest of the field closely. Tepidly played standouts seldom run to their prior good form.

According to long-standing tradition, the morning line—the odds posted on the tote board before the betting begins—is supposed to provide an estimate of the probable post-time odds for each horse in the race. The theoretical value of this line is to enable the player to spot overlays as well as to isolate those horses getting excessive betting action. I'm afraid it rarely does that.

In the days before pari-mutuel betting the morning line was a matter of professional pride. If an operating bookmaker in the track's betting ring didn't make a first-class morning line, the best bettors in the crowd would pounce on his mistakes. In those days a good morning line had to have value. It had to reflect a balanced book of percentages and reflect the realities of the race at hand. Frankly, I envy the players who had a chance to play the game in the age of the trackside bookmaker. It must have been great fun.

Today at the racetrack, in the age of pari-mutuel betting, the morning line is usually put together by a member of the mutuel department. Rarely does it do any more than suggest the probable betting favorites, although in "blind" betting situations—the daily double and exacta—it does exert an influence on the betting habits of uninformed bettors. Almost automatically the average horseplayer will include the top two or three morning-line choices in his double and exacta combinations. This has three predictable effects: (1) it tends to create lower double and exacta payoffs on morning-line choices regardless of their merits; (2) it forces higher payoffs on overlooked longshots; and (3) it sometimes helps to single out a betting stable's serious intentions with an otherwise lightly regarded horse.

Considering the reliability of low payoff possibilities for all morning-line choices in daily doubles and exactas, the player can conclude with reasonable certainty that a horse getting substantially greater play than his morning-line odds in these "blind" betting pools is getting play from informed sources. I know several professional handicappers who pay careful attention to the flow of money in daily doubles and exactas, and all of them say that the morning-line angle is fundamental to their calculations. Naturally, these players put their own money on the line only when a stable with a good winning history is involved.

One of the things that separates professional horse-players from the rest of the crowd is the ability to assign approximate yet realistic odds values to the horses in the race. This has nothing to do with post-time odds.

For example, when Riva Ridge, winner of the 1972 Kentucky Derby, went to Pimlico two weeks later for the Preakness Stakes, it was a foregone conclusion that his overall record and TV popularity would make him a prohibitive odds-on favorite. A good morning line would have surely pegged him at 1–2. A good value line might have been willing to accept 4–5 as a fair estimate of his winning chances—that is, until the rains began to fall on the eve of the Preakness.

Riva Ridge was no mud runner, by any stretch of the term. He had already been beaten in the Everglades Stakes by a common sort named Head of the River and had always worked below par on sloppy tracks. A professional handicapper who knew that about Riva Ridge could hardly have made him anything but third choice in the Preakness to No Le Hace and Key to the Mint, two horses that eventually did finish in front of him (Bee Bee Bee won).

Three weeks later Riva Ridge tackled most of these horses again on a fast racetrack in the 1½-mile Belmont

Stakes. A good value line on the race would have established the horse at even money or 4–5. There was nothing wrong with Riva Ridge. He was still in top form, far and away the best three-year-old in America. And he had trained brilliantly for the race. The only potential danger was Key to the Mint, who was on the comeback trail. With or without some fine-line handicapping of Key to the Mint's credentials (he worked much too fast for the race and, in a rare mistake for Elliott Burch, was somewhat short on distance preparation), the 8–5 post-time odds on Riva Ridge were a gift presented by national TV coverage of the Derby winner's horrible Preakness performance. Although horses are not robots, and it is dangerous to think that every race on paper will be run exactly to specifications in the flesh, there is money to be made betting the best horse in the race at generous odds. That is, in fact, the heart and soul of the game.

"If they ran this race 100 times, how many times would Riva Ridge win?" That's the kind of question that helps to establish the value line. On Belmont's fast racetrack Riva Ridge seemed strong enough and fit enough to have at least 50 percent of the race all to himself. That's the kind of answer that sets up prime betting possibilities, and it happens every day.

Had Andy Beyer and I been thinking in terms of the value line, Princess Doubleday to place would certainly have qualified as a value-line prime bet. And there are several other instances when the value-line concept works to the advantage of players who are capable of thinking second best.

The setting is an exacta event and there is an overwhelming odds-on favorite, a horse that deserves its lofty ranking, a horse that has every advantage over the competition. Although there are some players in the crowd who bet huge amounts of money on such "stickouts," only the very best handicappers among them will avoid betting the occasional phony that will break a bankroll in one shot. Those who have the skill to back 90 percent or more short-priced winners would do far better in the long run betting less money on good horses going to the post at good odds. But that's their problem. When I see a standout odds-on favorite in an exacta event, I will commit myself to a small action bet on it or perhaps bet another horse that I think might have a chance to spring an upset. There are two extremely important exceptions.

In some exacta races the betting public has trouble evaluating the contenders for second money. If sound handicapping turns up two, three, or four logical contenders for second place, a check of the exacta payoff possibilities on the closed-circuit TV system will sometimes open up the door to a maximum bet.

On the other hand, the public sometimes bets most of its exacta money on the dominant race favorite linked with one other apparently fit horse. In such circumstances it pays to take a close look at this "second best" horse. If it lacks convincing credentials, if there are sound reasons to bet against it, a wheel on the rest of the field could produce exciting payoffs. Indeed, this phenomenon occurs many times over in a season and produces a betting pattern that is extraordinarily predictable. Hundreds of illustrations could be given here, none more dramatic than the one facing the player lucky enough to have been at Belmont Park for the greatest performance in the history of Thoroughbred racing, Secretariat's 1973 Belmont Stakes.

Going into the Belmont, Secretariat was lord and master of the three-year-old division, a solid 1–10 shot to become the first Triple Crown winner in twenty-five years. Unlike Carry Back, Northern Dancer, Kauai King, Canonero II, and Majestic Prince—the five horses that failed to complete the Derby-Preakness-Belmont sweep—Secretariat came up to the 1973 Belmont at the peak of his powers, working faster and more energetically for the race than for any other race in his life. The same could not be said for Sham, the second-best three-year-old of 1973.

Sham had tried Secretariat twice and had failed both times. In the Derby Secretariat went very wide on both turns and with power in reserve outdrove Sham from the top of the stretch to the wire.

In the Preakness, while under no special urging, Secretariat made a spectacular move around the clubhouse turn—from last to first—passing Sham in the backstretch. For the final half of the race Pincay slashed his whip into Sham with wild fury. Turcotte, aboard Secretariat, never moved a muscle. But Sham never gained an inch. At the wire he was a tired horse.

Coming up to the 1973 Belmont, Sham had begun to show signs of wear and tear. He showed fewer workouts and they were not as brisk; this horse had been through a rough campaign. Nine route races in top company in less than eight weeks. Trips to California, Kentucky, Maryland, and New York. Actually, the only thing keeping Sham in the Triple Crown chase was trainer Frank Martin's stubbornness. A more objective view of his chances in the Belmont said that he would never beat Secretariat and could even go severely off form.

These were the win odds quoted on the race:

```
Secretariat  ----------$   .10–$1.00
Sham --------------- $  5.10–$1.00
Private Smiles -------- $14.30–$1.00
My Gallant  ---------- $12.40–$1.00
Twice a Prince ------- $17.30–$1.00
```

These were the exacta payoff possibilities as they were flashed on the closed-circuit TV system prior to post time:

Secretariat with Sham - - - - - - - - - - - - - - $ 3.40
Secretariat with Private Smiles - - - - - - - $24.60
Secretariat with My Gallant - - - - - - - - - - $19.80
Secretariat with Twice a Prince - - - - - - - $35.20

Eliminating Sham from the exacta play meant an investment of $6 (three combinations) and a minimum payoff
of $19.80 (My Gallant). What all this means is that the
track was offering three horses and excellent payoffs to beat
a tired Sham for second place. In fact, the payoffs were
almost identical to the odds in the win pool, the odds being
offered on each of these three horses to beat Sham *and*
Secretariat. By conceding the race to Secretariat, the player
had a chance to collect the same odds merely by beating
Sham. Now that's what I call value.

Through the weakness of the second betting favorite
and the availability of exacta wagering, an exciting but
seemingly unplayable race was turned into a very logical,
very promising prime bet. In a very real sense, it was like
being offered a bonus dividend for understanding the subtle-
ties of a great moment in racing history. It's times like that
when a horseplayer knows he is playing the greatest game in
the world.

105TH RUNNING—1973—SECRETARIAT

EIGHTH RACE
Belmont
JUNE 9, 1973

1 ½ MILES. (2.26⅗) 105th Running THE BELMONT $125,000 added. 3-year-olds. By subscription of $100 each to accompany the nomination; $250 to pass the entry box; $1,000 to start. A supplementary nomination may be made of $2,500 at the closing time of entries plus an additional $10,000 to start, with $125,000 added, of which 60% to the winner, 22% to second, 12% to third and 6% to fourth. Weights, Colts and Geldings 126 lbs. Fillies 121 lbs. Starters to be named at the closing time of entries. The winning owner will be presented with the August Belmont Memorial Cup to be retained for one year, as well as a trophy for permanent possession and trophies will be presented to the winning trainer and jockey. Closed Thursday, February 15, 1973 with 187 Nominations.
Value of race $150,200, value to winner $90,120, second $33,044, third $18,024, fourth $9,012. Mutuel pool $519,689, OTB pool $688,460.

Last Raced	Horse	Eqt	A Wt	PP	¼	½	1	1¼	Str	Fin	Jockey	Odds $1
19May73 ^{8}Pim^{1}	Secretariat	b	3 126	1	1^{hd}	1^{hd}	1^{7}	1^{20}	1^{28}	1^{31}	Turcotte R	10
2Jun73 ^{6}Bel^{4}	Twice A Prince		3 126	5	4^{5}	4^{10}	3^{hd}	2^{hd}	3^{12}	$2\frac{1}{2}$	Baeza B	17 30
31May73 ^{6}Bel^{1}	My Gallant	b	3 126	3	3^{3}	3^{hd}	4^{7}	3^{2}	2^{hd}	3^{13}	Cordero A Jr	12 40
28May73 ^{8}GS^{2}	Pvt. Smiles	b	3 126	2	5	5	5	5	5	$4\frac{3}{4}$	Gargan D	14 30
19May73 ^{8}Pim^{2}	Sham	b	3 126	6	2^{5}	2^{10}	2^{7}	4^{8}	$4^{1\frac{1}{2}}$	5	Pincay L Jr	5 10

Time, :23⅗, :46⅕, 1:09⅘, 1:34⅕, 1:59, 2:24, (Against wind in backstretch.). Track fast.
New Track Record.

$2 Mutuel Prices:				
	2-(A)-SECRETARIAT	2.20	2.40	—
	5-(E)-TWICE A PRINCE		4.60	—
	(No Show Wagering)			

Ch. c, by Bold Ruler—Somethingroyal, by Princequillo. Trainer Laurin L. Bred by Meadow Stud Inc (Va).
IN GATE AT 5:38; OFF AT 5:38, EDT. Start Good. Won Ridden out.

SECRETARIAT sent up along the inside to vie for the early lead with SHAM to the backstretch, disposed of that one after going three-quarters, drew off at will rounding the far turn and was under a hand ride from Turcotte to establish a record in a tremendous performance. TWICE A PRINCE, unable to stay with the leader early, moved through along the rail approaching the stretch and outfinished MY GALLANT for the place. The latter, void of early foot, moved with TWICE A PRINCE rounding the far turn and fought it out gamely with that one through the drive. PVT. SMILES showed nothing. SHAM alternated for the lead with SECRETARIAT to the backstretch, wasn't able to match stride with that rival after going three-quarters and stopped badly.

$2.00 EXACTA (2–5) PAID $35.00

18.
The Winning Horseplayer

Ideally, the most instructive way to illustrate the practical applications of the material in this book would be to present thousands of actual races, playable and nonplayable.

We would select several different racetracks, do post position studies for each, save and read result charts, compare the past performance records of all the important trainers, and be careful to note and measure the relative power of the racing surface as it influences the action on the track.

To get a fix on the local horses, we could construct classification codes, keep a record of purses, pay attention to the daily tabular workout listings, generate class pars, compute speed figures, hunt for Key Races, and watch whatever races we are privileged to see with eyes geared to detect the unusual as it happens.

Not all professional-class players do all of that.

Some rely strictly on speed figures or generally broad insights to uncover sound betting propositions. Some watch races with such skill that they are able to build a catalogue of live horses for future play. And some concentrate all serious play on one specific type of race—turf events, claiming races, sprints, routes, maidens, or stakes.

Frankly, I have no argument with players who are able to solve more than their share of racetrack riddles through a single window or two. Indeed, specialization according to individual strength makes excellent sense. Different strokes for different folks. On one level that is precisely what this book has been about. But on another level that is not the case at all.

I have been very fortunate. During my years around the racetrack I have been continuously exposed to the varied menu only an extensive itinerary can bring. Five years at Rutgers University, Garden State Park division. Two years of handicapping upward of fifty races a day at five or more tracks for the *Daily Racing Form*. Triple Crown coverage for the Mutual Radio Network. Five hundred daily five-minute seminars on handicapping for WLMD radio in Maryland. The editorship of *Turf and Sport Digest.* Trips to forty-two different racetracks. Serious assaults on eighteen. Summers at Saratoga. And conversations with some of the best thinkers and players in the game. People like Andy Beyer and Clem Florio in Maryland, Jules Schanzer and Saul Rosen at the *Form,* John Pricci of *Newsday* in New York, and Tom Ainslie, the man who gave me the most encouragement to commit to print all the insights I have thus far gained.

It has taken me almost 200 pages to do that. But I think it would help your focus if I reduced the essence of it all to a few key principles and a few key examples.

There are only two kinds of playable prime betting situations: easy ones and hard ones. The easy ones practically leap off the pages of the *Racing Form;* the hard ones require a bit of digging.

To the student of track bias, an easy one may come any time the bias is strong enough to prejudice the outcome of the race. The Travers Stakes on page 37 is a classic illustration of that. So is the Schuylerville Stakes on page 120.

To students of class, easy ones come in many forms. A hidden class dropdown like Caspar Milquetoast on page 98. A Key Race standout like Gay Gambler on page 89. A Shredder, a Secretariat, a Laplander, or a horse with significantly faster speed figures. (Yes, that too is an edge in class.)

Likewise, for those who pay attention to trainers and their methods, there is nothing very complicated about spotting a Mack Miller first-timer on the grass; much the same can be said for dozens of other horses whose past performance records signal the confidence of a winning horseman's best work.

Upsets? Of course. They happen every day. Horses and

the humans who handle them are always capable of throwing in a clunker or improving beyond previous limits of performance. Mistakes? Certainly. The player is no less governed by the same laws of nature. But to win at the racetrack, the player must not only learn from his own mistakes but avoid the trap of punishing himself for having made them. Usually, that kind of genuine confidence comes only from knowing that other straightforward opportunities will not be long in coming.

With no hesitation I can assure you that the tools, concepts, and research techniques contained in this book will isolate the probable race winner with minimum difficulty in hundreds of races each and every season. And two of the most frequently encountered betting situations will bear a striking resemblance to the following pair of examples.

There are many reasons why most players would not want to touch the above race with a ten-foot pole. Despite the grossly inflated purse—put up to encourage the New York State breeding industry—it would be difficult to find a weaker field of nonwinners at any major-class track. Nevertheless, there is a standout, maximum-limit prime bet in this race—the filly Flylet, a horse that embodies a classic winning pattern (see page 117).

In each of her prior races Flylet has shown considerably more early speed than any of her rivals has ever shown. Twice she even took a narrow lead at the first quarter call. On August 11 she met every member of today's field with the exception of No Empty Pocket and First Proof, and she was no less than half a dozen lengths in front of them all for much of the race. I'm sure you can imagine the ease with which she will therefore be able to sail to the front in today's race. And therein lies the heart and power of the pattern.

Except on a stretch-running track, whenever a horse figures to get a clear, uncontested lead on the field for the first time, the player should expect dramatic improvement

1st Saratoga

AUGUST 26, 1976

6 FURLONGS. (1:08). MAIDENS. CLAIMING. Purse $10,000. 2-year-olds, foaled in New York State and approved by the New York State-bred registry. (All purse money from New York Breeders' Fund). Weight, 122 lbs. Claiming price, $20,000; for each $1,000 to $18,000, allowed 2 lbs.

COUPLED: JOSH GOLDNER, RANDY'S CIL and NO EMPTY POCKET.

Listed According to Post Positions

Heidee's Cousin — **118** B. c (1974), by Flaneur II.—Buccanette, by Black Beard.
Breeder, Murray M. Garren (N. Y.). 1976 9 M 1 0 $3,090
Owner, Murray M. Garren. Trainer, Gilbert Puentes. $18.000

11 Aug76 1Sar 5½ f :223 :4631:054m 6½ 122 1011 86½ 810 916 VelezRI2 Mdn 72 RedSam 122 RagT meBelle 12
3 Aug76 3Sar 5½ f :223 :4631:053ft 6¼ 122 88 710 815 726 MapleE9 Mdn 63 VandySue119 TakeItAlong 9
25 Jly 76 9Aqu 5½ f :24 :49 1:083ft 3 120 62½ 53¾ 55½ 45½ MpleE1 M22500 64 Tacitus 122 Mad Jack 9
18 Jly 76 4Aqu 5½ f :232 :4741:063ft 6½ 122 95 95¾ 79 58¼ StgoA8 M25000 72 PrinceNoNme117 PictreShw 10
12 Jly 76 4Aqu 5½ f :232 :48 1:074ft 4½ 122 44 32 32½ 2nk MapleE6 Mdn 74 Ducky'sBolero122 Hdee'sCsn 8
30 Jun76 3Aqu 5½ f :223 :4631:06 ft 4 8 53 421 54 53½ StgoA2 M20000 79 HasAFuture120 ChairmanOx 8
27 Jun76 4Bel 5½ f :232 :4621:044ft 19 1135 41½ 58 68½ 68 MtnJE4 M40000 83 Peak Top 122 Proud Arion 9
11 Jun76 4Bel 5½ f :234 :48 1:064ft 30 118 75¾ 711 711 714 StgoA3 M 0000 67 Lancer'sPride122 PrizeNtive 9
31 May76 4Bel 5½ f :224 :4641:052ft 49 1175 98¾ 911 920 923 MartinJE9 Mdn 65 DukeWayne122 Turn ofCoin 9
Aug 24 Sar trt 4f ft :49⅗h   Aung 19 Sar trt 5f ft 1:03b   July 17 Bel trt 3f sy :36h

Ruddy Duck — **118** Ch. c (1974), by High Rank—Meadow Mole, by Egotistical.
Breeder, Mrs. Ann K. Morse (N. Y.). 1976 2 M 0 0 (——)
Owner, Ann K. Morse. Trainer, Thomas M. Waller. $18.000

11 Aug76 1Sar 5½ f :223 :4631:054m 2e*122 1111118½ 911 815 TurcotteR5 Mdn 73 RedSam 122 RagT meB le 12
12 Jly 76 4Aqu 5½ f :232 :48 1:074ft 4½e 122 56 59 58 57 TurctteR5 Mdn 67 Ducky'sBolero122 Hdee'sCsn 8
Aug 21 Sar 5f ft 1:05b   Aug 15 Sar trt 4f ft :54b   Aug 9 Sar 4f sy :48⅗h

First Proof — **122** Dk. b. or br. c (1974), by Only Once—Flora Bonda, by Auditing.
Breeder, Maxion Farms (N. Y.). 1976 2 M 0 0 (——)
Owner, William J. Maxion. Trainer, Everett F. Schoenborn. $20.000

19 Aug76 8Sar 6 f :222 :46 1:122ft 93 115 1617131511110109 TurcteR13 AlwS 69 FratelloEd115 Heidee'sPal 17
12 Jly 76 4Aqu 5½ f :232 :48 1:074ft 35 122 823 830 825 819 VeneziaM2 Mdn 55 Ducky'sBolero122 Hdee'sCsn 8
Aug 2 LD 3f ft :38bg   July 23 LD 49f ft :50⅖bg   July 9 FL 4f ft :50⅖bg

Flylet — **117** B. f (1974), by Flying Error—Whiglet, by Whig.
Breeder, Saverio Cardile (N. Y.). 1976 6 M 0 1 $1,440
Owner, Saverio Cardile. Trainer, Saverio Cardile. $19.000

19 Aug76 8Sar 6 f :222 :46 1:122ft 38 112 33 98¼12131112 SmithRC4 AlwS 66 FratelloEd115 Heidee'sPal 17
11 Aug76 1Sar 5½ f :223 :4631:054m 8¼ 119 33 33 66½ 69½ BaezaB11 Mdn 78 RedSam 122 RagT meBe e 12
3 Aug76 3Sar 5½ f :223 :4631:053ft 28 119 1½ 32 48 620 RujanoM1 Mdn 69 VandySue119 TakeItAlong 9
19 Jly 76 4Aqu 5½ f :223 :47 1:062ft 20 115 52¼ 86¼ 9131016 RjnoM5 M35000 65 ⒻRegal Jay119 Vandy Sue 10
12 Jly 76 4Aqu 5½ f :232 :48 1:074ft 16 119 11 2h 21½ 33¾ RujanoM4 Mdn 70 Ducky'sBolero122 Hdee'sCsn 8
6 May76 4Bel 5½ f :231 :4731:073ft 11 115 2h 64 716 822 DayP7 M45000 55 ⒻSly Grin 119 Rethread 8
July 18 Bel trt 3f ft :38⅘b   July 10 Bel trt 3f m :40b   July 3 Bel 5f ft 1:01hg

Randy's Cil — **119** B. f (1974), by Thomasville—Brimstar, by Mielleux.
Breeder, Dr. L. D. Star (N. Y.). 1976 3 M 0 1 $1,440
Owner, Winifred Star. Trainer, Adrien Gauthier. $20.000

19 Aug76 8Sar 6 f :222 :46 1:122ft 5½e 112 171712141109¾ 98¾ VelqezJ15 AlwS 69 FratelloEd115 Heidee'sPal 17
11 Aug76 1Sar 5½ f :223 :4631:054m 4e 119 99¾ 97 46 36 VelasqezJ9 Mdn 82 RedSam 122 RagT meBelle 12
3 Aug76 3Sar 5½ f :223 :4631:053ft 15 119 911 811 69¾ 517 VelasqzJ3 Mdn 72 VandySue119 TakeItAlong 9
July 29 Bel 5f ft 1:00⅗h   July 24 Bel 4f sy :49⅗bg   July 18 Bel trt 3f ft :36⅖h

Big Albert — **118** Ch. c (1974), by O'Hara—Lisl's Favor, by Noholme II.
Breeder, Dr. D. J. DeLuke (N. Y.). 1976 2 M 0 0 (——)
Owner, Assunta Louis Farm. Trainer, Ramon M. Hernandez. $18.000

11 Aug76 1Sar 5½ f :223 :4631:054m 7½ 122 1213129½10111016 HerndzR7 Mdn 72 RedSam 122 RagT meBe e 12
15 Jly 76 4Aqu 5½ f :224 :4711:054ft 36 122 111411141111310l3 HerndezR2 Mdn 71 Turn of Coin 122 Red Rolfe 12
Aug 21 Sar 4f ft :48⅖hg   Aug 7 Sar 3f ft :38h   Aug 5 Sar 5f ft 1:03⅘b

No Empty Pocket — **118** B. c (1974), by Zip Pocket—May Boss, by Boss.
Breeder, Dr. L. D. Star (N. Y.). 1976 7 M 1 0 $976
Owner, L. D. Star. Trainer, Adrien Gauthier. $18.000

19 Aug76 1Key 5½ f :224 :47 1:063ft 9½ 118 76¾ 78 510 57½ LogioA4 M10000 79 LimestoneCowby120 Lry'sLk 7
11 Aug76 4Mth 5½ f :23 :4631:054ft 5 114 42½ 55 55 57 MiceliM4 M8000 81 Night Games 118 Stangley 8
23 Jly 76 3Key 5½ f :224 :4721:071ft 4¾ 120 42½ 34½ 33½ 22½ LogcioA3 M5000 81 Manza117 NoEmptyPocket 6
18 Jly 76 4Aqu 5½ f :232 :4741:063ft 23e 118 1010108¾10151017 RhdsC1 M20000 63 PrinceNoNme117 PictreShw 10
11 Jly 76 4Aqu 5½ f :222 :47 1:07 ft 10e 122 911 911 87½ 86½ RchdsC4 M18000 71 BrghtJade122 Hl tothePrnce 10
21 May76 4Bel 5½ f :23 :4641:054ft 34 118 108 99¾ 915 816 RdsCH7 M30000 70 FlagOfficer122 WincomaLss 10
27 Apr76 4Aqu 5 f :234 :4?2 :591ft 11 118 68 610 718 722 RodrzJA4 20000 67 I Got Em 122 Translation 7
June 30 Bel trt 4f sy :50b

over recent performances. If the horse already rates close to the competition, as Flylet certainly does, the expected improvement is odds-on to result in victory. Odds-on is what I said and odds-on is what I meant. Give a horse like that a slow-breaking field or a front-running racetrack, and the only thing that will beat it is an act of god or war.

In the actual race Flylet went wire to wire, scoring a handy three-length victory, and paid a juicy $15.60.

MAY 3, 1975

9th Churchill Downs

1 1-16 MILES
CHURCHILL DOWNS
START FINISH

1 1/16 MILES. (1:41⅗). ALLOWANCES. Purse $25,000. 3-year-olds. Weight, 122 lbs. Non-winners of a race of $9,775 at a mile or over allowed 3 lbs.; a race of $6,000 at any distance, 5 lbs.; a race of $4,875 at any distance, 7 lbs.; a race of $3,900 at a mile or over in 1975, 9 lbs. (Maiden, claiming and starter races not considered.)

Jim Dan Bob **113** **B. c (1972), by Wa-Wa Cy—Legayle, by Bar Le Duc.**
Breeder, G. Begley (Ky.). 1975 10 0 3 3 $7,754
Owner, G. Begley. Trainer, A. Montano. 1974..11 4 2 2 $9,265

26 Apr75 7CD 7 f :234 :4711:25 ft 52 117 77¼ 714 615 512 ArroyoH1 Alw 70 Greek Answer122 Gatch 7
17 Apr75 7Kee 7 f :23 :46 1:234ft 92 1075 913 99¾ 910 96¾ TrsclairAJ7 Alw 80 HoneyMark114 Brent'sPrnce 11
3 Apr75 7Lat 1 :4711:1241:402ft 8-5e 114 78¾ 410 210 37½ McKnghtJ9 Alw 69 Some Dude 115 Count Paco 9
29 Mar75 7Lat 1 :48 1:1321:40 gd 7¼ 112 52½ 34½ 34½ 38 McKnhtJ2 AlwS 71 NaughtyJke119 PromndeLft 8
18 Mar75 8Lat 1 :4831:1441:433gd 3¾ 113 35 44½ 37 22 McKnghtJ6 Alw 59 ClarenceHenry120 JimDan 9
7 Mar75 7Lat 6 f :24 :4811:151gd 8-5 ▲116 2h 15 11½ 2no VasqzG1 A—— 72 MowingJoe113 JimDanBob 5
21 Feb75 7Lat 1 1/16 :4841:1441:494ft 2½ 113 33 2h 21 21½ VasquezG3 Alw 59 ClarenceHnry116 JmDanBob 6
1 Feb75 6Key 170 :4711:1441:47 gd 11 119 59 412 58½ 511 OrtizI3 Alw 54 Go Go Treniers 119 Prfct Gn 6
25 Jan75 8Key 6 f :222 :4611:132sy 11 112 58½ 48 511 619 OrtizI4 AlwS 56 Gallant Bob 119 Sgt. Hunt 7
17 Jan75 8Key 6 f :222 :4611:12 ft 17 117 66½ 51¾ 31½ 3¾ OrtizI3 Alw 81 SneakyWin 117 Dr.FrankB. 8
Dec28-747Cwl 6½ f 1:23⅘sy 1 ▲119 12 12 11 11 VasquezG2 Alw 79 JimDanBob119 Clar'nceH'ry B.J.King 6
April 24 CD 4f sy :52b **March 27 Lat 3f ft :39b** **March 5 Lat 3f ft :37h**

Ruggles Ferry **117** **Gr. c (1972), by Drone—Trotta Sue, by Promised Land.**
Breeder, F. Preston (Ky.). 1975 5 2 1 0 $12,075
Owner, Mrs. F. Preston. Trainer, H. Trotsek. 1974 13 2 2 6 $26,884

24 Apr75 7Kee 1⅛ :4711:12 1:49 sy 53 117 59 44 37 57¾ ArroyoH8 AlwS 84 MasterDerby123 HoneyMark 9
15 Apr75 7Kee 1 1/16 :47 1:11 1:423gd 6 115 56 54 23 25 ArroyoH5 Alw 88 MasterDerby123 RugglsFrry 6
22 Mar75 9FG 1⅛ :4611:1021:493ft 14 115 1020 914 911 98¼ BarrowT2 AlwS 88 MasterDrby123 ColonelPowr 11
14 Mar75 9FG 6 f :221 :46 1:104ft 1-2 ▲120 67¼ 54½ 22 11 BarrowT4 Alw 94 RugglesFrry120 ElectnSpecl 6
15 Feb75 6Hia 7 f :23 :4521:232ft 7 117 108¼ 79½ 32 1h BarrowT7 Alw 88 RgglsFerry117 BravestRman 11
Nov16-748CD 1 1:36 ft 5¾ 116 88½ 75 52½ 35¼ BarrowT2 HcpS 84 CircleHome116 MasterD'rby R'gl'sF'ry 9
Nov 6-748CD 7 f 1:25⅖sy 9 115 1118 1014 55 32½ BarrowT9 Alw 77 MasterD'rby122 W'yw'rdR'd R'gl'sF'y 11
Oct19-747Kee a 7 f 1:25⅘ft 8½ 122 109¾ 88½ 35 35½ BarrowT9 ScwS 88 Pack'rC'pt'n122 M'st'rD'by R'gl'sF'ry 11
Oct 9-747Kee 6 f 1:09⅗ft 5½ 115 65¾ 66½ 41½ 11½ BarrowT4 Alw 94 RugglesFerry115 Ga'ntBob Pack'rCa'n 6
Aug28-747AP 6 f 1:11⅗gd 2¼ ▲119 77 43½ 22½ 2¾ BarrowT6 Alw 84 CraftyD'ne119 R'gglesFerry DonOman 7
April 30 CD 5f ft 1:03⅖b **April 23 Kee 3f ft :36b** **April 20 Kee 5f ft 1:04b**

Dixmart **122** **B. g (1972), by Swoon's Son—Liz Piet, by Piet.**
Breeder, Copelan & Thornbury (Ky.). 1975 . 7 2 3 2 $29,800
Owner, C. O. Viar & R. Holthus. Trainer, R. Holthus. 1974..13 2 2 3 $11,085

22 Apr75 6Kee 7 f :23 :4541:23 ft 6½ 122 78 66½ 24 22 CampbllRJ1 Alw 89 Paris Dust 116 Dixmart 9
5 Apr75 7OP 170 :4611:1141:414ft 8 113 79 63¾ 2½ 1¾ CampbllRJ3 Alw 87 Dixmart 113 Doug 6
31 Mar75 5OP 6 f :22 :4541:112ft 6-5 ▲118 41¾ 52 41 32 CampbllRJ3 Alw 86 Jay'sGig114 BourrePadnah 9
26 Mar75 6OP 6 f :22 :4511:104ft 5¾ 113 32 23½ 22½ 2no CmpblRJ10 Alw 91 Pleasure Prize 113 Dixmart 10
11 Mar75 6OP 6 f :221 :4611:131sl 8¾ 112 86¾ 77½ 43 11½ CmpblRJ3 22500 79 Dixmart 112 Kayjo 11
4 Mar75 6OP 6 f :214 :4511:12 ft 3¼ 114 54 54¼ 3nk 2nk RiniA9 15000 85 Warrior Knight 112 Dixmart 10
18 Feb75 6OP 5½ f :222 :4641:053ft 4¾ 116 84 53¼ 41½ 36½ RiniA9 15000 83 BourrePadnh111 GrtRhythm 12
Oct19-745Haw 6½ f 1:16⅕ft 8-5e▲114 87½ 814 714 711 LivelyJ1 Alw 81 Str'teMiss114 J'dgeBol'm'r Hon'yM'rk 9
April 29 CD 6f ft 1:18b **Mar 25 OP 3f ft :37⅖b** **Mar 20 OP 5f ft 1:02⅗b**

Marauding 119

Gr. c (1972), by Warfare—Juliet, by Nearctic.
Breeder, Barrett M. Morris & Virginia M. Morris (Ky.). 1975 . . 8 2 2 2 $32,450
Owner, Bromagen Cattle Co. Trainer, G. P. Bernis. 1974 10 1 3 0 $7,955

22 Apr75 ^{6}Kee 7 f :23 :45^{4}1:23 ft 3¾ 122 3^{2} 5^{4}½ 3^{4}½ 3^{3} LouvereGE^{7} Alw 88 Paris Dust 116 Dixmart 9
5 Apr75 ^{9}OP 1⅛ :46^{4}1:10^{2}1:51^{4}ft 17 123 5^{3}½ 9^{4}½ 8^{5}¼ 8^{5}¼ McHrgeD^{7} AlwS 79 PrmisedCity126 BldChapeau 14
15 Mar75 ^{9}OP 1^{70} :47^{2}1:13^{1}1:44^{2}gd 2e 119 3^{1} 2^{h} 4^{1}¾ 5^{4}¾ MelncnL^{2} HcpO 69 PromisedCity120 Me n'Mine 12
8 Mar75 ^{7}OP 1^{70} :23 :47^{2}1:42 ft 4½ 117 1½ 1^{h} 1^{h} 1^{h} MelanconL^{1} Alw 86 Maraudng117 CountryByJim 7
28 Feb75 ^{8}OP 6 f :21^{3} :45^{1}1:11^{1}ft 4¾ 122 5^{1}¾ 4^{4} 5^{3}¾ 2^{2}¾ MelnconL^{8} Alw 86 PoorOldJoe 114 Marauding 8
14 Feb75 ^{8}OP 6 f :21^{4} :44^{3}1:10^{2}ft 2½e▲120 5^{3}½ 4^{7} 3^{1} 3^{1} MelconL^{4} HcpO 92 King Jody 112 Untwine 11
7 Feb75 ^{8}OP 5½ f :22^{1} :46^{2}1:06 gd 27 117 5^{2}½ 4^{2}½ 3^{1}½ 1¾ MelnconL^{4} Alw 88 Marauding 117 Peto'sFellow 12
24 Jan75 ^{8}LaD 6 f :23^{1} :48^{2}1:14^{2}m 9-5 ▲115^{5} 1^{1}½ 1^{6} 1^{3} 2½ WolfCG^{6} Alw Hot Paque 111 Marauding 6
Nov30-74^{9}FG 6 f 1:^{1}3⅖sgd 68 112 4^{2}½ 3^{3} 5^{8}½ 5^{11} Mel'onL^{6} HcpO 70 HoneyM'k117 RusticRuler MidniteR'o 14
April 28 CD 1m ft 1:45⅖b April 21 Kee 3f ft :37⅗b April 16 Kee 5f ft :59h

Naughty Jake 122

Dk. b. or br. c (1972), by Gallant Romeo—Matrona, by Terra Firma.
Breeder, S. Turner (Ky.). 1975 . . 8 2 0 1 $25,650
Owner, Mildred Bachelor. Trainer, J. Bachelor. 1974 . . 7 3 1 0 $17,675

29 Apr75 ^{8}CD 1 :46^{4}1:11 1:36^{2}ft 4½ 122 2^{1}½ 2½ 3^{1}½ 3^{3}¼ VasqzG^{4} AlwS 94 RoundStake122 RushingMan 5
15 Apr75 ^{7}Kee 1$\frac{1}{16}$:47 1:11 1:42^{3}gd 9½ 123 3^{3}½ 4^{3}½ 5^{5}½ 4^{12} VasquezG^{1} Alw 81 MasterDerby123 RugglsFrry 6
29 Mar75 ^{7}Lat 1 :48 1:13^{2}1:40 gd 1-3 ▲119 1½ 1^{3} 1½ 1^{1} VasqzG^{3} AlwS 79 NaughtyJke119 PromndeLft 9
22 Mar75 ^{5}Lat 6 f :23 :47^{1}1:12^{4}sy 2-3 ▲122 2^{6} 2^{3} 1^{1} 1^{4} VasquezG^{7} Alw 84 NaughtyJake122 ColonialPnt 7
20 Feb75 ^{3}Hia 1$\frac{1}{16}$:46^{3}1:11 1:42^{4}sy 5¼ 117 7^{11} 5^{11} 4^{8} 4^{9}¾ ValdizanF^{1} Alw 79 CircleHome119 Administratr 7
29 Jan75 ^{9}Hia 7 f :22^{2} :44^{4}1:22 ft 30 115 6^{8} 5^{8} 5^{8} 6^{5}½ ValdiznF^{5} AlwS 89 Ascetic 115 Ellora 11
18 Jan75 ^{9}Hia 6 f :22 :44^{3}1:10^{1}sy 74 115 7^{5}¾ 5^{6}½ 4^{5} 4^{1}¾ ValdiznF^{6} AlwS 90 Ricks Jet 114 Prevailer 11
Jan 9-75^{9}Crc 6½ f 1:19⅗ft 15 122 6^{7} 6^{8}¾ 6^{7} 4^{5}½ ValdizanF^{4} Alw 87 Strateaway113 Prevailer IrishRing 6
April 27 CD 3f ft :35h

Mr. Snow Cap 113

B. g (1972), by One More Chorus—Orange Ice, by Iceberg II.
Breeder, H. G. Tilson (Ky.). 1975 . . 6 2 2 1 $9,210
Owner, Audley Farm Stable. Trainer, D. Smith.

24 Apr75 ^{4}Kee 6 f :22 :45 1:10^{1}sy 4 114 6^{8} 5^{6}¼ 4^{9} 5^{14} DelahyeE^{10} Alw 77 BearerBond112 CmmrclPilot 11
18 Apr75 ^{6}Kee 7 f :23^{3} :46^{3}1:24^{2}ft 6-5 ▲112 2^{1}½ 2½ 2½ 1^{2}½ DelahsyeE^{2} Alw 84 Mr. Snow Cap 112 Easabaya 10
9 Apr75 ^{7}Kee 6 f :22^{2} :45^{4}1:10^{3}ft 8-5 ▲114 4^{3} 4^{3} 2^{1} 2¾ DelahsyeE^{3} Alw 88 RushingMan118 Mr.SnwCap 9
12 Mar75 ^{7}FG 6 f :22^{2} :46^{4}1:12^{2}ft 3-2 120 5^{4}¾ 4^{4} 3^{1}½ 2no DelahsyeE^{1} Alw 86 FlwlssFinish120 Mr.SnwCap 7
26 Feb75 ^{8}FG 6 f :21^{4} :45^{3}1:11^{1}ft 1-2e▲120 4¾ 1^{h} 2^{1} 3^{4}½ AndersnJR^{8} Alw 87 Tailor'sTack120 BoldChapau 9
16 Feb75 ^{2}FG 6 f :22^{4} :48^{1}1:14^{1}sl 3-2 ▲120 1½ 1^{1} 1^{2} 1^{5} DsyeE^{11} M10000 77 Mr.SnwCap120 BrtherBadBy 12
April 17 Kee 3f ft :35⅗b April 7 Kee 3f ft :36b March 28 FG 3f ft :37b

Victory Judge 113

B. c (1972), by Traffic Judge—Choiseul, by Victory Morn.
Breeder, R. C. Kyle (Can.). 1975 . . 8 1 0 0 $1,452
Owner, Sacred Stable. Trainer, A. Battaglia. 1974 4 M 1 1 $1,050

17 Apr75 ^{9}GP Ⓣ a 1 1:39^{2}fm 90 114 8^{13} 8^{11} 8^{13} 8^{23} RamosR^{6} Alw 61 TooCordial 114 StepForward 8
10 Mar75 ^{9}GP 7 f :22 :44^{1}1:21^{3}ft 239 110 5^{5}½10^{16}10^{23}11^{28} DennieD^{10} AlwS 68 GreekAnswer122 FashinSale 11
1 Mar75 ^{6}Hia 6 f :22^{2} :45^{4}1:10^{2}ft 54 119 9^{7}¼ 8^{10} 9^{14} 9^{13} ArroyoH^{7} Alw 78 SwingLbrSwing117 Zinglng 10
5 Feb75 ^{8}Hia 7 f :23^{1} :45^{3}1:22^{4}ft 66 122 3^{2}½ 5^{4}½ 9^{17}11^{18} BrumfelcD^{9} Alw 73 Directory 117 Jimbosanda 11
29 Jan75 ^{9}Hia 7 f :22^{2} :44^{4}1:22 ft 299 112 5^{7} 9^{15}11^{20}11^{17} ArroyoH^{11} AlwS 78 Ascetic 115 Ellora 11
18 Jan75 ^{3}Cwl 6½ :24^{2} :48^{3}1:23^{4}m 2 ▲120 1^{5} 1^{6} 1^{5} 1^{9} SaylerB^{5} Mdn 79 VictoryJudge120 ZperGgette 8
Jan10-75^{8}Cwl 5½ f 1:08⅖sy 5 105 6^{14} 5^{11} 5^{4}¼ 4^{1}½ ClinchT^{1} Alw 81 Mike'sPal 116 PrinceArc NoDate 7
Jan 2-75^{8}Cwl 6½ f 1:25⅗m 13 116 6^{3}½ 3^{1}½ 3^{1}½ 8^{18} GastonR^{6} Alw 53 Donda'sMir'e122 CoolItB'e Jan't'sDe't 10
Dec21-74^{3}Cwl a1 1:42⅗gd 2-3 ▲120 1^{4} 1^{1} 2^{h} 3^{5}½ SaylerB^{1} Mdn 61 Cool ItBabe117 BrightM'ch V't'ryJ'ge 10
Dec 7-74^{8}Cwl 1$\frac{1}{16}$ 1:54⅕sy 29 111 2^{1}½ 1^{h} 1^{h} 2^{1}½ SaylerB^{4} Alw 65 Clar'ceH'ry113 Vict'yJ'ge JimDanBob 6
April 21 GP 7f ft 1:28⅗h

Greek Answer 122

B. c (1972), by Northern Answer—Greek Victress, by Victoria Park.
Breeder, E. P. Taylor (Can.). 1975 5 3 0 1 $57,707
Ownr, W P. Gilbride. Trainer, F. H. Merrill. 1974 . . 11 5 2 2 $187,261

26 Apr75 ^{7}CD 7 f :23^{4} :47^{1}1:25 ft 1-3 ▲122 1½ 1^{2}½ 1^{2} 1¾ SolomneM^{7} Alw 82 Greek Answer122 Gatch 7
19 Mar75 ^{9}GP 1$\frac{1}{16}$:46 1:10^{1}1:42^{4}ft 6-5 ▲122 1^{5} 1^{6} 1^{3} 1^{4} SolmneM^{6} AlwS 87 Greek Answer 122 Decipher 8
10 Mar75 ^{9}GP 7 f :22 :44^{1}1:21^{3}ft 3-5 ▲122 1½ 1½ 1^{4} 1^{5} CstdaM^{11} AlwS 96 GreekAnswer122 FashinSale 11
29 Jan75 ^{9}Hia 7 f :22^{2} :44^{4}1:22 ft 3½ 122 1½ 1^{1}½ 2^{2} 4^{4}¾ CastaM^{10} AlwS 90 Ascetic 115 Ellora 11
18 Jan75 ^{9}Hia 6 f :22 :44^{3}1:10^{1}sy 3-5 ▲122 1^{h} 1^{h} 2^{h} 3^{1} CstndaM^{4} AlwS 91 Ricks Jet 114 Prevailer 11
Oct19-74^{8}Bow 7 f 1:24⅘ft 2-3 ▲119 2^{2}½ 2^{2} 1^{h} 2¾ Hin'j'saH^{6} AlwS 80 Gall'tBob113 Gr'kAnswer ParvaHasta 10
Sep15-74^{8}WO 1-70 1:42⅕ft 7-5 122 1^{1}½ 1^{1} 2^{2}½ 3^{6}½ C'st'daM^{7} HcpS 85 L'Enjol'r122 N'r t'eHighS'a G'kAnsw'r 11
Sep 2-74^{8}AP 6½ f 1:17⅘ft 3¼ 122 1^{2}½ 1^{1} 1^{1}½ 1¾ C'st'daM^{2} ScwS 86 Gr'kAnsw'r122 Col'lP'w'r TheB'g'lPr'e 7
Au~24-74^{8}Sar 6½ f 1:15 ft 13 121 1^{2}½ 1^{2} 1½ 2^{3}¾ Cas'daM^{8} ScwS 92 F'lishPl's're121 G'kAnsw'r OurT'lism'n 8
Aug 5-74^{6}FE 6½ f 1:21⅕sl 2-5 ▲120 1^{h} 2^{h} 1^{h} 4^{8} GreenW^{2} AlwS 65 Col'sCl'rion115 OnaP'dSt'l'g P'sleyPal 8
Jly 21-74^{6}FE 6½ f 1:17 ft 1-3 ▲122 1½ 1^{2} 1^{3} 1¾ GreenW^{2} AlwS 94 Greek Answer 122 L'Enjoleur Hagelin 5
Jun28-74^{6}WO 6 f 1:10⅗ft 4-5 ▲120 2^{h} 1½ 1^{3} 1^{7} GreenW^{4} AlwS 90 Gr'kAnswer120 N'r t.HighSea R'lS'ari 6
Jun 9-74^{6}WO 6 f 1:10⅖ft 1-2 ▲114 1^{h} 1^{2} 1^{3}½ 1^{5}½ GreenW^{7} AlwS 91 GreekAnswer114 Sgt.Hunt RunJay 7
April 21 CD 1m ft 1:41h

As I explained in Chapter 4, the position of the starting gate relative to the first turn is very important in middle-distance route races at most racetracks. Churchill Downs is one of those tracks.

The favorite in this race—the Twin Spires Purse, an annual fixture on the Derby Day program—is Greek Answer at 3–5. There are several reasons why this choice is out-rageously out of line with reality.

One of those reasons is named Ruggles Ferry, who has run only one subpar race (March 22) while meeting some of the best three-year-old routers in America (Master Derby, Colonel Power, Honey Mark, Circle Home). He has also shown enough speed in several of his races to suggest he can take advantage of his inner post position.

The other reasons lie with Greek Answer himself. This is a colt that has shown a tendency to tire in the late stages at 6½ furlongs and beyond; a colt whose lone win around two turns was scored on Gulfstream Park's notorious front-running track; a colt that will have to use much of his early speed to get clear of this field in the short run to the first turn. These are serious problems for a 3–5 shot to overcome. I make him 6–1.

The crowd made Ruggles Ferry 5–2. I make him even money, a 250 percent overlay. The key to this betting situa-tion is more subtle than that of a Flylet-type front runner, but it is nevertheless there for all to see. The favorite is breaking from a disadvantageous post position, and his past performance history suggests he can ill afford to race under a handicap. The chief competition is easily identified and is set to race from a favorable post.

In the race Greek Answer raced four wide in the run to and through the clubhouse turn, struggled to get the lead on the backstretch, and tired steadily thereafter to finish fourth. Ruggles Ferry saved ground, held a striking position to the far turn, and rallied in the upper stretch to win by seven widening lengths. Had the post positions been reversed, I am sure Greek Answer would have given a much better account of himself.

Learning to recognize the straightforward betting opportunity is fundamental to the player's ambitions for profit. There will be countless other times, however, when the player will have to use all the tools in his bag to uncover the probable race winner. As often as 80 percent of the time, the only conclusion to be drawn from the effort is that no single horse in the field deserves a significant edge. There is great joy, however, in the exception.

SEPTEMBER 24, 1976

7th Tdn

$3 PERFECTA WAGERING ON THIS RACE

6 FURLONGS (chute). (1:09⅘). CLAIMING. Purse $2,300. Fillies and mares. 3-year-olds and upward. 3-year-olds, 115 lbs.; older, 121 lbs. Non-winners of three races since June 30 allowed 2 lbs.; two races since then, 4 lbs.; a race since then, 6 lbs. Claiming price, $2,500; if for $2.250, allowed 2 lbs.

Sultan Sue Sis **112** Ro. f (1972) by Venetian Jester—Sultan s Sue, by Strokkr.
Br. Edward & J. Armstrong. Jr (Okla.) 1976 15 5 3 1 $8,642
Owner, R. F. Zupanc. Trainer. Ida Zupanc. $2.500 1975 6 M 3 2 $1 680

11 Sep76	4Tdn	6 f	:233 :4821:142sl	2½	1085	42	41	3nk	1½	BordenD2	c2000	77	SultanSueSis108	TurningShy	8
3 Sep76	7Tdn	6 f	:23 :4811:151ft	6-5	▲1115	86¼	41¼	31½	21½	BordenD4	2000	71	Ⓕ AmberComt116	SltnSeSis	8
19 Aug76	6Tdn	6 f	:23 :47 1:124ft	2½	▲1115	34	23	33½	36	BordenD2	2500	79	Ⓕ AprilFrost120	MissJeerful	7
15 Aug76	3Tdn	5½ f	:223 :4741:08 m	7½	1125	86¼	86¼	74	64½	BordenD2	2500	74	JazzDancer111	BridgePatrl	8
24 Jly 76	10Tdn	6 f	:224 :4711:142ft	6½	117	51¾	31	41½	2nk	GraellA3	2500	77	WrkAndTrn120	SltanSueSis	10
15 Jly 76	10Tdn	6 f	:222 :4611:13 ft	5½	117	86¼	65½	53½	45½	FelinoBR8	2500	78	ClayPigeon122	GreekWhiz	12
17 Jun76	2Tdn	6 f	:224 :4721:144sl	3½	117	74½	57	41½	24	FelicoBR1	2500	71	OverlandWay120	SltnSueSis	10
11 Jun76	6Tdn	6 f	:232 :4741:134gd	12	117	96¾	87	55	57½	KelleyBA4	3500	72	Blocklamur 122	Count Adam	9
3 Jun76	5Tdn	6 f	:222 :4611:131ft	3	117	32	21½	1h	12	FelicoBR2	2500	83	SultanSueSis117	HevnlyRosa	9
26 May76	5Tdn	6 f	:223 :4721:133ft	5	120	43	22	15	110	FelicoBR1	2000	81	Ⓕ SultanSueSis120	HwieToo	11

Shad Pac **110** B. m (1971), by Clem Pac—Star Shadow, by Stella Aurata.
Breeder. C. P. Blake & S. Laser (Ark.). 1976 15 3 1 1 $6,141
Owner, Lela Mellinger. Trainer, Edward H. Mellinger III. $2.500 1975 21 2 1 2 $4.28/

19 Sep76	1Tdn	5½ f	:224 :4731:071ft	18	1085	83¼	63¾	66	57½	FranscoD8	2500	75	GallowayBay116	ShrLovelins	8
5 Sep76	8Com	4½ f	:233 :473 :54 ft	10	114	4	53½	67½	44¼	AntusLJ5	2500	89	Hollie'sPaxton115	HenryH.	7
29 Jun76	6Com	6½ f	:23 :47 1:193ft	2½	114	614	513	411	47¼	LydaR2	2500	84	EasyMission117	G.J.Frmlwy	6
6 Jun76	5RD	170	:48 1:1341:464ft	3	109	45½	42½	3½	31¾	NewkirkT7	2500	64	Humbjo 116	Make Me Gone	8
31 May76	3RD	6 f	:221 :4631:133m	3	1077	310	37½	31½	11½	TalricoM1	2500	75	Shad Pac 107	Althen	7
22 May76	3RD	6 f	:221 :4621:123ft	17	1087	88½	87½	74½	61¼	TalaricoM1	2500	79	Liberal Man 116	Hesourpet	12
14 May76	2RD	6 f	:222 :4621:114ft	41	119	65½	98½	97½	811	WingoR9	3500	73	Ⓕ AntherPluck116	Buxomby	10
13 Apr76	6HP	1	:4921:1521:424ft	30	115	98¼	109	916	915	GilbtCJJr5	3200	54	HotShotDor115	AkepotSask	10
5 Apr76	6HP	6½ f	:23 :48 1:202ft	9½	1105	57½	58	69½	67	RodgzJD3	3200	72	CocntRow115	Kg of theOzks	10
29 Mar76	5Lat	1	:4741:15 1:44 m	10	1127	45	22½	11½	15	NewkirkT4	2500	58	Ⓕ ShadPac112	QueerVashti	8

Crafty Vodelia **115** Dk. b. or br. f (1972), by Noble Commander—Crafty Love, by Crafty Admiral. Breeder, F. Wiercioch (Fla.). 1976 24 3 2 2 $5,954
Owner, L. R.Benshoff, lessee. Trainer, L. R. Benshoff. $2,500 1975 22 0 0 1 $2,529

18 Sep76	3Tdn	6 f	:231 :4741:141m	31	114	43	33½	21½	22	RiniA4	2000	76	Rick'sBuckeye120	CrftyVdlia	8
11 Sep76	4Tdn	6 f	:233 :4821:142sl	67	114	83¼	77	53¾	45½	RiniA3	2000	71	SultanSueSis108	TurningShy	8
14 Aug76	5Tdn	6 f	:224 :4711:141sl	63	114	42	75½	66½	69¼	RiniA3	2000	69	King's Levy 122	Fast Arab	8
4 Aug76	7Tdn	6 f	:232 :4731:144ft	93	118	52¾	45	66	67½	InfanteF8	2000	67	Ⓕ TouchO'Ri113	April Silvrs	8
28 Jly 76	5Tdn	5½ f	:221 :48 1:083ft	21	1117	74¾	87	710	68	StaffordA7	2000	68	Ⓕ Confetti 118	Lady's Hat	8
8 Jly 76	7Tdn	140	:4911:1541:47 sl	25	115	21½	44½	86½	813	RiniA4	2000	47	EarlyLady117	CertnlyMntrip	9
30 Jun76	4Tdn	6 f	:24 :49 1:163sy	2½	115	21	1h	11	12	RiniA7	2000	66	CraftyVodelia115	FirstBurst	7
24 Jun76	5Tdn	140	:4811:1541:482sy	5¾	117	12	21	53	610	CooperG3	2000	43	PrceBravos122	StlTheRoses	7
17 Jun76	7Tdn	6 f	:222 :4621:142sl	39	117	87¼	76½	64¼	48½	CooperG2	2500	68	Greek Whiz 118	Our Pirate	8

Sept j Tdn 5f ft 1:03⅘b

Kin O Mine

115 Ch. m (1969), by Mighty Mine—Kimeo, by Ozbeg.
Breeder, J. A. Davis (Cal.). 1976 12 4 1 1 $6,345

Owner, Bunny Coatney. Trainer, Bunny Coatney. $2,250 1975 14 2 3 2 $5,020

4 Aug76 7Tdn	6 f :232 :4731:144ft	4½	120	42½	65¼	43	44½	MunsterL3	2000	70	ⒻTouchO'Ri113	April Silvrs	8
24 Jly 76 2Tdn	6 f :224 :4721:142ft	2½	117	32½	31	42	78½	MunsterL5	2000	68	Part Western 120	Fleet Pac	8
8 Jly 76 6Tdn	6 f :231 :4731:142sl	8-5	▲118	21	1h	1h	11	SosaR8	2000	77	ⒻKin O Mine 118	Tiz A Joy	8
23 Jun76 7Tdn	6 f :223 :4641:14 ft	8-5	▲116	73¾	41½	3½	11	SosaR9	2000	79	ⒻKinOMine 116	MissJeerful	9
5 Jun76 5Tdn	6 f :232 :4711:131ft	8	115	3½	2½	21	14	SosaR1	2000	83	Kin O Mine 115	Extinguisher	12
26 Mar76 6Tdn ▣	a 5 f :234 :4841:014ft	2¾	118	1h	2h	2½	43¼	CooperG6	2000	83	ⒻIndianCojo120	AtollsMiss	6
20 Mar76 7Tdn ▣	a 5 f :224 :48 1:011ft	3¼	118	54½	53½	33	24½	GraellA5	2500	84	ⒻTrafficGun113	KinOMine	7
13 Mar76 10Tdn ▣	a 5 f :24 :49 1:02 gd	9-5	113	85¼	34½	32½	11	GraellA5	2000	85	Kin O Mine 113	Alfie O	10
6 Mar76 3Tdn ▣	a 5 f :242 :4831:012ft	5	115	22½	31½	33½	34	PlackeD9	2000	84	Hub 118	Smart David	9

Sheer Loveliness

112 B. m (1971), by Molino—Mischief Miss, by Don Mike.
Breeder, Mrs. J. P. Strain (Ohio). 1976 13 3 1 1 $3,492

Owner, J. P. Strain, Jr. Trainer, J. P. Strain, Jr. $2.500 1975 5 M 0 0 $161

19 Sep76 1Tdn	5½ f :224 :4731:071ft	28	1087	11	11	12	22	ShewellJ1	2500	81	GallowayBay116	ShrLovelins	8
29 Aug76 2Tdn	6 f :231:4721:124gd	19	115	62¾	56½	47	616	D'AmicoA9	2500	69	Angl'sPlsre118	Freemn'sMn	9
12 Aug76 9Tdn	6 f :224 :4641:131ft	54	117	1½	21	66½	615	VaughnJ5	6000	68	ⒻBaryVible115	VincesDr'm	7
31 Jly 76 5Com	6½ f :243 :4841:214ft	16	117	1h	22½	13	11½	PhillipsD10	2000	80	SheerLoveliness117	MsPnRn	10
22 Jly 76 5Com	4½ f :232 :471 :534ft	2½	117	1	21½	24	36¼†	HussrMW9	2000	88	Time ofEmprrs122	MissLrgrs	9

†Disqualified and placed seventh.

15 Jly 76 4Com	6½ f :234 :4731:211ft	4½	117	12	11	1½	45	HussrMW2	2000	78	JolliPassage114	MissPanRun	7
1 Jly 76 10Tdn	6 f :231 :4821:16 m	39	118	11½	1h	1h	45½	HussrMW4	2500	63	SandyLathe102	CrtyDestino	10
1 Jly 76 10Tdn	6 f :231 :4821:16 m	39	118	11½	1h	1h	45½†	HussrMW4	2500	63	SandyLathe102	CrftyDestino	10

†Placed third through disqualification.

21 Jun76 2Com	5 f :233 :4731:011ft	2¾	118	11½	12	11	11½	HussrMW1	1500	82	ShrLovelinss118	GenrlMateo	8

Bibi Mine

115 Ch. m (1971), by O'Bibi—Condamine, by Deliberator.
Breeder, J. W. Mecom (Tex.). 1976 16 3 4 1 $10,521

Owner, Miller Farm. Trainer, Edward Collins. $2.500 1975 14 1 2 3 $4.285

11 Sep76 6Lat	6½ f :24 :48 1:211ft	6½	116	41¼	42½	54¼	65	TennbmM8	5000	70	Tosoro 113	Circus Act	10
5 Sep76 10RD	6 f :221 :4541:113ft	8¼	111	42	42	35	45½	TnnbmM5	05000	79	ResJudicada113	MmySowrd	11
28 Aug76 6Tdn	140 :4711:1341:45 sl	6¾	113	22	23	86	811	MunsterL8	6000	59	Reasontodare113	BritishRed	8
12 Aug76 9Tdn	6 f :224 :4641:131ft	3	116	41	31	32	31¼	MunsterL6	6000	82	ⒻBaryVible115	VincesDr'm	7
1 Aug76 7Tdn	6 f :223 :4631:13 ft	27	115	31	52½	42	53¼	MunsterL1	7000	81	Dad'sReflction116	BrlyVsble	10
24 Jly 76 7RD	5½ f :223 :4621:063sy	7¼	117	87¼	912	68½	68¾	SorezW5	A2500	73	Triptique 116	Shaded Silver	10
27 Jun76 8Tdn	6 f :23 :4621:12 ft	19	116	42½	54	55½	510	MunsterL2	Alw	79	ⒻGoOnDrmng116	Mrge'sPck	7
9 Jun76 9Tdn	6 f :223 :46 1:122ft	8½	114	22	23	2½	13	MunsterL2	Alw	87	ⒻBibi Mine 114	Lark Star	10
1 Jun76 5CD	6 f :223 :4541:122ft	31	117	31½	1½	11½	2nk	SoirezW8	5000	84	ⒻHelen'sMusic117	BibiMine	9
21 May76 8Tdn	6 f :231 :47 1:131ft	3½	116	1h	1h	1h	11	MunsterL3	3500	83	ⒻBibiMine116	GoDancerGo	7

Pajone's Hostess

115 Ch. f (1972), by Pajone—Anchorette, by My Host.
Breeder, W. J. Kosterman (Wash.). 1976 13 0 0 1 $558

Owner, W. Kosterman. Trainer, John Myers. $

15 Sep76 10Tdn	6 f :23 :47 1:132ft	33	115	62½	43	98¾	1014	PlackeD5	3500	68	SkyLock111	Work and Turn	11
5 Sep76 3Tdn	140 :4741:1331:43 ft	42	1085	43½	69	817	836	BordenD8	3500	44	LookWho'sHere 122	DuroT	[illegible]
26 Aug76 6Tdn	6 f :23 :4631:13 ft	5	1095	51¼	22	54½	612	KelleyBA9	3500	72	ⒻGrandElm116	April Frost	9
19 Aug76 9Tdn	6 f :222 :4541:124ft	19	1085	33½	21	4¾	65¼	KelleyBA9	3500	80	InfieldHomer117	AbilityPls	10
6 Aug76 7Tdn	6 f :223 :4611:123ft	23	113	32½	34	67	715	SackettR3	4500	71	LookWho'sHere118	SkyLock	8
28 Jly 76 7Tdn	6 f :222 :4621:131ft	15	1085	63¾	43½	43½	78	KelleyBA5	4500	75	Urticante116	Whatawaytogo	8
22 Jly 76 9Tdn	6 f :222 :4631:133ft	18	1095	42	1h	1h	34½	KelleyBA6	4500	76	ⒻMillennum115	Wally'sSisr	9
15 Jly 76 9Tdn	6 f :224 :4631:121ft	26	115	31½	2h	75	714	GraellA5	5000	74	IndianSpeed 120	EarlsMeldy	7
19 Jun76 7Tdn	6 f :224 :4711:14 m	22	117	71½	31½	52¾	610	FelicnoBR6	Alw	69	BoldTom122	Great [illegible]bridge	7

Aug 2 Tdn 3f ft :37⅘bg

Foolish Lola

117 Ch. m (1970), by Venetian Jester—Lassa Gal, by Gallahadion.
Breeder, C. Sawyer (Okla.). 1976 10 2 1 1 $2,689

Owner, G. Mancuso. Trainer, Joseph Mazur. $2,500 1975 25 6 4 5 $10,446

10 Sep76 5Tdn	6 f :233 :4821:152sl	2	▲114	1h	11½	13	14½	D'AmicoA1	2000	72	ⒻFoolishLola114	IndianLil	7
27 Aug76 7Tdn	6 f :231 :47 1:141sl	28	113	2½	73¾	55	55½	D'AmicoA4	2500	72	DriveJoy122	LadofPrtsmuth	10
31 Jly 76 6Com	5 f :232 :4731:002ft	4½	117	31½	33	35	35¼	RamosW5	2500	84	Sharpsville 115	Base Fiddle	7
17 Jly 76 6Com	5 f :23 :4731:001ft	3	117	54¼	68	67	65	RamosW7	2500	82	OpenWind122	KamsinWind	7
26 Jun76 8Com	6½ f :233 :4731:212ft	2¾	▲112	1½	1½	21	22½	RamosW4	2500	79	Wild Boss 117	Foolish Lola	7
18 Jun76 9Com	6½ f :241 :4821:22 ft	3¾	▲115	12	12	15	112	RamosW1	2000	79	FoolishLola115	RennieBee	10

Confetti

112 Dk. b. or br. f (1972), by Roman Line—Starstruck, by Dark Star.
Breeder W. H. May (Ky.). 1976 16 4 0 4 $6,147

Owner, K. E. Strickler. Trainer, Homer Dewey. $2.500 1975 16 0 2 3 $2,148

29 Aug76 7RD	6 f :22 :4611:121ft	21	1107	87	811	813	819	MysJRJr8	02500	63	TriplicateCopy 111	BushHoc	8
28 Jly 76 5Tdn	5½ f :221 :48 1:083ft	9¾	118	54½	34	32	13	InfanteF6	2000	76	ⒻConfetti 118	Lady's Hat	8
9 Jly 76 zFL	5½ f :233 :48 1:081ft	6	114	31½	3½	13	13½	VedilgoW4	2000	81	Confetti 114	Northen Proof	7
3 Jly 76 7FL	5½ f :224 :4641:081ft	7	113	63¾	65¼	66¼	56½	VedilgoW6	2000	74	Tisha Bell 115	Grossecat	7
26 Jun76 5FL	6 f :223 :4641:142ft	4	114	42½	2h	2h	44	VedilgoW1	2000	78	Prove It Su 106	Easy Mike	6
15 Jun76 6FL	6 f :23 :4611:122ft	13	112	67	57½	67	76½	WingoR5	A1750	85	Barborian 112	Petit Homme	8
5 Jun76 6FL	5½ f :222 :4631:061ft	29	111	74¾	76½	76	65½	WingoR7	3000	85	Misget 111	Anar Kali	7
22 May76 6FL	5½ f :223 :47 1:071ft	18	111	77¾	67	65	78	RinconR7	3500	78	RuthlessCount116	ShoeTax	8

Using only the past performance records above, the handicapper would have a hard time justifying a confident selection. Several horses in the field appear to be in good form, while a few others are ostensibly dropping in class. Yet the past performance records do not contain sufficient clues to make conclusive comparisons. The same is true for the majority of claiming races run throughout the country.

There is no track bias, no known trainer pattern, and no unusual betting activity to consider. But there are result charts, and classification codes, and speed figures.

Using speed figures or result-chart time comparisons, we would begin our detective work by determining that Sultan Sue Sis ran the fastest recent race.

On September 11, in an open-grade $2,000 claiming race, Sultan Sue Sis completed six furlongs in 1:14⅖, not very impressive time on first glance. But compared with several other races that day, the time was extraordinary. These were some of the other six-furlong times posted:

$5,000 claiming - - - - - - 1:14⅕
$4,500 claiming - - - - - - 1:14⅘
$3,500 claiming - - - - - - 1:14⅖
$3,000 claiming - - - - - - 1:14⅗

Obviously, Sultan Sue Sis ran a big race last time out and is ready to step up sharply in class. But what about the rest of the field? What about 4–5 favorite Bibi Mine, who is getting play mostly on the basis of her sharp drop in claiming price?

In my judgment, this is not a negative class drop in the classic sense. Considering Bibi Mine's inability to win at the higher claiming level, the drop in class may be what she needs to get back on the winning track. In order to make a clearer determination of that judgment we need to discover more information about the caliber of horses she faced at Latonia. Again, result charts and comparative race times will prove very useful to this end.

The first race on the September 11 Latonia card was a $3,500 maiden claiming race. The fractions and final time were identical to Bibi Mine's $5,000 claiming race, a race for proven winners: .24 . . . .48 . . . 1:14⅕ . . . 1:21⅕. Two conclusions are possible: Either the maiden race was run very fast or Bibi Mine's race was run very slow.

Two other races run that day say Bibi Mine was in a slow field:

$3,500 claiming - - - - - - 1:14⅖
$3,500 claiming - - - - - - 1:14...1:20⅘

Indeed, Bibi Mine may once have been a much better horse and will probably appreciate the drop in class today, but at present she is not faster than Sultan Sue Sis and has no right to be favored over her.

Crafty Vodelia was recently trounced by Sultan Sue Sis and then came back to race very creditably in an open-grade $2,000 claimer. Another meeting with Sultan Sue Sis will not be what the doctor ordered.

Shad Pac recently returned to competition but gave no indication that she is fit enough to catch these horses in a six-furlong race.

Kin O' Mine has been absent from competition for seven weeks and is stepping up in claiming price. A good performance is likely, considering the interval that preceded her win over a weak field on June 5; but it would be asking too much to have her step into this field of multiple winners to win first crack out of the box.

Sheer Loveliness has shown good early speed on several occasions, but she couldn't hold onto a clear lead in a shorter race last time out. A time-comparison study of the races run that day will also show that Sheer Loveliness was in a slow $2,500 race.

Pajone's Hostess is winless this year and desperately needs a drop in class. Signs of early lick in her recent past performances are valid indicators of improving physical condition; but a win seems unlikely.

Foolish Lola won her last race the same way she scored her only other victory this season: wire to wire. A review of the Thistledown charts for September 10 will make light of her chances to repeat that today. Although she had the rail from start to finish on a track that was extremely biased toward the inside, her fractional times were slower than those for most of the other races on the card. Moreover, she is stepping up sharply in company from a C-class $2,000 claimer to an open-class $2,500 race.

Confetti was in top form at the tail end of July but spent a month in the barn before making her next start. That's a clear sign of physical problems, fully confirmed by her August 29 performance, the worst race on her chart. She now returns with another four-week vacation behind her. If this horse wins, the knowledgeable horseplayers in the crowd should give trainer Homer Dewey a standing ovation; but few if any of them will wager on her chances. Short of clear-cut evidence in the post parade, there is no logical reason to conclude that this horse is back in top competitive form.

EXACTA PAYOFF FOR SULTAN SUE SIS WITH	
Bibi Mine	$ 52
Shad Pac	$ 96
Foolish Lola	$158
Pajone's Hostess	$190
Crafty Vodelia	$210
Sheer Loveliness	$275
Kin O'Mine	$275
Confetti	$390

On the basis of the material that our detective work has uncovered, we may now conclude that Sultan Sue Sis has a decided edge over every horse in the race. Indeed, she need only run within two lengths of her most recent race to win in a walk. For added confidence, her honest record, including five prior wins, suggests that she is likely to do that and more. Given 7–2 odds on Sultan Sue Sis, we should forgive the player who is now making a mad dash to the win windows, but anyone contemplating a wager larger than $30 would be better off investing in the exacta pool.

At $3 per ticket, a straight wheel would cost $24, but it would also leave the player open to two less profitable results (Bibi Mine or Shad Pac). However, there are other alternatives to consider, and the following is only the simplest.

By purchasing two *extra* combinations with Bibi Mine and one with Shad Pac, the player would automatically increase the minimum odds on Sultan Sue Sis to 4–1 ($33 invested, $156 minimum possible payoff) and give himself a chance for considerably greater rewards without additional risk. In a game that taxes the player 20 cents for every dollar wagered, 50 cents extra profit on the dollar is nothing to sneeze at.

SEVENTH RACE
Tdn
Sept'ber 24, 1976

6 FURLONGS (chute). (1:09⅘). CLAIMING. Purse $2,300. Fillies and mares. 3-year-olds and upward. 3-year-olds, 115 lbs.; older, 121 lbs. Non-winners of three races since June 30 allowed 2 lbs.; two races since then, 4 lbs.; a race since then, 6 lbs. Claiming price, $2,500; if for $2,250, allowed 2 lbs.

Value to winner $1,380; second, $460; third, $230; fourth, $115; fifth, $69; sixth, $46. Mutuel Pool, $14,296. Perfecta Pool, $32,082.

Last Raced	Horse	EqtAWt	PP	St	¼	½	Str	Fin	Jockeys	Owners	Odds to $1
11 Sep76 4Tdn1	Sultan Sue Sis	b4 117	1	7	2h	2h	11	13	RSackett	R F Zuanc	3.60
11 Sep76 6Lat6	Bibi Mine	b5 115	6	8	61½	31½	21	21	LMunster	Miller Farm	.80
15 Sep76 10Tdn10	Jajone's Hostess	b4 115	7	2	4h	4½	41	3no	DPlacke	W Kosterman	16.80
4 Aug76 7Tdn4	Kin O Mine	7 115	4	4	7h	51	3½	4½	BMWilson	Bunny Coatney	21.30
18 Sep76 3Tdn2	Crafty Vodelia	b4 115	3	9	8h	9	5h	51	ARini	L R Benshoff lessee	12.70
19 Sep76 1Tdn5	Shad Pac	b5 110	2	5	3r	61	61	61	BAKelley5	Mrs L Meltinger	5.60
10 Sep76 5Tdn1	Foolish Lola	6 117	8	3	51	7h	81½	71	AD'Amico	G Mancuso	12.50
19 Sep76 1Tdn2	Sheer Loveliness	b5 112	5	6	9	82	9	82	JShewell7	J P Strain Jr	23.30
29 Aug76 7RD8	Confetti	b4 112	9	1	13	1h	7½	9	RJMyres7	K E Strickley	82.40

OFF AT 4:08 EDT. Start good. Won driving. Time, :23, :47⅖, 1:14. Track slow.

$2 Mutuel Prices:

1-SULTAN SUE SIS	9.20	3.60	2.80
6-BIBI MINE		3.40	2.80
7-PAJONE'S HOSTESS			6.00

$3 PERFECTA (1-6) PAID $52.80.

Ro. f, by Venetian Jester—Sultan's Sue, by Strokkr. Trainer, Ida Zupanc. Bred by Edward and J. Armstrong, Jr. (Okla.).

SULTAN SUE SIS, with the pace all the way while saving ground along the rail, had to be steadied at the five-sixteenths pole while waiting for an opening, got through along the rail to make the lead and won under steady pressure. BIBI MINE circled horses on the middle of the turn to go up to challenge for the lead, then finished evenly. PAJONE'S HOSTESS lacked the needed response KIN O' MINE closed some ground late. SHAD PAC was through early. FOOLISH LOLA had brief speed CONFETTI set the pace for a half and stopped to a walk.

Before we leave this step-by-step illustration—indeed, before we part company altogether—I would like to point out that Sultan Sue Sis was not preordained to win the above race. There was, in fact, one major clue that could well have destroyed all our expectations. The little *c* next to Sultan Sue Sis' claiming price on the September 11 past performance line indicates she was claimed by the trainer of record—Ida Zupanc.

Considering the extraordinary impact trainers have on the performance potential of all horses, it would be a mistake to bet serious money on a horse whose trainer had given any evidence of incompetence. In the case of Ida Zupanc, no such evidence is revealed in a review of recent result charts. Moreover, her excellent judgment in claiming this improving racehorse ten or fifteen minutes prior to the September 11 race is reason enough to give her the benefit of the doubt. I am not that conservative to pass up 4–1 odds on a 50–50 proposition. But I am also not that foolish to forget that 50 percent winners means 50 percent losers as well. To win at the racetrack the player has to be alert, flexible, and fully in touch with his own limitations. The future may be predictable, but it is never predetermined.

Appendix

Guide to past performance profiles and the
DAILY RACING FORM—*List of North American
tracks—"Points of call" in charts—How to
set up a post position survey—Percentage table
for morning line—How to compute place and
show payoffs—Parallel time chart—Class pars—
Speed figures and track variants—
Recommended reading list*

Guide to

PAST PERFORMANCES

WITH FRACTIONAL TIMES

Position in Race and Margin Behind Leading Horse

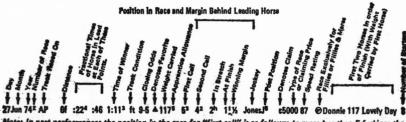

27 Jun 74² AP   6f :22⁴ :46 1:11³ ft 9-5 ▲117⁵ 5³ 4² 2ʰ 1¹½ JonesJ⁵   c5000 87 ⊙Donnie 117 Lovely Day 8

Note: In past performances the position in the race for "first call" is as follows: In races less than 5 furlongs the first call is the start; at 5 furlongs the first call is the three-sixteenths; from 5½ to 7½ furlongs the first call is the quarter mile; at 1 mile or more the first call is the half.

		Points of Call				Fractional Times Given At These Points of Call		
	Distance of Race	1st Call	2nd Call	3rd Call	4th Call			
2	Furlongs	Start	—	Stretch	Finish	—	—	Finish
5/16	Mile	Start	—	Stretch	Finish	—	—	Finish
3	Furlongs	Start	—	Stretch	Finish	1/4	—	Finish
3 1/2	Furlongs	Start	1/4	Stretch	Finish	1/4	3/8	Finish
4	Furlongs	Start	1/4	Stretch	Finish	1/4	—	Finish
4 1/2	Furlongs	Start	1/4	Stretch	Finish	1/4	1/2	Finish
5	Furlongs	3/16	3/8	Stretch	Finish	1/4	1/2	Finish
5 1/2	Furlongs	1/4	3/8	Stretch	Finish	1/4	1/2	Finish
6	Furlongs	1/4	1/2	Stretch	Finish	1/4	1/2	Finish
6 1/2	Furlongs	1/4	1/2	Stretch	Finish	1/4	1/2	Finish
7	Furlongs	1/4	1/2	Stretch	Finish	1/4	1/2	Finish
1	Mile	1/2	3/4	Stretch	Finish	1/2	3/4	Finish
1	Mile, 70 yards	1/2	3/4	Stretch	Finish	1/2	3/4	Finish
1 1/16	Miles	1/2	3/4	Stretch	Finish	1/2	3/4	Finish
1 1/8	Miles	1/2	3/4	Stretch	Finish	1/2	3/4	Finish
1 3/16	Miles	1/2	3/4	Stretch	Finish	1/2	3/4	Finish
1 1/4	Miles	1/2	1 mile	Stretch	Finish	1/2	3/4	Finish
1 5/16	Miles	1/2	1 mile	Stretch	Finish	1/2	3/4	Finish
1 3/8	Miles	1/2	1 mile	Stretch	Finish	1/2	3/4	Finish
1 1/2	Miles	1/2	1 1/4	Stretch	Finish	1/2	3/4	Finish
1 5/8	Miles	1/2	1 3/8	Stretch	Finish	1/2	3/4	Finish
1 3/4	Miles	1/2	1 1/2	Stretch	Finish	1/2	3/4	Finish

Key to Symbols, Abbreviations in Past Performances

FOREIGN-BRED HORSES
An asterisk (*) preceding the name of the horse indicates foreign-bred. (No notation is made for horses bred in Canada and Cuba.)

MUD MARKS
*—Fair mud runner   ✕—Good mud runner
⊗—Superior mud runner

COLOR
B.—Bay   Blk.—Black   Br.—Brown   Ch.—Chestnut
Gr.—Gray   Ro.—Roan   Wh.—White
Dk. b. or br.—Dark bay or brown
(Lt. before color denotes Light)

SEX
c—colt   h—horse   g—gelding   rig—ridgling
f—filly   m—mare

PEDIGREE
Each horse's pedigree lists, in the order named, color, sex, year foaled, sire, dam and grandsire (sire of dam).

BREEDER
Abbreviation following breeder's name indicates the state, place of origin or foreign country in which the horse was foaled.

TODAY'S CLAIMING PRICE
Claiming prices for horses entered today appear in bold face type to right of trainer's name.

RECORD OF STARTS AND EARNINGS
The horse's racing record for his most recent two years of competition appears to the extreme right of the name of the breeder. This lists the year, number of starts, wins, seconds, thirds and earnings. The letter "M" in the win column of the upper line indicates the horse is a maiden. If the letter "M" is in the lower line only, it indicates the horse was a maiden at the end of that year.

DISTANCE
a—preceding distance (a6f) denotes "about" distance (about 6 furlongs in this instance.)

TURF COURSES
①—before distance indicates turf (grass) course race.
①—before distance indicates inner turf course.
⊙—before distance indicates inner dirt course.

TRACK CONDITIONS
ft—fast   fr—frozen   gd—good   sl—slow
sy—sloppy   m—muddy   hy—heavy
Turf course races, including steeplechase and hurdles:
hd—hard   fm—firm   gd—good   yl—yielding   sf—soft
Note: SC in place of track condition indicates Synthetic Course in use at various tracks. The condition of this synthetic course is fast at all times.

CLOSING ODDS
2ᴬ—favorite   2e—entry   15f—mutuel field

APPRENTICE OR RIDER WEIGHT ALLOWANCES
Allowance (in pounds) indicated by superior figure following weight—117⁵.

ABBREVIATIONS USED IN POINTS OF CALL
no—nose   h—head   nk—neck

POST POSITION
Horse's post position appears after jockey's name—WilsonR⁴.

RACE CLASSIFICATIONS
10000—Claiming race (eligible to be claimed for $10,000). Note: The letter c preceding claiming price (c10000) indicates horse was claimed.

M10000—Maiden claiming race (non-winners—eligible to be claimed).

10000H—Claiming handicap (eligible to be claimed).

ᵒ10000—Optional claiming race (entered NOT to be claimed).

10000ᵒ—Optional claiming race (eligible to be claimed).

Mdn—Maiden race (non-winners).

AlwM—Maiden allowance race (for non-winners with special weight allowance for those having started in a claiming race).

Alw—Allowance race.

HcpO—Overnight handicap race.

SpiW—Special weight race.

Wfa—Weight-for-age race.

Mtch—Match race.

A10000—Starter allowance race (horses who have started for claiming price shown, or less, as stipulated in the conditions).

H10000—Starter handicap (same restriction as above).

S10000—Starter special weight (restricted as above).
Note: Where no amount is specified in the conditions of the "starters" race dashes are substituted, as shown below:
A———   H———   S———

STEEPLECHASE AND HURDLE RACES
[S—Steeplechase   [H—Hurdle race

STAKES RACES
AlwS—Allowance stakes.
HcpS—Handicap stakes.
ScwS—Scale weight stakes.
SpwS—Special weight stakes.
WfaS—Weight-for-age stakes.
50000S—Claiming stakes (eligible to be claimed).

INVITATIONAL RACES
InvA—Invitational allowance.
InvH—Invitational handicap.
InvSc—Invitational scale weight.
InvSp—Invitational special weights.
InvW—Invitational weight-for-age.

RACES EXCLUSIVELY FOR FILLIES, MARES
℗—Immediately following the speed rating indicates races exclusively for fillies or fillies and mares.

SPEED RATINGS
This is a comparison of the horse's time with the track record established prior to the opening of the meeting. The track record is given a rating of 100 and one point is deducted for each one-fifth second slower than the record. When a horse breaks the track record one point is added to the par 100 for each one-fifth second faster than the record. One-fifth of a second is considered the equivalent of one length.

No ratings are given for hurdle or steeplechase events, for races less than three furlongs, for races where the horse's speed rating is less than 25.
Note: Speed ratings for new distances are computed and assigned when adequate time standards are established. At Caliente, Mexico, which operates throughout the year, rating changes are made whenever a track record is broken.

EACH HORSE'S MOST RECENT WORKOUTS APPEAR DIRECTLY UNDER THE PAST PERFORMANCES
For example, July 30 Bel 3f ft :38b indicates the horse worked on July 30 at Belmont Park. The distance of the trial was 3 furlongs over a fast track and the horse was timed in 38 seconds, breezing. The following abbreviations are used to describe how each horse worked:
b—breezing   d—driving   e—easily   g—worked from stall gate   h—handily   bo—bore out
trt following track abbreviation indicates horse worked on training track.   tc—turf course   TR—trial race
HC—Hillside Course

ABBREVIATIONS FOR NORTH AMERICAN TRACKS

Abbreviations below designate tracks in DAILY RACING FORM charts and past performances.

AC	— Agua Caliente, Mex.	**Hag**	—*Hagerstown, Md.	**San**	—*Sandown Park, Can.
Aks	— Ak-Sar-Ben, Neb.	**Haw**	— Hawthorne, Ill.	**Sar**	— Saratoga, N. Y.
Alb	— Albuquerque, N. Mex.	**Hia**	— Hialeah Park, Fla.	**ScD**	— Scarborough Downs, Me.
AP	— Arlington Park, Ill.	**Hol**	— Hollywood Park, Calif.	**Sem**	—*Seminole Downs, Fla.
Aqu	— Aqueduct, N. Y.	**HP**	—*Hazel Park, Mich.	**SFe**	— Santa Fe Downs, N. Mex.
AsD	—*Assiniboia Downs, Can.	**JnD**	—*Jefferson Downs, La.	**ShD**	— Shenandoah Downs, W.Va.
Atl	— Atlantic City, N. J.	**Jua**	— Juarez, Mex.	**Sol**	—*Solano, Calif.
Ato	—*Atokad Park, Neb.	**Kee**	— Keeneland, Ky.	**Spt**	—*Sportsman's Park, Ill.
BB	—*Blue Bonnets, Can.	**Key**	— Keystone Race Track, Pa.	**SR**	—*Santa Rosa, Calif.
BD	—*Berkshire Downs, Mass.	**LaD**	— Louisiana Downs, La.	**Stk**	— Stockton, Calif.
Bel	— Belmont Park, N. Y.	**LaM**	—*La Mesa Park, N. Mex.	**StP**	—³*Stampede Park, Can.
Beu	— Beulah Park, Ohio	**Lat**	— Latonia, Ky.	**Suf**	—*Suffolk Downs, Mass.
BF	—*Brockton Fair, Mass.	**Lbg**	—*Lethbridge, Can.	**Sun**	— Sunland Park, N. Mex.
Bil	—*Billings, Mont.	**LD**	—*Lincoln Downs, R. I.	**Tdn**	— Thistledown, Ohio
BM	— Bay Meadows, Calif.	**Lga**	— Longacres, Wash.	**Tim**	— Timonium, Md.
Bmf	— Bay Meadows Fair, Calif.	**Lib**	— Liberty Bell Park, Pa.	**TrP**	— Tropical Park, Fla.
Boi	— Boise, Idaho	**LnN**	—*Lincoln State Fair, Neb.	**TuP**	— Turf Paradise, Ariz.
Bow	— Bowie, Md.	**Lrl**	— Laurel Race Course, Md.	**Was**	— Washington Park, Ill.
CD	— Churchill Downs, Ky.	**Mad**	—*Madison, Neb.	**Wat**	— Waterford Park, W.Va.
CdA	— Coeur d'Alene, Idaho	**Mar**	—*Marlboro, Md.	**Wey**	—*Weymouth Fair, Mass.
Ceg	—*Victoria Park, Can.	**MD**	—*Marquis Downs, Can.	**Win**	—*Windsor Raceway, Can.
Cen	— Centennial Race Track, Colo.	**Mex**	— Mexico City, Mex.	**WO**	— Woodbine, Can.
Cka	—*Cahokia Downs, Ill.	**MF**	—*Marshfield Fair, Mass.	**YM**	— Yakima Meadows, Wash.
Cls	—*Columbus, Neb.	**Mol**	—*East Moline Downs, Ill.		
Com	—*Commodore Downs, Pa.	**Mth**	— Monmouth Park, N. J.		**HUNT MEETINGS**
Crc	— Calder Race Course, Fla.	**Nar**	— Narragansett Park, R. I.	**Aik**	— Aiken, S. C.
CT	—*Charles Town, W. Va.	**Nmp**	—*Northampton, Mass.	**AtH**	— Atlanta, Ga.
Cwl	—¹*Commonwealth	**NP**	—*Northlands Park, Can.	**Cam**	— Camden, S. C.
	Race Course, Ky.	**OP**	— Oaklawn Park, Ark.	**Clm**	— Clemmons, N. C.
DeD	—*Delta Downs, La.	**Pen**	— Penn National, Pa.	**DR**	— Deep Run, Va.
Del	— Delaware Park, Del.	**Pim**	— Pimlico, Md.	**Fai**	— Fair Hill, Md.
Det	— Detroit Race Course, Mich.	**Pit**	—*Pitt Park, Pa.	**Fax**	— Fairfax, Va.
Dmr	— Del Mar, Calif.	**PJ**	—*Park Jefferson, S. D.	**FH**	— Far Hills, N. J.
Dov	—*Dover Downs, Del.	**Pla**	—*Playfair, Wash.	**Gln**	— Glyndon, Md.
EIP	— James C. Ellis Park, Ky.	**Pin**	— Pleasanton, Calif.	**GN**	— Grand National, Md.
EP	—*Exhibition Park, Can.	**PM**	— Portland Meadows, Ore.	**Lex**	— Lexington, Ky.
EvD	—*Evangeline Downs, La.	**Pmf**	— Portland M'd'ws Fair, Ore.	**Lig**	— Ligonier, Pa.
FD	—²Florida Downs, Fla.	**Poc**	—*Pocono Downs, Pa.	**Mal**	— Malvern, Pa.
FE	— Fort Erie, Can.	**Pom**	—*Pomona, Calif.	**Med**	— Media, Pa.
Fer	—*Ferndale, Calif.	**PR**	— Puerto Rico	**Mid**	— Middleburg, Va.
FG	— Fair Grounds, La.	**Pre**	—*Prescott Downs, Ariz.	**Mon**	— Monkton, Md.
FL	— Finger Lakes, N. Y.	**RaP**	—*Raceway Park, Ohio	**Mtp**	— Montpelier, Va.
Fno	— Fresno, Calif.	**RD**	— River Downs, Ohio	**Oxm**	— Oxmoor, Ky.
Fon	—*Fonner Park, Neb.	**Reg**	—*Regina, Can.	**Pur**	— Purchase, N. Y.
FP	— Fairmount Park, Ill.	**Ril**	—*Rillito, Ariz.	**PW**	— Percy Warner, Tenn.
GaD	—*Gator Downs, Fla.	**Rkm**	— Rockingham Park, N. H.	**RB**	— Red Bank, N. J.
GBF	—*Great Barrington, Mass.	**Rul**	—*Ruidoso Downs, N. Mex.	**SH**	— Strawberry Hill, Va.
GF	—*Great Falls, Mont.	**SA**	— Santa Anita Park, Calif.	**SoP**	— Southern Pines, N. C.
GG	—*Golden Gate Fields, Calif.	**Sac**	— Sacramento, Calif.	**Try**	— Tryon, N. C.
GM	—*Green Mountain, Vt.	**Sal**	—*Salem, Ore.	**Uni**	— Unionville, Pa.
GP	— Gulfstream Park, Fla.			**War**	— Warrenton, Va.
Grd	—*Greenwood, Can.			**Wel**	— Wellsville, Pa.
GS	— Garden State Park, N. J.				

*Indicates tracks less than one mile in circumference. ¹Formerly named Miles Park.
²Formerly named Sunshine Park. ³Formerly named Victoria Park.

'Points of Call' in Thoroughbred Charts

Following is a tabulation listing the "points of call" for the various distances in charts of thoroughbred racing:

Distance							
3 Furlongs	PP	Start				Str	Fin
3½ Furlongs	PP	Start	¼			Str	Fin
4 Furlongs	PP	Start	¼			Str	Fin
4½ Furlongs	PP	Start	¼			Str	Fin
5 Furlongs	PP	Start	3-16	⅜		Str	Fin
5½ Furlongs	PP	Start	¼	⅜		Str	Fin
6 Furlongs	PP	Start	¼	½		Str	Fin
6½ Furlongs	PP	Start	¼	½		Str	Fin
7 Furlongs	PP	Start	¼	½		Str	Fin
7½ Furlongs	PP	Start	¼	½		Str	Fin
1 Mile	PP	Start	¼	½	¾	Str	Fin
1 Mile, 30 Yards	PP	Start	¼	½	¾	Str	Fin
1 Mile, 70 Yards	PP	Start	¼	½	¾	Str	Fin
1 1/16 Miles	PP	Start	¼	½	¾	Str	Fin
1 1/8 Miles	PP	Start	¼	½	¾	Str	Fin
1 3/16 Miles	PP	Start	¼	½	¾	Str	Fin

Note: In races at 1 1/4 Miles to 1 11/16 Miles, the Start call is eliminated and the ¼ mile call is substituted (as shown below):

Distance							
1 1/4 Miles	PP	¼	½	¾	1	Str	Fin
1 5/16 Miles	PP	¼	½	¾	1	Str	Fin
1 3/8 Miles	PP	¼	½	¾	1	Str	Fin
1 7/16 Miles	PP	¼	½	1	1¼	Str	Fin
1 1/2 Miles	PP	¼	½	1	1¼	Str	Fin
1 9/16 Miles	PP	¼	½	1	1¼	Str	Fin
1 5/8 Miles	PP	¼	½	1	1⅜	Str	Fin
1 11/16 Miles	PP	¼	½	1	1⅜	Str	Fin

In races at 1 3/4 Miles or more, the first call is at the ½ mile (as shown below):

Distance							
1 3/4 Miles	PP	½	1	1¼	1½	Str	Fin
1 13/16 Miles	PP	½	1	1¼	1½	Str	Fin
1 7/8 Miles	PP	½	1	1⅜	1⅝	Str	Fin
1 15/16 Miles	PP	½	1	1⅜	1⅝	Str	Fin
2 Miles	PP	½	1	1½	1¾	Str	Fin
2 Miles, 70 Yards	PP	½	1	1½	1¾	Str	Fin
2 1/16 Miles	PP	½	1	1½	1¾	Str	Fin
2 1/8 Miles	PP	½	1	1½	1¾	Str	Fin
2 3/16 Miles	PP	½	1	1½	1¾	Str	Fin
2 1/4 Miles	PP	½	1	1½	2	Str	Fin
2 5/16 Miles	PP	½	1	1½	2	Str	Fin
2 3/8 Miles	PP	½	1	1½	2	Str	Fin
2 1/2 Miles	PP	½	1	1½	2	Str	Fin

THE PROPER WAY TO SET UP A POST POSITION SURVEY

For the period involved, note at each distance charted: (1) the number of races from each post position, (2) the number of wins per post, and (3) the win percentage per post. A separate category should be maintained for "outside post position" for all races. *Optional:* At the same time, record the number of wire-to-wire winners.

Several sample post position surveys appear below.

ROCKINGHAM

July 5 — Sept. 21, 1975 (67 days)

POST POSITION
SPRINTS (5 furlongs — 6 furlongs)

Post Position	Starters	Wins	Win Percentage
1	477	57	11.9
2	477	55	11.5
3	477	60	12.6
4	477	62	13.0
5	477	53	11.1
6	475	55	11.6
7	454	57	12.6
8	380	33	8.7
9	288	21	7.3
10	191	14	7.3
11	122	6	4.9
12	73	4	5.5
outside	477	40	8.4

Wire-to-wire winners — 27.3%

POST POSITION
ROUTES (1 mile 40 yds. — 1 ½ miles)

Post Position	Starters	Wins	Win Percentage
1	164	24	14.6
2	164	24	14.6
3	164	21	12.8
4	164	24	14.6
5	164	15	9.1
6	163	18	11.0
7	151	14	9.3
8	118	17	14.4
9	66	1	—
10	39	2	—
11	23	3	—
12	12	1	—
outside	164	13	7.9

Wire-to-wire winners — 15.2%

DETROIT RACE COURSE

April 1 — July 13, 1975 (90 days)

POST POSITION
Sprints (2 fur. — 6 fur., inclusive)

Post Position	Starts	Wins	Win Percentage
1	682	71	10.4
2	682	75	11.0
3	682	64	9.4
4	682	82	12.0
5	682	75	11.0
6	678	90	13.3
7	663	82	12.4
8	567	59	10.4
9	398	35	8.8
10	278	27	9.7
11	179	14	7.8
12	103	8	7.8
outside	682	84	12.3

Wire-to-wire winners — 24.8%

POST POSITION
Routes (1 mile and longer)

Post Position	Starts	Wins	Win Percentage
1	154	34	22.1
2	154	15	9.7
3	154	24	15.6
4	154	20	13.0
5	154	15	9.7
6	154	15	9.7
7	150	15	10.0
8	124	7	5.6
9	70	6	8.6
10	30	3	10.0
11	11	0	0.0
12	8	0	0.0
outside	154	10	6.5

Wire-to-wire winners — 14.9%

HOLLYWOOD PARK

DEL MAR

April 11 - July 21, 1975 (76 days)

Post Position
Turf Course (all distances)

Post Position	Starters	Wins	Percentage
1	199	33	16.6
2	199	16	8.0
3	199	21	10.5
4	199	26	13.1
5	199	28	14.1
6	197	21	10.7
7	179	19	10.6
8	143	18	12.6
9	105	7	6.7
10	75	7	9.3
11	24	1	4.2
12	19	2	10.5
outside	199	20	10.1

Front-running winners — 8.5%

July 23 — Sept. 10, 1975 (43 days)

**POST POSITION
TURF RACES (all distances)**

Post Position	Starters	Wins	Win Percentage
1	69	18	26.1
2	69	12	17.4
3	69	8	11.6
4	69	8	11.6
5	69	7	10.1
6	68	10	14.7
7	54	1	—
8	43	3	—
9	21	1	—
10	5	1	—
11	2	0	0.0
12	1	0	0.0
outside	69	4	5.8

Wire-to-wire winners — 20.3%

Post Position
Sprints (up to seven furlongs)

Post Position	Starters	Wins	Percentage
1	344	32	9.3
2	344	31	9.0
3	344	36	10.5
4	344	41	11.9
5	344	36	10.5
6	343	48	14.0
7	316	33	10.4
8	271	30	11.1
9	220	27	12.3
10	172	16	9.3
11	130	7	5.4
12	98	7	7.1
outside	344	35	10.2

Front-running winners – 25.3%

**POST POSITION
SPRINTS (6 furlongs)**

Post Position	Starters	Wins	Win Percentage
1	203	33	16.3
2	203	27	13.3
3	203	26	12.8
4	203	25	12.3
5	203	27	13.3
6	200	9	4.5
7	178	22	12.4
8	143	13	9.1
9	95	8	8.4
10	74	3	4.1
11	54	6	11.1
12	28	4	14.3
outside	203	18	8.9

Wire-to-wire winners – 30.5%

Post Position
Routes (one mile and over)

Post Position	Starters	Wins	Percentage
1	178	19	10.7
2	178	22	12.4
3	178	24	13.5
4	178	27	15.2
5	178	21	11.8
6	174	13	7.5
7	161	15	9.3
8	135	15	11.1
9	103	8	7.8
10	79	6	7.6
11	45	5	11.1
12	31	3	9.7
outside	178	18	10.1

Front-running winners — 15.2%

**POST POSITION
ROUTES (1 mile — abt. 1¼ miles)**

Post Position	Starters	Wins	Win Percentage
1	115	15	13.0
2	115	13	11.3
3	115	13	11.3
4	115	22	19.1
5	115	16	13.9
6	114	15	13.2
7	99	9	9.1
8	69	8	11.6
9	35	1	—
10	21	3	—
11	9	0	0.0
12	3	0	0.0
outside	115	12	10.4

Wire-to-wire winners – 26.1%

PERCENTAGE TABLE FOR COMPUTING
A MORNING LINE

The following table provides a reference for computing a morning line. The percentage totals for the field should equal 118 to 125 points. This allows for the pari-mutuel tax.

ODDS	PERCENTAGE POINTS	ODDS	PERCENTAGE POINTS
1 – 5	83	2 – 1	33
1 – 4	80	5 – 2	28
1 – 3	75	3 – 1	25
1 – 2	67	7 – 2	22
3 – 5	62	4 – 1	20
2 – 3	60	9 – 2	18
3 – 4	57	5 – 1	16
4 – 5	55	6 – 1	14
even	50	8 – 1	11
6 – 5	45	10 – 1	9
7 – 5	41	12 – 1	8
3 – 2	40	15 – 1	6
8 – 5	38	20 – 1	4
9 – 5	35	30 – 1	3

Below are two sample morning lines with percentage points.

HYPOTHETICAL RACE 1—1¼ MILES		
HORSE	ODDS	POINTS
Run Dusty Run	7 – 5	41
Royal Ski	2 – 1	33
Banquet Table	5 – 1	16
Sail to Rome	6 – 1	14
Sanhedrin	12 – 1	8
For the Moment	20 – 1	4
Ali Oop	20 – 1	4
		120 *total*

HYPOTHETICAL RACE 2—1¼ MILES

HORSE	ODDS	POINTS
Seattle Slew	3 – 5	62
Royal Ski	7 – 2	22
Banquet Table	6 – 1	14
Sail to Rome	10 – 1	9
Sanhedrin	20 – 1	4
Ali Oop	20 – 1	4
Bob's Dusty	20 – 1	4
Something Rotten	30 – 1	3
		122 *total*

COMPUTING APPROXIMATE PLACE AND SHOW PAYOFFS

Short of using the most sophisticated electronic equipment, no player can hope to generate all the possible place and show payoffs in a race. Place and show payoffs are determined by the order of finish itself, or more correctly, by the money bet in the place pool and the money bet in the show pool on each horse involved in the top two and three finishing positions. The player's best course is to compute the lowest possible place and show payoff—a single calculation—because the lowest possible payoff is statistically the most likely payoff. It is the one produced by the favorites in the race finishing in the money. The following example shows how this is done.

HORSE	PLACE POOL	SHOW POOL
Carry Back	$ 4,000	$ 2,500
Buckpasser	$ 8,500	$ 6,000
Count Fleet	$12,000	$ 7,000
Tom Fool	$ 9,000	$ 4,000
Native Dancer	$10,000	$ 5,000
Round Table	$ 5,500	$ 1,500
Swaps	$10,000	$ 8,000
Silky Sullivan	$ 1,000	$ 1,000
Totals	$60,000	$35,000

QUESTION: *How much will Native Dancer pay to place?*

ANSWER: Minimum payoff is computed in four steps.

STEP 1: Deduct 20 percent pari-mutuel takeout tax from place pool total (20 percent of $60,000 or $12,000). Net pool = $48,000.

STEP 2: Combine the amount of money bet on Native Dancer to place with the amount of money bet on the horse getting the most play in the race. In this case, Count Fleet with $12,000 is the favorite in the place pool; thus the combined total equals $22,000.

STEP 3: Subtract the $22,000 from the $48,000 net place pool to determine the amount of money available for profit. In this case, $48,000 − $22,000 = $26,000 profit.

STEP 4: Divide the $26,000 profit into two equal parts to determine the amount of profit available to Native Dancer place pool bettors. In this case

$$\frac{\$26,000}{2} = \$13,000$$

THUS: The odds on Native Dancer to place are $13,000 profit to $10,000 invested, or 13–10 ($1.30–$1.00). Native Dancer will pay a minimum place price of $4.60 (includes original $2 investment).

QUESTION: *How much will Tom Fool pay to show?*

ANSWER: Minimum show payoff is computed in four steps.

STEP 1: Deduct 20 percent pari-mutuel takeout tax from show pool total (20 percent of $35,000, or $7,000). Net pool = $28,000.

STEP 2: Combine the amount of money bet on Tom Fool to show ($4,000) with the amount of money bet on the two horses getting the most play in the race. In this case, Swaps is getting $8,000; Count Fleet,

$7,000. Thus the combined total for all three horses is $19,000.

STEP 3: Subtract $19,000 from the $28,000 net show pool to determine the money available for profit. In this case, $28,000 − $19,000 = $9,000 net profit.

STEP 4: Divide the net profit into three equal parts to determine Tom Fool's show pool profit. In this case

$$\frac{\$9,000}{3} = \$3,000$$

THUS: The odds on Tom Fool to show are $3,000 profit to $4,000 invested, or 3–4 ($.75–$1.00). Tom Fool will pay a minimum show price of $3.40 (includes breakage to nearest dime and original $2 investment).

With some practice, the place and show payoffs for any horse can be computed in this manner in a matter of seconds. *Hint:* Round off to convenient whole numbers.

The parallel time chart on page 204 includes a speed-rating system that is consistent with the value of one-fifth of a second at all rates of speed at all distances. The time values incorporated in the chart were developed mathematically through class-par research at New York racetracks. With some important exceptions, described in the following material, this parallel time chart is adaptable for use at any racetrack with a circumference of one mile or more. Because of the unique nature of smaller tracks (more turns, shorter straightaways), the time values for minor tracks can be generated only through class-par research.

CLASS PARS AND PARALLEL TIME CHARTS

The idea behind the Beyer-Kovitz speed-figure method is to compare the final times of main-track races run on a

PARALLEL TIME CHART

SPEED FIG-URE	5½ FUR-LONGS	6 FUR-LONGS	7 FUR-LONGS	1 MILE	BEL-MONT (ONE TURN) 1⅛ MILES	AQUE-DUCT (TWO TURNS) 1⅛ MILES
136	1:02⅘	1:09	1:21⅖	1:33⅘	1:46⅖	1:48⅕
132	1:03	1:09⅕	1:21⅗	1:34⅕	1:46⅘	1:48⅗
128	1:03⅕	1:09⅗	1:22	1:34⅗	1:47⅕	1:49
124	1:03⅗	1:09⅘	1:22⅖	1:35	1:47⅗	1:49⅖
120	1:03⅘	1:10⅕	1:22⅘	1:35⅖	1:48	1:49⅘
116	1:04	1:10⅖	1:23	1:35⅘	1:48⅖	1:50⅕
112	1:04⅖	1:10⅗	1:23⅖	1:36⅕	1:49	1:50⅘
108	1:04⅗	1:11	1:23⅘	1:36⅗	1:49⅖	1:51⅕
104	1:04⅘	1:11⅕	1:24⅕	1:37	1:50	1:51⅘
100	1:05⅕	1:11⅗	1:24⅗	1:37⅗	1:50⅗	1:52⅕
96	1:05⅖	1:11⅘	1:24⅘	1:37⅘	1:50⅘	1:52⅗
92	1:05⅗	1:12⅕	1:25⅕	1:38⅕	1:51⅕	1:53
88	1:06	1:12⅖	1:25⅖	1:38⅗	1:51⅗	1:53⅖
84	1:06⅕	1:12⅘	1:25⅘	1:39	1:52⅕	1:54
80	1:06⅖	1:13	1:26⅕	1:39⅖	1:52⅗	1:54⅖
76	1:06⅘	1:13⅕	1:26⅗	1:39⅘	1:53⅕	1:55
72	1:07	1:13⅗	1:27	1:40⅕	1:53⅗	1:55⅖
68	1:07⅕	1:13⅘	1:27⅕	1:40⅗	1:54	1:55⅘
64	1:07⅗	1:14⅕	1:27⅗	1:41	1:54⅖	1:56⅕
60	1:07⅘	1:14⅖	1:28	1:41⅖	1:55	1:56⅗

given day with a valid set of standards (par times). The parallel time chart above is an essential ingredient in that process. For absolute accuracy, such a chart might well be constructed by researching the average winning times for each class and distance run at the track in question. Fortunately, there are several mathematical relationships that can be relied upon to shorten the research effort.

ITEM: There is a natural, mathematical relationship between final times at various distances. For example, if a horse travels six furlongs in 1:13, it will have to travel the seven-furlong distance in 1:26⅕ to earn equal credit. This additional 13⅕ seconds for the extra furlong is based on considerable research, is mathematically sound, and incorporates the normal loss of speed we would expect for the added difficulty of a longer distance. Given a faster rate of speed, say 1:10 for six furlongs, the equivalent seven-furlong time would be 1:22⅗, or a difference of 12⅗ seconds. Given a slower rate of speed, say six furlongs in 1:14⅗, the equivalent seven-furlong time would be 1:28, or a difference of 13⅖ seconds.

ITEM: The above relationship assumes the presence of only one turn at each distance, and a similar mathematical relationship could be shown to exist for all other one-turn distances. For example, at Belmont Park, where a chute extends the track's ability to card one-turn races up to 1¼ miles, the following times are approximately equal to each other:

	6 FURLONGS	7 FURLONGS	1 MILE	1⅛ MILES
	1:14⅗ =	1:28 =	1:41⅖ =	1:55
	1:13 =	1:26⅕ =	1:39⅖ =	1:52⅘
	1:10 =	1:22⅗ =	1:35⅕ =	1:48

ITEM: The equivalent time for a race involving a half-furlong (i.e., 6½ furlongs or 1¹⁄₁₆ miles) can be interpolated from the above table. For instance, 1:39⅖ at one mile equals 1:46⅕ at 1¹⁄₁₆ miles.

ITEM: The presence of an extra turn destroys the mathematical relationship as represented by the table. Thus at Aqueduct, where 1⅛-mile races are contested around two turns, the only way to establish equivalent times is to conduct class-par research. To refresh your memory (Chapter 11), that means finding the average winning time (fast tracks only) for each class of race at each distance. What I am suggesting below is a shortcut.

STEP 1: For the most popular sprint distance (one turn), find the average winning time for every major race classification. At Belmont Park and Aqueduct, for instance, the class pars for older horses traveling six furlongs are as follows. The approximate speed-figure ratings can be obtained by consulting the parallel time chart.

CLAIMING RACES			
$50,000+	1:10⅗	$11,000+	1:11⅗
$35,000+	1:10⅘	$ 8,000+	1:11⅘
$25,000+	1:11	$ 6,000+	1:12
$20,000+	1:11⅕	$ 5,000+	1:12⅕
$15,000+	1:11⅖		

MAIDEN CLAIMING		ALLOWANCE RACES	
$30,000+	1:12	$25,000 purse	1:10⅕
$20,000+	1:12⅖	$20,000 purse	1:10⅖
$12,000+	1:12⅘	$15,000 purse	1:10⅗
$ 8,000+	1:13	$12,000 purse	1:11
		$10,000 purse	1:11⅖

MAIDEN SPECIAL WEIGHT			
All ages	1:11⅘	Stakes races	1:10

STEP 2: Repeat the above class-par research for as many two-turn distances as you wish to include in the parallel time chart. Because the relationship between final time and class is an orderly one, someone handy with numbers may reduce the required research by skipping several class levels and filling in the missing time values through interpolation.

STEP 3: Using the following example as a guide, match the class pars for each distance so that each horizontal line represents an equivalent measure of speed. It is in this manner that the parallel time

chart can be adjusted to reflect the true value of
the extra turn.

AQUEDUCT—$25,000 CLAIMING

6 FURLONGS		1⅛ MILES
1:11	=	1:51⅕

AQUEDUCT—$15,000 CLAIMING

6 FURLONGS		1⅛ MILES
1:11⅖	=	1:52

SPEED FIGURES AND TRACK VARIANTS

Using class pars and the parallel time chart on page
204, we are now ready to compute a track variant.

PAR	ACTUAL SPEED FIGURE	VARIANT
88	91	−3
83	88	−5
90	92	−2
96	96	0
108	112	−4
turf	no figure	no variant
1½ miles	no figure	no variant
120	126	−6
108	109	−1
		Average variant = −3 (−21 for 7 races)

STEP 1: After today's races are run, compare the final times
with the par time for the distance and class. At Belmont the par time for a $25,000 claiming race is 1:11
for six furlongs. On the parallel time chart that is
worth 108 speed-figure points. If, however, the race was
run in 1:10⅗, the winner has actually earned 112

speed-figure points. What we want to find out is whether the horse actually earned the high figure or whether he was helped to some extent by the speed conduciveness of the racetrack. For this we will need to compare all the speed figures and par times for main-track races run at Belmont Park that day.

STEP 2: At this point, deduct 3 speed-figure points from each horse's earned figure. It is obvious that the track contributed to the final times. When we enter the net speed figures in our permanent record, we will note the variant and the adjusted speed figures in the following manner:

				RACES						
DATE	VARIANT	1	2	3	4	5	6	7	8	9
6/11	−3	88	85	89	93	109	T	none	123	106

Of course, not every racing day is so easily compared. Sometimes the times will be much faster than par for the first few races and not as fast for the remainder of the card. Sometimes the one-turn races will be faster or slower than the two-turn races. It is for this reason that the player should set up the par time comparisons in the following manner (S = sprint, R = route).

PAR	ACTUAL SPEED FIGURE	VARIANT
90 – S	95	−5
84 – S	90	−6
100 – R	100	0
106 – S	112	−6
80 – R	77	+3
turf	no figure	no variant
94 – S	100	−6
120 – R	118	+2
88 – R	85	+3
	Sprints = −6 (−23 for 4 races)	
	Routes = +2 (+ 8 for 4 races)	

Deduct 6 speed-figure points from each sprint race speed figure. Add 2 speed-figure points to each route race speed figure. Enter the adjusted speed figures on the permanent record.

STEP 3: After a few weeks of compiling speed-figure ratings, you will be able to employ speed figures for handicapping purposes. To determine the speed figure of any horse, consult the permanent record and adjust the figure according to the beaten-lengths chart below.

STEP 4: (Optional) Andy Beyer's advanced speed-figure method eliminates the par times as a standard once the permanent record becomes functional. Instead of par times, Andy substitutes *projected* times based on the actual speed figures earned by the horses in prior races. In other words, if a race is run in 1:11 flat, instead of comparing the time to the expected par Andy compares the actual speed figure to the speed figure the horse's prior record indicates it should have run. Indeed, he projects speed figures for several horses in each race in order to get a valid standard. Obviously, this procedure is more accurate, but it is difficult to master. It should not be attempted until the player has complete familiarity with the class-par version of the method, which by itself provides an adequate *track* variant.

The interested handicapper should note these additional facts about speed figures:

1. Speed figures may be generated for turf races only at those racetracks where an electronic timing device is known to be accurate and in regular use.
2. The class pars for races carded exclusively for fillies are usually one-fifth of a second slower for each class at six furlongs.
3. The six-furlong class pars for three-year-olds are three-fifths of a second slower in January, two-fifths slower in June, and one-fifth slower in September.

BEATEN-LENGTHS CHART
(*Deduct Points from Winner's Rating*)

MARGIN	5 FUR-LONGS	6 FUR-LONGS	7 FUR-LONGS	1 MILE	1⅛ MILES
neck	1	1	1	0	0
½	1	1	1	1	1
¾	2	2	2	1	1
1	3	2	2	2	2
1¼	4	3	3	2	2
1½	4	4	3	3	3
1¾	5	4	4	3	3
2	6	5	4	4	3
2¼	7	6	5	4	4
2½	7	6	5	4	4
2¾	8	7	6	5	5
3	9	7	6	5	5
3¼	9	8	7	6	5
3½	10	9	7	6	6
3¾	11	9	8	7	6
4	12	10	8	7	7
4¼	12	10	9	8	7
4½	13	11	9	8	8
4¾	14	11	10	9	8
5	15	12	10	9	8
5½	16	13	11	10	9
6	18	15	12	11	10
6½	19	16	13	12	11
7	20	17	14	13	12
7½	22	18	15	13	13
8	23	20	17	14	13
8½	25	21	18	15	14
9	26	22	19	16	15
9½	28	23	19	17	16
10	29	24	20	18	17
11	32	27	23	20	18
12	35	29	25	21	20
13	38	32	27	23	22
14	41	34	29	25	23
15	44	37	31	27	25

4. Speed figures earned on severely biased racetracks should be regarded suspiciously for handicapping purposes.

RECOMMENDED READING LIST

STATISTICS AND GENERAL RACING INFORMATION

The American Racing Manual, published annually by the *Daily Racing Form.*

The Blood Horse's annual statistical review.

The Thoroughbred Record's annual statistical review.

Turf and Sport Digest (monthly magazine).

BREEDING AND TRAINING

The Blood Horse (weekly magazine).

Breeding the Racehorse, by Federico Tesio; tr. Marchese E. Spinola. British Book Center, 1973. $12.50.

The Thoroughbred Record (weekly magazine).

Training Thoroughbred Horses, by Preston M. Burch. The Blood Horse Library, 1953. $6.00.

Typology of the Racehorse, by Franco Varola. British Book Center, 1974. $37.50.

RACING HISTORY

Big Red of Meadow Stable: Secretariat, The Making of a Champion, by William Nack. Arthur Fields Books, 1975. $10.00.

The History of Thoroughbred Racing in America, by William H. Robertson. Bonanza Books, 1964. $25.00.

In the Winner's Circle, by Joseph A. Hirsh and Gene Plowden. Mason Charter, 1974. $7.95.

Run for the Roses: 100 Years of the Kentucky Derby, by Jim Bolus. Hawthorn Books, 1974, $12.95.

This Was Racing, by Joe H. Palmer. Henry Clay, 1973. $7.95.

HANDICAPPING

Ainslie's Complete Guide to Thoroughbred Racing, by Tom Ainslie. Simon and Schuster, 1968. $14.95.

Picking Winners, by Andrew Beyer. Houghton Mifflin, 1975. $7.95.